Divine Interventions

Personal Testimonies of the Miraculous

DENISE SAMUELS

ISBN 978-1-0980-9522-2 (paperback)
ISBN 978-1-0980-9523-9 (digital)

Christian Faith Publishing, Inc.
832 Park Avenue
Meadville, PA 16335
www.christianfaithpublishing.com

Printed in the United States of America

This book is dedicated to my mother and best friend, Beverley Elaine Walcott, who went on to be with the Lord on May 8, 2017, at the age of seventy-three.

Mom, you were present when I received the prophetic word many years ago to write this book, which will be one of many. I am your miracle and you were mine. You not only taught me about Jesus but you also showed Him to me through your selfless love.

Words are inadequate to express my love for you. You were my confidant and shoulder to cry on. Your love for me was always unwavering, and no matter how rough things were, I always knew that you had my back.

I will miss you forever. You are irreplaceable, I love you endlessly, and I still cry although I know that you are now with the one you revered most, Jesus Christ.

The one thing that was most constant in your prayers was "I need to make it to heaven," and that you did. We will meet again to be together forever.

CONTENTS

Preface...7

Chapter 1: Created for God's Glory 9
Chapter 2: A Miraculous Rescue 28
Chapter 3: Desire, Disappointment, Decision...........41
Chapter 4: Something Big Is Coming Out of This....61
Chapter 5: Jesus Has Need of You...............................86
Chapter 6: It Should Have Killed You, But! 93
Chapter 7: Fight Like a Girl!.....................................112
Chapter 8: Break Up with the Flesh 136
Chapter 9: Don't Let the Stone Stop You! 157
Chapter 10: If You Can Have It, God Can Heal It.....178
Chapter 11: Forever I Do...188
Chapter 12: Provoke Your Rainfall 209
Chapter 13: Lord, Give Me a Double Portion............224
Chapter 14: Live Full, Die Empty...............................249
Chapter 15: Expect God to Do the Unexpected.........274

PREFACE

Merriam-Webster Dictionary says that a miracle is "an extraordinary event manifesting divine intervention in human affairs." This definition sums up my life story, which has been and continues to be a manifestation of divine interventions.

Throughout the years, I have preached way over one hundred sermons, the majority of which were birthed from either a personal experience or a divine revelation.

This book reveals some of the personal experiences and miracles that gave birth to some of my sermons.

It is my prayer that you will not only be blessed but that your lives will also be transformed.

CHAPTER 1

Created for God's Glory

I still remember my first altar call response. I was only six years of age, and I had attended an outdoor crusade with my mom and brother at a Baptist church.

The preacher's message of salvation had reached deep into my soul, and before I knew it, I had found myself walking up to the altar with tears streaming down my face. I knew from that very moment that there was a higher source.

No one in my family had been saved at the time, but my mother had been raised by a father who, although not saved, insisted that she and her younger sibling attended Sunday school every week. The lessons had planted the seed in her heart that made Proverbs 22:6—"Train up a child in the way he should go: and when he is old, he will not depart from it"—become a reality.

My mom started taking my brother and I to a Pentecostal church every Sunday soon after that, and I had found myself telling her at every opportunity that I got that I wanted to get baptized at the age of seven years. The requests had flustered my mom because she had felt that I was too young to fully understand the requirements of the commitment and to therefore be baptized.

A few days after my seventh birthday, my mom was baptized. A couple weeks thereafter, I fell ill, and my mom and dad took me to the hospital. I was given penicillin injections as the treatment.

Whilst leaving the hospital, I started feeling almost as if I was going to pass out, and I told my mom. Thank God she was always an avid reader, and so immediately she suspected that I was having an allergic reaction to the penicillin and told my father to lift me up and help her take me back to the doctor. My father responded that by the time I was placed in the back of the car and the wind started blowing in my face, I would feel better. My mother rebutted and insisted that I be brought back to the doctor.

The next thing I knew was that we were asked to sit and wait as the doctor was otherwise engaged, but my mother wasn't about to wait, and so she went to have strong words with the nursing staff.

Whilst waiting, I remember I kept feeling nauseous and the need to sleep. Then I remember being lifted by my father and placed on a bed, and then I passed out.

In what seemed like a few minutes, I was awakened by voices telling me to wake up and asking me if I knew where I was and what my name was. I opened my eyes to find that the bed that they had laid me in was surrounded by doctors and nurses, with two of them injecting me with drugs (which I later found out was intended on counteracting the effects of the penicillin) and telling me to fight to stay awake.

This was the first of my many miracles, because I stayed awake!

A few weeks after, my mother decided to allow me to get baptized as she reasoned if I was not too young to die, then I was not too young to get saved. I was created for God's glory.

The Sermon

In the beginning God created the heaven and the earth.

And God said, Let us make man in our image, after our likeness: and let them have dominion over the fish of the sea, and over the fowl of the air, and over the cattle, and over all the earth, and over every creeping thing that creepeth upon the earth.

So God created man in his own image, in the image of God created he him; male and female created he them. (Gen. 1:1, 26–27)

But now thus saith the LORD that created thee, O Jacob, and he that formed thee, O Israel, Fear not: for I have redeemed thee, I have called thee by thy name; thou art mine.

When thou passest through the waters, I will be with thee; and through the rivers, they shall not overflow thee: when thou walkest through the fire, thou shalt not be burned; neither shall the flame kindle upon thee.

I will say to the north, Give up; and to the south, Keep not back: bring my sons from far, and my daughters from the ends of the earth;

Even every one that is called by my name: for I have created him for my glory, I have formed him; yea, I have made him.

Bring forth the blind people that have eyes, and the deaf that have ears.

Remember ye not the former things, neither consider the things of old.

Behold, I will do a new thing; now it shall spring forth; shall ye not know it? I will even make a way in the wilderness, and rivers in the desert.

The beast of the field shall honour me, the dragons and the owls: because I give waters in the wilderness, and rivers in the desert, to give drink to my people, my chosen.

This people have I formed for myself; they shall shew forth my praise. (Isa. 43:1–2; 6–8; 18–21)

It doesn't matter how messed up your life is right now. You were created for God's glory!

I don't care if right now you are a sinner or a saint. You were created for God's glory!

God created you to display His glory. It may not look that way to you or you may not feel that way, but you were created for His glory.

HOW do I know? Well, first of all, the Bible says, "In the beginning God created the heaven and the earth."

GOD was in the beginning, and God was prior to the beginning. He always was, He always will be, and He doesn't exist in time. So much so that way back then, God was able to see today, and in seeing today, He saw you and me.

HE saw us before He made us. He saw our ending before He initiated our beginning. He saw everything we would have gone through before we went through it. And yet in us, God saw His beauty, His Reflection. In us, God saw potential and great possibilities.

GOD was able to see us because He is omnipresent. He is everywhere at once, and there is nowhere that He is not!

When God saw us, He decided to create the heaven and the earth because He said, "Surely, these people will need a place to live and a place to retire to." God is a spirit, which means that He does not have flesh and bones. However, He knew that those with flesh and bones would need a place like earth and eventually heaven.

HE knew this because He is Omniscient. He knows all things, and there is nothing that He does not know.

God made the heaven and the earth and everything in between, such as the trees, animals, birds of the air, and fish of the sea. AFTER God made the heaven and the earth, He decided to create human bodies that would produce after its kind. SO God the Father turned to God the Son and to God the Holy Spirit and said, "Let us make man in our own image and after Our own likeness.

"Let us make man as creative beings. Let us make man with the ability to love like we can. Let us make man with the ability to display patience like we can. Let us make man with the ability to forgive like we can. Let us make man with the ability to be kind and faithful like we are."

You see, God is a creative being, and it gives Him pleasure, it gives Him glory, and it gives Him splendor to create.

We were made in the image and likeness of God. We have the ability to know God and to therefore love Him, worship Him, serve Him, and fellowship with Him. Yet without human beings, God would still be God. It was only for His glorification that He made man.

He said in His word, "And let us give man dominion over the earth" so that they can have power over the earth and rule the things of the earth, and not the things of the earth rule them.

God was able to make the heaven and the earth and everything in between. He was able to make male and female and give them dominion, because God is Omnipotent. He is all powerful. He is able to do whatever He will.

Now despite the fact that man was created for God's glory, man messed up. As a people, we oftentimes stray from our purpose, and instead of man utilizing its dominion and rule over the things of the earth, man allowed the things of this earth to rule and dominate its existence.

A perfect example of a people who messed up and failed to live the life God intended were the children of Israel. In the chapter of Isaiah 43, which we read earlier, the children of Israel had become a sinful, rebellious generation.

Many had taken up into idol worshipping. They were disobedient, just like many persons are today.

The children of Israel's disobedience led to them becoming captives to their enemies and exiled in a foreign land.

Many persons here today are captives to the devil, and you have been exiled in a world of sin.

It is a terrible thing to know that although you were created in the image of the Sovereign God, created to be a conqueror and to rule over the things of the earth, you find that rather than conquering, you have been conquered!

The Israelites had lost everything, including their homes and temples, and as their years in exile became many decades, the questions that burned in their hearts were the following: (1) Will we ever be saved? (2) Will we ever be rescued and restored? (3) Is there a way out of this impossible and difficult time? (4) Are we ever going to make it back home?

The questions contemplated by the children of Israel back then are no different from the many questions being pondered in many persons' hearts today. Many of you here today feel like your life is just not getting anywhere.

Many of you feel like you are stuck in the same routine day after day. You have lost so much that your hope of recovery is failing. Many of you have done so much wrong, and you have done wrong for so long that you often find yourselves wondering if God even loves you.

In the passage of scripture that we read, the children of Israel had found themselves at the point of sinfulness and hopelessness.

Some had felt that for all the wrong that they had done, there was no way God would have wanted anything else to do with them. Many had reached the breaking point, and many were broken, but that's exactly where God wanted them to be.

Brokenness reminds us of our need for God. Brokenness reminds us that we are nothing without God. Brokenness opens the door of our hearts to God, and it gives God the opportunity to be God in our lives.

Just when the children of Israel thought that it was over for them, just when they thought that God was through with them, just when they thought that they were beyond the point of recovery, God stepped in!

Life may have been unkind to you. Your mother forsook you. Your father disowned you. Your children rebelled against you. However, don't you ever forget that God is for you, and He will step in!

God stepped in at a time when the Israelites needed Him most, and He spoke to them. He reintroduced Himself to them. The children of Israel needed to start over. They needed a fresh start because they were mixed up in sin, mixed up in gossiping, mixed up in jealousies, mixed up in controversies, and mixed up in stubbornness that they needed to start over.

They had lost everything. They had lost their freedom, their earthly possessions, and most importantly, they had lost their relationship with God, and so they needed a new beginning, because "in the beginning, God..."

If you would like to experience a new beginning in your life, your relationships, your finances, your business, you have to get back to the basics.

If you have experienced setbacks and failures that have caused much heartache and pain, if you are experiencing guilt and shame that burdens your souls, if you have been delaying your dreams and your destiny, and deep within your heart you know that your only solution is a new beginning, then you have to go back to the beginning, because "in the beginning, God..."

God stepped in at a time of greatest need, and He spoke to the children of Israel who were lost in sin and were being held in captivity, and in verse 1 of Isaiah 43, God says, **"Fear not: for I have redeemed thee, I have called thee by thy name; thou art mine."**

In other words, He was saying to the children of Israel, "For your sinful condition, you deserve to die, but don't worry. Fear not. The price for your sins has been paid so that you can live!"

Redemption means that God has paid something for us. It says in 1 Corinthians 6:19–20, "What? Know ye not that your body is the temple of the Holy Ghost which is in you, which you have of God, and ye are not your own? For you were bought with a price: therefore glorify God in your body, and in your spirit, which are God's."

Sin broke our relationship with *the* God of "in the beginning," but because He is the creator of man, and because we were created for His glory, He decided that there is no way that He could just sit still and do nothing about restoring our relationship with Him.

Sin comes with a high price tag. The reward for sin leads to death. And in order for life to overpower and conquer death, the shedding of sinless blood was necessary to suffice the payment, because sinless blood gives life!

So God did the ultimate! God paid the price for our sins with the blood of His son Jesus Christ, thus redeeming us, and because He paid for us, He now owns us!

Whether you like it or not, you belong to God! You can run from God all you want, but there is no getting away from Him. He knows your name. He knows everything about you; even the hairs on your head are numbered. You belong to God because He paid the ultimate price for you. Sin stole you, but God bought you back!

God has a bounty out on your life! You belong to Him, and He is not taking no for an answer! You have to serve God, whether freely or by force, because He owns you.

If I were to ask you right now how many of you wanted to be anointed; I think that almost all—if not everyone—would raise their hands, including the unsaved, because we covet the anointing. It is the anointing that makes us better.

If you sing, you want to be anointed because it makes you sing better. If you preach, you want to be anointed because it makes you preach better. If you play an instrument, play ball, or work in the secular field, you want the anointing because it makes you better.

The anointing makes you more effective and more successful. The anointing applied to natural abilities and gifting make us better than we usually are. And the fact is, it is good to yearn for the anointing, because if ever there is a generation that needs to be anointed and filled with power, it is this one!

God is in desperate need for men and women who have more than talent, more than ability, more than gifting. God wants us to operate at a higher level of excellence, power, and deliverance. Plus, more than ever, we need to be able to walk into demonic, hopeless, and against-all-odds situations and bring breakthroughs.

Somebody should be able to take a microphone and produce a sound that will set the captives free. But too many people want the anointing with no relationship. They want to experience the power, but they don't want to go any deeper.

Too many want to sing, but they don't want to be consecrated. Too many want to work for God, but they don't want to be disciplined. Too many want the favor of God, but they don't want to make the commitment. However, having said that, I believe that much more than the anointing, what is really needed is a bloodbath!

More than you need to be anointed, you need to be bathed and washed in His blood. Many of you look anointed, but what would be much better is if you looked like you were bathed in His blood!

The truth is that oil follows blood. The oil cannot and will not go where the blood has not gone. We have to go through the process. Before we get the oil, the blood must first be applied.

It is the blood of Jesus that saves you and keeps you saved.

It is the blood of Jesus that sanctifies you and keeps you sanctified.

It is the blood of Jesus that preserves your relationship with God.

In fact, Exodus 29 gives us the prescribed method of consecrating priests. In 1 Peter 2:9, it tells us that whether we like it or not, we are priests: "For we are a chosen generation, a royal priesthood, an holy nation, a peculiar people; that ye should shew forth the praises of Him who hath called us out of darkness into His marvelous light."

As priests, we must go through the purification process, similar to that which is outlined in Exodus 29. The purification process requires a bloodbath. It requires us applying **blood to our ears** so that it may be consecrated to continually hear from God.

Please understand that if you have problems obeying the voice of God, it means that you need a bloodbath. If you struggle with listening to the teachings of God, you need a bloodbath! If you love to listen to gossip more than truth, you need a bloodbath. Your ears need to be bathed and consecrated with the blood of Jesus Christ!

Exodus 29 also tells us that we must **apply the blood to our thumb.** Blood must be applied to the thumb to signify that our hands are to be set apart as holy hand.

DAVID asks us the question in Psalm 24, "Who can ascend unto God? Who can be used by God? Who can handle the Oil? Those who have clean hands and pure hearts."

I am concerned that many persons who so badly want the anointing allow their hands to be used for evil rather than good. If you use your hands to do evil, you need a bloodbath! If you use your hands to write letters of mischief, you need a bloodbath!

Your hands must work to be a blessing and not a curse! Let God consecrate your hands with a bloodbath!

Thirdly, the Word of God says that we must **apply blood to our toe**. We are commanded to walk circumspectly—to walk straight.

You need to be careful where your feet have been taking you. You need to be careful where you go. If you find that your feet have been taking you down a path of destruction, you need a bloodbath. If your feet keep taking you to the nightclub, to the gambling den, to the house of promiscuity, you need a bloodbath!

King Saul was anointed. He had oil running down his head. He was talented. He was gifted. He was handsome. However, he had one problem—no blood, no discipline, no consecration. There are too many persons running around claiming to be anointed, even showing signs of being anointed, but they are in desperate need of a bloodbath.

You are ministering but still shacking up. You never miss a service, but you still live like a rebel. In church, you act and look like a saint, but outside of church, you act and live like a sinner. You need a bloodbath! He that hath an ear to hear let him hear what the Spirit of God is saying to His church!

In verse 2 of Isaiah 43, God says something that is so remarkable. It is remarkable because I believe that this verse is not only intended for the saved but also for the unsaved, as it will become a testament, an evidence against them if they don't act before it is too late.

The verse says, "When thou passest through the waters, I will be with thee; and through the rivers, they shall not overflow thee: when thou walkest through the fire, thou shalt not be burned; neither shall the flame kindle upon thee."

To the believing Christian, this is a remarkable word of encouragement. It is encouraging and comforting just to know that regardless of what life throws your way, God will be right there with you, protecting you, shielding you, and guiding you.

You can't help but remember the thee Hebrew boys in the fiery furnace and how God showed up as the fourth man in the fire. He loosed them, walked around in the fire with them, and then caused the same fire that could not harm them to destroy the ones that meant them harm.

You can't help but remember Daniel in the lion's den and how God showed up and caused the lions to lose their appetite so that Daniel could keep on praying.

So to the true child of God, this verse of scripture brings joy and comfort in knowing that God is always with them. But to the unsaved, this same verse of scripture takes on another role. It becomes public evidence against them.

> Whither shall I go from thy spirit? or whither shall I flee from thy presence?
> If I ascend up into heaven, thou art there: if I make my bed in hell, behold, thou art there.
> If I take the wings of the morning, and dwell in the uttermost parts of the sea;
> Even there shall thy hand lead me, and thy right hand shall hold me.
> If I say, Surely the darkness shall cover me; even the night shall be light about me.
> Yea, the darkness hideth not from thee; but the night shineth as the day: the darkness and the light are both alike to thee. (Ps. 39:7–12)

In other words, if you are *not* saved, the only reason that you are alive today is because God wants to give you another chance to amend your ways. No matter what you do or where you go, God is watching you. You cannot hide from Him.

We can't see your hearts and your intentions, and we may never witness some of your actions, but nothing is hidden from God!

God has kept you alive for this day to give you one more chance to make it right with Him. God has kept you alive for this day to give you another opportunity to hear of His saving grace and mercy. If you refuse to listen, if you refuse to obey, it will be a testament against you, because the scriptures already made it clear in Psalm

139. That even in your lowest state of sinful living, God has been working behind the scenes to bring you to Him.

The truth of the matter is that you should have been dead a long time ago! You were held up at gunpoint and at knifepoint. You were beaten up pretty badly. You tried to commit suicide. They sent evil darts against you, but you are still alive!

You are still alive, not because you did anything good, not because you deserve to live, but only because of the grace and mercies of God!

Somebody needs to know that you should have lost your mind when the man left you. You should have lost your mind when you couldn't pay your bills, had no food to eat, and couldn't pay the rent, but you are still in your right mind. Not because of anything good that you did but only because God chose to allow you another opportunity to make the right choice and to surrender your life to Him.

Don't take God's mercies for granted! Time is running out! You are here today by *His* choice! You were created for His glory, and He chose to give you one more chance today to live a life that glorifies Him.

Today may be your last chance, because tomorrow is not promised to any man. Choose ye this day whom you will serve. Serve the devil and go to hell or serve God and live life eternal.

God is here for you! He said in **VERSE 6 of the chapter**:

> I will say to the north, Give up; and to the south, Keep not back: bring my sons from far, and my daughters from the ends of the earth;
> Even every one that is called by my name: for I have created him for my glory, I have formed him; yea, I have made him.

In other words, God is letting us know that He will speak to the situations in the earth—the situations that have been dominating your lives and have been keeping you captive.

Spirits of homosexuality and lesbianism, God is speaking to you, and He says, "Give up my sons and my daughters! Release them back to Me! They were created for My glory!"

I was shocked when I viewed an advertisement on television just this past week. It was an advertisement where a professed Christian pastor and his wife admitted that they struggled for years with whether or not homosexuality was wrong. They said that after much thought, they were now convinced that nothing was wrong with it, so much so that the pastor recently officiated the marriage of his homosexual son. But the devil is still a liar!

SPIRITS of rape, incest, and child molestation, God is speaking to you. He says, "Release the hearts and minds of mankind back to conscious thinking!"

SPIRIT of adultery, God is speaking to you! He says, "Take your hands off marriages. Release them to wholesome family living."

SPIRIT of abortion, God is speaking to you! He says, "Take your hands off the unborn. They were created to live for My glory!"

SPIRIT of suicide, God is speaking to you! He says, "Take your hands off My people. That female was created to give Me glory through song. That male was created to give Me glory through the preached word. Take your hands off my children. They belong to Me!"

SPIRITS of oppression, hatred, envy, and strife. SPIRITS of crime and violence, God is speaking to you! He says, "Come out of the north, come out of the south, come out of the east, come out of the west, and release people and be destroyed!"

I believe that God is releasing you right now! You need to begin to praise Him!

God says in verse 8, "Bring forth the blind people that have eyes, and the deaf that have ears."

SINNERMAN/BACKSLIDER/CHURCHGOER, God is talking to you right now. He is releasing you to hear this word, because you have eyes but cannot see. You have ears but cannot hear!

In the name of Jesus Christ of Nazareth, I command that your eyes be opened so that you can see the troublesome state that you are in! In the name of Jesus Christ of Nazareth, I command that your ears be opened so that you can hear the urgent plea of God for your life.

He that hath an ear to hear, let him hear what the Spirit of God is saying to you right now! God wants to do a new thing in the lives of the saved and of the unsaved, because God is far more interested in your future than your past.

In verse 18 of the chapter, God says, "Forget the former things. Don't dwell on the past." And we know that the word *dwell* means "to reside." Where you dwell is where you live. But God says, "Don't live in the past." Don't live in the past hurt and pain. Don't live in the past shame and disdain. Stop making excuses for your failures! Stop blaming other people. Stop seeing yourself as the victim of your circumstance.

People can hurt us, they can harm us, and they can scar us, but the only person that can ruin your life is you. So forget about the past failures, because the mishaps, the turning aside, and the misunderstandings are yesterday's news. Today is a new day!

Change your focus! You may be living in sin. You may have messed up, but God can make you whole. So change your address! Move away from the street of unforgiveness and resentment. Move away from the street of loneliness. Move away from the street of rejection.

Change your address, because God wants to do a new thing in your life.

Start looking ahead. If you keep looking back, you will never see where you are going.

The apostle Paul is a perfect example of a man who lived his life looking forward and not looking back. That was good for Paul because he had a pretty nasty history to look back on. He had made some horrible mistakes. It was the apostle Paul who watched and did nothing to stop the stoning of Stephen, a servant of God, to death. The apostle Paul was a persecutor of the church. He was so greatly feared that Christians scattered to get away from him. But one day on the road to Damascus, Paul had an experience with God. A blinding light came down from heaven, and Paul fell to the ground.

God spoke to Paul that day, and Paul repented of his sins, and in that moment, Paul received the gift of salvation. And in that moment, Paul was changed forever!

Today can be your Damascus road experience. God wants to do a new thing in your life.

Paul could not have accomplished all that he did if he was focused on the terrible things that he had done before he got saved. No wonder he wrote in Philippians 3:14, "I press on to reach the end of the race, and receive the heavenly prize for which God, through Christ Jesus, is calling us."

It is okay to recall what you went through to be where you are today, but don't dwell there! It is okay to recall the good old days, the past victories, but you cannot live on past victories because that's what they are—the past.

Just like the children of Israel, many here today have had many victories and glorious times in the past. The children of Israel experienced victory in their defeat of the Egyptians. They experienced the victory of God opening the Red Sea so that they could cross over on dry land, and then the closing of the Red Sea so that their enemies would be destroyed.

The children of Israel experienced the victory of seeing Jericho defeated, simply because they obeyed God and marched around it for seven days. They had many victories on their way to Canaan. They conquered Canaan, and they won many battles against their enemies. But now that they were in captivity, their past victories were of no use to them. It couldn't set them free. They needed a new beginning, a new portion of faith, a new miracle, a new victory. There are people who can tell you what went on in their lives thirty or fifty years ago, but they can't tell you what God is doing in their lives today. You cannot depend on your past victories and glory to take you out of your present condition.

Yesterday's victories will not save us today. Your future is not based on what God has done in your life. Your future is based on what God is going to do in your life, starting today.

God is not a God of the past. He refuses to live five minutes ago because there are too many things that He has for His people now! God is a now God! He lives in the now zone, which is designed to propel you into your future, to propel you into your destiny. You were created to live forward, and that is why God sent me to tell you that starting today, He is going to do a new thing in your life.

By the unction of the Holy Spirit and with the assurance of God's Word, God says to tell you that the good news today, the good news at this moment, is that it is not over. He is giving you another chance. It may be your last chance, but at least you are getting another chance for God to do something new in your life.

It's not over! God has a plan for your life, and He is about to do something new in you. What God is about to do in you is so great and so important and so impressive that it will make what He did in the past pale in comparison.

Haggai 2:9 says, "The glory of this present house will be greater than the glory of the former house." This is who God is. He is not content to do one great thing and stop. He continues to outdo Himself.

God says, "I will do a new thing; now it shall spring forth," which means that you are going to see the change and experience the change almost immediately. According to verse 19 of the chapter, God wants to "make a way in the wilderness, and rivers in the desert," and that's why you have got to understand that the wilderness, the desert, is not a location. It is a condition.

It speaks to the confused condition of your mind, the barren condition of your life, and the dry and thirsty condition of your soul. However, the good news is that the Hebrew verb translated as "make" in this passage means "to turn something into something else." So the Lord is not saying that He will make rivers in the desert. What He is actually saying is that He will turn the desert into rivers.

You see, anybody can carve out makeshift rivers in a desert. These days, you find a lot of man-made ponds. You have pools where no water freely flows, so making rivers into the desert is a possible thing to do. But God our Creator specializes in things that are impossible, and so God says that He is going to turn your desert into rivers, and your life will become a stream of life and fields of blessings and abundance.

Abraham had experienced this firsthand. Lot and Abraham had a misunderstanding, and so Lot selected the plains of Jordan for his cattle, and Abraham was left with the desert, having no way to feed his cattle. The vegetables and plants for his people could not grow in the desert, and so Abraham felt dry and lost.

In Genesis 13, the Lord said to Abraham, "Lift up your eyes from where you are and look north and south, east and west. All the land that you see I will give to you and your offspring forever." In other words, God was saying, "Abraham, the desert that you are left with is not your future. Look up. Lift up your eyes. Look to the future. The future is where I am leading you!"

We should be excited that God can take a dried-up, useless life and transform it into a life of purpose and grace!

God is going to turn your desert into rivers as an act of renewal. To renew is to bring something back to its former state or condition. Remember, you were created in God's image and for His glory!

GOD is going to turn your desert into rivers as an act of revival. To revive is to restore or to put back what has been depleted or used.

You were created for God's glory, and God wants to restore your relationship with Him. But in order to receive what God wants for you, see yourself as God sees you and commit yourself to God's plan!

In Isaiah 43, we see that God had already set into motion the events and people who would lead Israel out of captivity, but it was still up to them to decide if they wanted what God had offered and to have acted accordingly. If they had refused to follow where God was leading, then they would have been doomed to remain in captivity.

A story is told where a young boy said, "Daddy, if three frogs are sitting on a limb hanging over a pool and one frog decides to jump, how many frogs are left on the limb?"

His dad replied, "Two."

"No!" the son said. "Listen carefully, Daddy. There are three frogs, and one decides to jump. How many are left?"

Dad says, "Oh, I get it. If one decides to jump, the others would too. So there are none left."

"No, Daddy!" the young boy said. "There are **three** left on the limb! The first frog only decided to jump, but he never did!"

You can sit in your seats this morning and you can decide to jump. You can decide to change your living. You can decide to allow

God to do a new thing in your life. But if you don't put your decision into action, you will remain in the place of bondage.

God is building a people! Verse 21 of the chapter says, "He is building a people to show forth His Praise!" God wants your life to show forth His praise!

All that you need to do is to repent by sorrowfully turning away from sinful living and allow God to do a new thing in *and* with your life!

> Come now, let us reason together, says the Lord. Though your sins are like scarlet, they shall be as white as snow; though they are red as crimson, they shall be like wool. (Isa. 1:18)
>
> Let the wicked forsake his way, and the evil man his thoughts. Let him turn to the Lord, and he will have mercy on him, and to our God, for he will freely pardon. (Isa. 55:7).

If you believe that God created *you* for His glory, please stand.

Now I am going to make another request, and I don't want anybody to lie to the Spirit of God. Ananias and Sapphira did it, and they dropped dead in church before everyone!

If you know that without a shadow of a doubt your life testifies of God's glory, if you know that if Jesus were to come right now, heaven would be your home because there is no sin in your life, you are not a backslider. You are not a sinner. You are not living a double life as a Christian. You know that you have been living as a saved, sanctified, and believing child of God. You are a Christian and you know it. Take your seats.

Those of you who are still standing, please come to the altar. God wants to do a new thing in your life, and He told me to give something to you. I have in my hand strips of red wool that have been prayed over, saturated in olive oil, and left to dry.

Jesus asked me to place a strip in the hand of every person who comes forward for prayer. These red strips represent the blood of Jesus, and as I place them in your hand, just know that it signifies the blood of Jesus that was shed thousands of years ago for the remission—the forgiveness of our sins.

As I place a strip in your hand, just know that it serves as a reminder that you were bought with a price. Sin shall not have any more dominion over you. You belong to Jesus!

I want you to keep the strip for as long as you live, because it will serve as a reminder of the day when you took the bold step for Jesus.

You took the bold step for Jesus because you were created for His glory!

CHAPTER 2

A Miraculous Rescue

It began with the cramping of my left leg. Initially, I thought nothing of it and would simply shake the leg and say, "Devil, you are a liar!" and went about my normal business. However, as the days went by, the cramping intensified to the point that I had to seek medical attention on a number of occasions, all the while praying that God would provide the healing. Numerous tests and x-rays failed to reveal the source of the cramping, which eventually led to the noticeably shrinking of the leg and me walking with a slight limp.

A group of women committed to joining forces with my family to pray for my healing. We fasted, we prayed, we believed, and yet the cramping, which increasingly progressed to a consistent pain in the leg, remained. A dear friend of the family, Sis. Dorothy McKenzie (now a pastor), took my crisis personally, and even when it seemed like others took a break on praying for me, she remained consistent.

One Sunday morning about eight months after the initial cramping in my leg, I was in the process of getting dressed for the early service at church when suddenly, I sneezed three times. And with each sneeze, the pain in my leg got worse, so much so that after the third sneeze, the intensity of the pain forced me to lay in bed, crying out, "Jesus!" During that time, I kept thinking that by faith, I was still going to go to church. But as the hours passed by, the pain got so excruciating that it prevented me from sitting up, much less getting out of bed.

The cries of my pain took a hold on my father, who was not saved at the time. When it seemed he had enough, as the day was far spent, he came into my room and asked for a pair of my stockings or a foot of my socks so that he could go have it checked out to determine the source of my pain. I immediately knew what he meant, because he was an avid believer in the powers of witchcraft. I unhesitatingly responded by saying, "No, Dad, I believe in the miraculous power of God, and I prefer to give God a chance to work in my life."

During the course of the night, the pain continued to the extent that it prevented me from sleeping. At one point, I literally saw a host of demons with party hats on gathered around my bed, drinking and laughing at me. The experience was such that I cried out to the Lord and said, "Jesus! Talk to the Father for me. Let the Father know what pain feels like because you have experienced pain before." After a few minutes, the pain subsided to the point where I fell asleep.

The dawn of morning came, and physically, I felt drained, so much so that I decided that I would go and get medically examined one more time. At that point, Sister McKenzie called, and I told her of my decision. She asked that I delay my going to allow her the opportunity to pray with me once more, and I agreed. She came, and she prayed in tongues this time. Immediately, I felt the power of God lifting me out of the bed, and I was able to run around, giving praise to God for having healed me by His miraculous power. I was also able to go and pick my son up from school.

The following Sunday, I went to church and shared my testimony with a women's group that had been constantly praying for me. However, by the Tuesday of that week, the pain started coming back. I prayed and asked the Lord if He was going to allow His name to be brought to shame, because I had shared the testimony of Him healing me. The pain kept increasing, and by Thursday of that week, I decided to fast and pray one more time for God to reveal to me exactly what was happening.

That morning, I got up and sat on the edge of my bed to pray to commence my fast when I noticed the pair of my flat black shoes (which I had been wearing very often because of the pain) on the floor in the middle of the room, and it looked funny.

Usually, I don't leave my shoes lying on the floor. I had attended church the night before and had somehow left it there. I really can't recall doing so, but there it was lying on the floor looking funny.

I shouted to my mother, who was in the living room, "Mommy, my shoes look funny!" And while she was on her way down to my bedroom to look at the shoes, the house phone rang, and she turned back to answer it. When she answered, it was the same lady, Dorothy McKenzie, who had been faithful in crying out to God on my behalf. She was on the phone, and my mother brought the phone to me.

She asked, "Denise, do you own a pair of flat black shoes?"

I said, "Yes, why?"

And she said, "I was just praying, and the Lord showed me a pair of flat black shoes, and He said that I should burn it."

I shouted out, "Oh my god! I just saw the shoes lying on the floor in my bedroom, and it looked funny. And I shouted it out to my mother, and she was on her way to look at the shoes when the telephone rang."

Sister McKenzie said, "Okay, I am coming over to look at it to see if they are the same shoes that the Lord showed me."

Within minutes, she arrived at the house, and when she looked at the shoes, she shouted out, "It is the same one!" She took the shoes and set it on fire in the back of the yard. We then went back inside of the house, and she anointed my foot again. She prayed in both English and tongues again. Within weeks, my leg returned to its normal size, and after twenty-one years, I am still a walking miracle.

The Sermon

Acts 12:1–16

The text provides a clear pattern of the church and how it should be modeled. It provides an example of the desperate situations that people often find themselves in and an example of what the church usually does when faced with a desperate situation.

Acts 12:1–16 also shows how God responds to the cry of His people who walk humbly before Him during desperate times.

Embodied within this passage of scripture, we see that Peter had been placed in a seemingly hopeless situation. It was his midnight hour, and he was in a truly humbling position, and he needed to experience God's best.

If you know anything about being in a midnight hour, you know that it is the time when things are the darkest. You know that it is the time when you need to be rescued, because you are virtually blinded by your situation. You know that it is the time when you need a miracle, because only a miracle can bring you the urgent relief that you so desperately need.

The theme **"A Miraculous Rescue"** is therefore appropriate in describing what transpired in this passage of scripture and in describing what many have been trusting God to do.

I don't know what you are going through, but what I do know is that God is going to miraculously rescue you.

The truth is that all hell may be breaking loose around you, but God has a provision to miraculously rescue you.

It is good to remember that although you may be going through the most humbling experience of your life, although you may feel like God has forgotten you, that your friends have forsaken you, and you feel abandoned and alone, God will always make a way to provide for a miraculous rescue.

You are not forgotten. Get ready for the miraculous!

You Shall Be Delivered

Now if we are talking about "A Miraculous Rescue," we need to know what it really means to be rescued.

There are three biblical meanings of the word *rescue*.

Firstly, to be *rescued* means to be "delivered." *Deliverance* means to be "set free from whatever is holding you down or holding you in bondage." When you are delivered, you won't have to deal with the issues that kept you bound in the first place.

In the text, we see that Peter was imprisoned by Herod. King Herod was a wicked ruler. He was a persecutor of Christians, and he even had the apostle James, John's brother, put to death. When King Herod saw that the Jews were pleased about it, Herod had Peter arrested and put in prison to stand trial, which reconfirms that Satan will make trouble for you just because you are a Christian. The devil will make trouble for you, and it is not because you did anything wrong. It is not because you stepped out of line. It is just because you chose to serve God in Spirit and in truth. It is because you chose to walk humbly before God.

Satan will also use people against you. He will use people to create havoc in your lives and to imprison you just because you chose to stand for holiness and for righteousness. But God told me to tell you that He positioned you for a miraculous rescue. Right there in your imprisoned state, you are positioned for a miraculous rescue. That situation that keeps plaguing you from last year into this year is an opportunity for a miraculous rescue.

God also told me to tell you that He is going to miraculously rescue you from the bondage of joblessness. He is going to miraculously rescue you from the bondage of poverty. He is going to miraculously rescue you from the bondage of sexual sins. He is going to miraculously rescue you from the bondage of sickness and disease.

If you believe it, say to out loud: "I am positioned for a miraculous rescue!" Get ready for a supernatural move of God!

You Shall Be Loosed.

Secondly, to be *rescued* means to be "loosed from…"

In the text, Peter was loosed from his chains and his shackles in a way that could only be done by God.

Herod wanted to make sure that Peter didn't escape, and so he placed guards in the prison to guard him.

There were four rotating shifts of four guards, which equated to sixteen guards in all! It would then seem that there would have been no way for Peter to have left the prison. Peter would surely have had to stand trial the next day. But during that time, the church was praying.

While Peter was locked up, the church was praying that God would take care of Peter. The church was praying that God would rescue Peter.

We should never stop praying. If we have to go all night praying, we should, but we should never stop praying.

The saints of God prayed without ceasing for Peter. They were not criticizing him. They were not laughing at his demise. They were praying! And I believe that they must have been saying, "Lord, You see Peter down there in that prison cell. Loose him, Jesus!" They must have been saying, "Lord, You see Peter bound by chains. Break him free, Jesus!" Undoubtedly, the saints must have been praying, "Lord, it is not that we don't have needs of our own, but we believe that when we put other person's needs before ours, You will also show up on our behalf. Show up, Jesus!"

Peter was asleep in the prison, and the church was praying.

There were chains on each of Peter's wrists, and there was a guard on each side of him and more guards at the doorway, but there is nothing too hard for God to do.

If you desire to be loosed, if you are in need of a divine intervention, God is able to meet you at your point of need.

Herod imprisoned Peter, but that wasn't enough. He had to also chain him, possibly thinking that his mechanisms could override the power of the Almighty God. But Satan's chains are no match for God's power.

Prayer Changes Things

While the church folks were praying, a bright light appeared in the prison cell where Peter was, and an angel appeared. The angel appeared to find Peter fast asleep!

Now can you imagine the assurance that Peter must have had in God? Because here Peter was, imprisoned and chained. He was about to be tried and possibly executed the next morning, but he found rest. Peter was at peace. He was fast asleep during his midnight hour.

You may be experiencing midnight, but you should rest easy, as the difference between midnight and a new day is just sixty seconds.

In sixty seconds, you can go from past failures to present success. In sixty seconds, you can go from past hurts to present cure. In sixty seconds, you can be free, because God always shows up in our midnight hour!

Peter was so fast asleep that the angel had to poke Peter hard and say, "Wake up! Get up! You are about to be rescued!"

As a people, it is time for us to get up as we are about to be rescued!

Sometimes our situations can drain us and push us to sleep, but we need to get up. God is about to change our situation.

I believe that God divinely appointed this time for a change. Your season is about to change. Your deliverance has come. Your breakthrough is here.

The angel said to Peter, "Get up quickly!"

You see, when God shows up on your behalf, you have got to move quickly. When God shows up on your behalf, you have to move at His command.

Someone who is being rescued cannot stay in the same place of bondage. You can't stay in the same place of imprisonment. If you stay there, you will remain bound, so you have to get up.

Church, it is getting up time! It is time for you to get up in your spirit, get up in your mind. Change your position, because it is getting up time!

The minute that Peter got up, the Bible says that the chains fell off from his hands, and then the angel told Peter to put on his clothes and sandals and to wrap his coat around him, and this got me to be thinking. Why would the angel of God tell Peter to put on his clothes and sandals and to then wrap his coat around him? As I thought about this, the Lord began to show me that Peter's clothes represented his spiritual covering.

You Are Covered

If Peter was to get out of the prison alive, he had to be spiritually covered.

Undoubtedly, Peter must have had on some prison clothes, but the Angel instructed him to cover himself—to use *his* clothes as a spiritual covering so that not even the guards who were around could recognize him!

Listen, when Jesus recues you, He covers you! You are covered!

You are covered by the blood of Jesus Christ of Nazareth. You are covered by Jesus's blood from the crown of your head to the soles of your feet.

When the enemy looks at you, he doesn't see you. He sees the blood of Jesus!

The blood of Jesus covers you and sets you free. The blood of Jesus is a blessing to you but a deterrent to the enemy. You are covered!

Follow Jesus

So the angel told Peter to get up, then the angel told him to put on his spiritual covering, and the third thing that the angel told Peter to do was to *follow him.*

Your see, we will never be rescued until we follow Jesus. You can go your own way if you want to. You can do your own thing if you want to. But you will never be rescued until you follow Jesus!

We have to follow Jesus's teachings, we have to follow Jesus's leadings, and we have to follow Jesus!

Peter obeyed the angel's command, although at first he wasn't even sure it was happening in the real. At first, Peter thought it was just a vision, but it was the real thing.

Miracles are real! They happened in the past, and they are still happening today. They are not gimmicks! They are real!

Leave the Baggage Behind

When God rescues you, He looses you from whatever chains that are binding you. God not only frees you, but he also looses you completely! He looses you completely because note this: Peter didn't take any part of his shackles or chains with him. He left them behind, and he followed God's lead!

When God looses you, He wants you to leave the baggage behind. He doesn't want you to carry it with you!

The angel took Peter past the first guard, and then the second guard, and the guards didn't even see them. The guards were blinded by Peter's covering. However, there was still one more barrier to his freedom. The iron gate that led to the city was in front of them, but then suddenly, without pushing on it, the gate swung open by itself!

Obstacles Shall Be Removed

When Jesus miraculously rescues you, you don't have to do a thing, because Jesus will break down barriers, He will tear down walls, He will destroy obstacles, and it will happen suddenly.

Think about it. How many doors has God opened wide for you in the past? You didn't have to push, you didn't have to turn a knob or pry, but the door just flung open, and you walked right through it.

You should see yourselves just walking through an open door right now—a door that God has just flung wide open for you as He miraculously rescues you!

See God clearing the way for you. See God creating opportunities for you. See God delivering you!

Suddenly, the gate swung wide open for Peter to go through. Your miracle is going to happen suddenly!

God Provides a Way of Escape

Peter escaped from prison, and the reason he *escaped* from prison was because there was no other way out!

When God rescues you, it is an escape because there is no other way out!

Sometimes, God allows us to be placed in situations that only He and He alone can rescue us. God doesn't want us giving the glory to man, so He causes us to find ourselves in situations that when we get rescued, we know without a shadow of a doubt that it had to be God and God alone who brought us out!

The angel then led Peter through the gate and went the length of one street, and then suddenly, just as he had appeared, the angel left.

Verse 11 of the chapter says, "And when Peter was come to himself, he said, now I know of a surety, that the Lord hath sent His angels, and hath delivered me."

In other words, when Peter looked back at what the Lord did for Him, when Peter looked back at how the Lord miraculously rescued him from the hands of the enemy, Peter began to worship God. He began to give God the praise. Peter said, "Surely it was God who delivered me."

When you look back at what the Lord did for you last year or last night, when you look back at how the Lord miraculously rescued you in the past, when you consider that it will indeed take another miraculous rescue to get you out of the situation that you are now in, are you willing to do as Peter did and begin to give God the praise?

You should praise God regardless of your circumstance. You should praise God regardless of how you feel. The scripture reminds us to bless the Lord at all times! Men ought to always praise God!

The Answer Is at the Door

Now there is something remarkable in this story that I don't want you to miss. After Peter got through praising God, Peter went to the house where the saints had gathered praying for his deliverance, and he knocked at the door. *Knock, knock, knock!* A damsel, a servant girl named Rhoda, came to the door, and inquired who it was.

Peter must have answered, "It is me" without stating his name, because the Bible said that "she recognized that it was the voice of Peter."

The damsel Rhoda got excited, yet she failed to let Peter into the house. Instead, she ran back to the others who had gathered and were still praying for Peter's deliverance, and she said to them, "Peter is at the door!"

But the praying church folks, the church folks who had gathered at a prayer meeting, the church folks who love to pray *but* had failed to believe, said, "You must be mad! Peter couldn't be at the door. It must be an angel!" And they kept on praying, and the Bible said, "Peter kept on knocking."

When I read this, the Lord said, "Tell My people that the answer is at the door!" God said, "Tell My people that the miracle that they have been praying for, that thing that they have been trusting Me for, that healing that they have been fasting for, the answer is at the door!"

God said, "You have prayed, but it is now time to believe! The answer is at the door!"

The people had been praying for God to deliver Peter. They had been praying for God to set Peter free, and God had answered their prayers. God delivered Peter. He set Peter free and sent Peter to them, but the prayer meeting folks had failed to believe. They kept the answer to their prayers waiting at the door!

But God says, "Open the door and let the answer in!"

OPEN the door and take ahold of your miracle.

> For God shall supply all your needs according to His riches in glory in Christ Jesus. (Phil. 4:19)

OPEN the door and take ahold of your deliverance.

> When the righteous cry for help, the Lord hears and delivers them out of all their troubles. (Ps. 34:17)

OPEN the door and take ahold of your breakthrough.

> Remember not the former things, nor consider the things of old. Behold, God is doing a new thing; now it springs forth, do you not per-

ceive it? He will make a way in the wilderness and rivers in the desert. (Isa. 43:18–19)

OPEN the door and take hold of your peace.

Fear not, for God is with you; be not dismayed, for He is your God; He will strengthen you, He will help you, He will uphold you with His righteous right hand.

Behold, all who are incensed against you shall be put to shame and confounded; those who strive against you shall be as nothing and shall perish. You shall seek those who contend with you, but you shall not find them; those who war against you shall be as nothing at all.

For the Lord your God, hold your right hand; it is He who say to you, "Fear not, He is the one who helps you." (Isa. 41:10–13)

OPEN the door and take ahold of a greater anointing.

The Spirit of the Lord is upon you, because he has anointed you to proclaim good news to the poor. He has sent you to proclaim liberty to the captives and the recovering of sight to the blind, to set at liberty those who are oppressed. (Luke 4:18)

OPEN the door and take hold of your salvation.

For "everyone who calls on the name of the Lord will be saved." (Rom. 10:13)

For God so loved the world, that He gave His only begotten son, that whosoever believeth in Him shall be saved! (John 3:16).

The answer is at the door!

God is performing a miraculous rescue right now.

Somebody is getting their healing right now.

Somebody is being restored right now.

Somebody is being rescued right now.

God is bringing somebody out right now.

Because the answer is at the door!

This nation shall experience the greatest revival ever, because the answer to this nation's problems is at the door!

In 2 Chronicles 7:14, God says, "If my people, which are called by my name, shall humble themselves, and pray, and seek my face, and turn from their wicked ways; then will I hear from heaven, and will forgive their sin, and will heal their land."

If you believe it, praise God and receive the answer to your prayers. Praise God and receive God's best into your lives!

Keep walking humbly before God. The answer is at the door!

Whatever you have been praying for, believing God for, waiting for, God says, "He has answered your prayers, and your answer is at the door. Open the door and receive your answer!"

Believe the word that God is giving to you right now—the answer is at the door!

CHAPTER 3

Desire, Disappointment, Decision

All my life, all that I have known is that of the life of a Christian. It was mine as it was every young girl's dream to meet and marry the man of her dreams, have a family, and live happily ever after.

At the age of twenty, I met a man whom I married two years after. We were both active in our churches. However, after marriage, I started attending his church. It had ripped my heart apart because he had initially promised to have us attend my church. It was a sign for things to come.

After the honeymoon and the settling then came the reality that I had made the biggest mistake of my life. The man that I had known to be his pastor's armor bearer, men's president, and choir member was proving to be a pretender in every way.

His extramarital affairs while remaining active in the church caused me to often wonder if I was dreaming, and I was wishing someone would quickly wake me from the horrible dream.

As every young wife, I tried to do everything possible to make the marriage work. And when my efforts failed, I asked the Lord what I needed to do. God told me that I was not in His will. This was when I learned for the first time about being in the permissive will and the perfect will of God. I was in God's permissive will but not His perfect will, and there was only one way out.

The birth of our son two years after our marriage had only provided a temporary distraction for him because by the time our son turned three years of age, I had to ask him to move out of the house as I was not prepared to live the rest my life being unhappy. I wanted to be in the perfect will of God for my life.

I still remember like it was yesterday the day that he moved out. For one week starting from the night he moved out, the presence of God was so heavy and real in my room that it would wake me from my sleep. I would be sitting up in bed, looking around the room to see God. When I didn't see Him and only feel His presence, I would give Him thanks for His presence and went back to bed. It would happen again the next night for seven days. It was like God was telling me, "Welcome back, my daughter. You are now in my perfect will."

After seven years of marriage, I was back in God's perfect will to include returning to the church of my spiritual development. The road thereafter still wasn't easy, but it was worth it.

Romans 8:28 says, "All things work together for my good, for them who love the Lord, to them who are the called according to His purpose." Although my desire had led to my disappointment, my decision continues to work for my good!

The Sermon

Genesis 29:16–31

The Lord led me to a typical story of tragedy. It was a tragedy that happened in a different form, but nonetheless a tragedy and one filled with lessons to be learned—lessons that can long be remembered as we continue the tradition of celebrating mothers.

> And Laban had two daughters: the name of the elder was Leah, and the name of the younger was Rachel.
> Leah was tender eyed; but Rachel was beautiful and well favoured.

And Jacob loved Rachel; and said, I will serve thee 7 years for Rachel thy younger daughter.

And Laban said, It is better that I give her to thee than that I should give her to another man: abide with me.

And Jacob served 7 years for Rachel; and they seemed unto him but a few days, for the love he had to her.

And Jacob said unto Laban, Give me my wife, for my days are fulfilled, that I may go in unto her.

And Laban gathered together all the men of the place and made a feast.

And it came to pass in the evening that he took Leah his daughter, and brought her to him; and he went in unto her.

And Laban gave unto his daughter Leah Zilph his maid for an handmaid.

And it came to pass, that in the morning, behold, it was Leah: and he said to Laban, What is this thou hast done unto me? Did not I serve with thee for Rachel? Wherefore then hast thou beguiled me?

And Laban said, It must not be so done in our country, to give the younger before the firstborn.

Fulfill her week, and we will give thee this also for the service which thou shalt serve with me yet 7 other years.

And Jacob did so, and fulfilled her week; and he gave him Rachel his daughter to wife also.

And Laban gave to Rachel his daughter Bilhah his handmaid to be her maid.

And he went in also unto Rachel, and he loved also Rachel more than Leah, and served with him yet 7 other years.

And when the Lord saw that Leah was
hated, he opened her womb: but Rachel was barren. (Gen. 29:16–31)

THE STORY that we have just read is a story that would break
any one's heart, particularly the hearts of women and more so mothers. IT speaks about two sisters in rivalry against each other. But this
morning, I want to first and foremost highlight the struggles and
triumphs of one of the sisters, the one named Leah.

LEAH was involved in an Old Testament love triangle.

ASK your neighbor, "Do you know what a love triangle is?"

LEAH, as we have read, was the oldest daughter of Laban, the
sister to Rachel, and the first wife of Jacob.

BUT Leah was what many would call today a plain Jane. She
did not possess the physical attractiveness that her younger sister
possessed.

AND to really give you a graphic picture of what she looked
like, Leah probably looked like God *did not* spend enough time on
her.

AND added to that, it would have seemed that although she
was the firstborn—and the custom at the time was that the firstborn was to be given in marriage first—Leah did not get a proposal.
Instead, it was her sister, Rachel, the beautiful one, who got the proposal. SO FAR, we see two things stacking up against Leah. For one
thing, she was ugly. She was unattractive. And secondly, although she
was the eldest of the two daughters, no man seemed to have wanted
to marry her. She was a reject as far as men were concerned!

LEAH'S father then went on and did the unthinkable thing—
HE decided that he would trick a man into marrying her.

LISTEN. Let me just pause to say this: ALL those women
who are thinking of tricking a man into marrying them, you better
be careful. It may well just backfire on you!

ALL those women who have already tricked a man into marrying you, you must be feeling the pain! But all is not lost! God's mercy
is able to rescue you!

LEAH'S father, Laban, must have thought that if Leah, his first-born, was ever going to get married, he would have had to use her as a ploy to trap Jacob into marrying her.

BUT don't forget that the name Jacob means "deceiver."

SO Leah was married to a deceiver!

TELL somebody, "That is a horrible situation to be in!"

LEAH already had to deal with the fact that she was unattractive. She was already dealing with the fact that no man wanted to marry her.

AND now on top of that, she was being made to deal with the fact that she was married to a deceiver!

I FEEL like asking somebody, "WHO are you married to in the spirit?"

ARE you married to the deceiver, the devil, OR are you married to God?

WHO are you spiritually married to?

JACOB was forced to marry Leah.

AND now LEAH found herself in a relationship with a man who did not love her. DO you know what that feels like?

Living with a man that does not love you?

Married to a man that could not care less about you?

DO you know what that feels like?

LEAH found herself in a stressful situation—a situation that made her feel unwanted and unloved. And so in an attempt to win her husband's affection, in an attempt to feel loved, LEAH decided to become a mother.

YOU see, being a mother is a beautiful thing.

THERE is nothing more precious than knowing that you brought a life into this world. THERE is nothing more precious than knowing that you nurtured and cared for a life that is flesh of your flesh. BEING a mother is a beautiful thing.

Even if you were not the one to have given birth to the child.

BECAUSE I know that some of the mothers here today became mothers by adoption. Physically OR spiritually.

SO LEAH decided to make the best of her situation.

She refused to roll over and die.

She refused to throw in the towel.

LEAH decided that she had to do something to change her situation, AND that something had to be with God's help.

YOU SEE, verse 31 of the chapter that we read said, "Now the Lord saw that Leah was unloved, and He opened her womb, but Rachel was barren."

NOW BEFORE we move on, I WONDER IF YOU can catch this in the spiritual realm and cry out, "Lord, open my womb!"

SAY, "Lord, I am unloved, but open my womb! LORD, I feel rejected by family and society. I don't seem to fit in. But open my womb! I NEED a change in my situation, Lord. I need to become productive. I need to produce some children in the Spirit. LORD! MAKE me a spiritual mother and open my womb!"

GOD opened the womb of the rejected Leah and caused Rachel, the one who was accepted based on man's opinion of beauty, to be barren.

AND THIS tells me something.

IT tells me that GOD has a heart for those who are rejected by men.

GOD has compassion for those who have found themselves in an uncomfortable place.

WHEN others have turned their backs on you, God will cause His favor to shine upon you.

YOUR outward beauty does not automatically qualify you to be a mother.

Your outward beauty does not pass you fit to be a mother.

TELL YOUR neighbor, "IT takes more than outward appearance to be a mother!" (Repeat.)

YOU may dress right. You may look right. BUT if your heart is not in the right place, you may as well be barren!

IF your heart is not in the right place, GOD will close up your spiritual womb!

LEAH was a woman of prayer.

She did not have outer beauty, but her heart was in the right place.

SHE understood GOD to be a faithful source.

AND she had a DESIRE to be loved!

TELL somebody, "I have a desire to be loved. I want to feel a part of the scheme of things! I want to belong! I want to know that purpose is on my life!"

EVERY human being will admit that they desire to be loved.

They desire to be loved unconditionally, unreservedly, unmistakenly, passionately, and completely.

THEY want to be loved for who they are rather than for what they have OR have not.

ASK your neighbor, "Whose love do you desire?"

IS IT the love of your children?

Is it the love of a spouse?

Is it the love of your own mother?

"WHOSE love do you desire?"

DESIRE speaks of a longing, a craving, a yearning for something that you do not have.

WHOSE love have you been wishing for?

Whose love have you been begging for?

"WHOSE love do you desire?"

I FEEL like pausing and asking you to say to your neighbor, "I know that I have made a lot of mistakes, but do you love me?

"Neighbor, I know that I don't dress quite right, but do you love me?

"Neighbor, I know that I don't seem to fit in, but do you love me?

"Neighbor, I know that I seem unlovable, but do you love me?"

SAY, "Neighbor, I DESIRE to be loved. I am barely hanging on for a glimpse of hope. SO just ANSWER me. Do you love me?"

IT WAS Leah's desire to be loved.

That pushed her into becoming a mother.

LEAH became pregnant and started having children.

THE first child that she had, she named him **Reuben.**

REUBEN means "behold a son" OR "a gift is given."

BECAUSE LEAH thought, *Surely the Lord had seen my affliction.*

LEAH named her son Reuben in honor of God, because for God to have opened up her womb, it must have been that He had seen her affliction.

I WONDER if we have anybody here this morning who believes that the Lord has seen their affliction?

YOU have been feeling the pain of having lost your own mother.

YOU don't even feel like celebrating today because you are still grieving your mother's persistent illness or death.

ANYBODY here this morning who believes that the Lord has seen their affliction?

You have been feeling the pain of having lost your child or children in childbirth.

You have been feeling the guilt of having aborted your child.

You have been feeling the pain of having lost your child or children at the hands of gunmen.

YOU have been struggling with a wayward child.

ANYBODY here this morning believes that God has seen their affliction?

YOU have been crying day in and day out over your children who Have forsaken you. They have turned their backs on you.

WELL, DON'T lose hope. JUST give birth to your Reuben!

GOD said, "THIS is the morning to give spiritual birth!"

I HOPE we have some doctors in the house and prayer warriors in the house who are ready to help you deliver.

IT IS time to give birth to your spiritual Reuben.

IT IS time to give birth to your spiritual son, to your spiritual gift.

GOD HAS seen your affliction.

And for that He has blessed your womb!

TELL your neighbor, "God has blessed me in spite of my affliction!"

OUT OF evil has cometh good!

> FOR many are the afflictions of the righteous, but the Lord delivereth them out of them all. (Ps. 34:19)

TELL somebody else, "Get out the scissors. YOU will soon have to cut the umbilical cord!"

A spiritual Reuben is being born!

LEAH then decided to have another child.

Because although the Lord had seen her affliction, she still required more.

YOU see, it wasn't just enough for God to have seen her affliction.

She also wanted God to hear her cries!

IT IS one thing to see something.

But when it's possible to also hear what you have seen, it can make a big difference.

IT IS one thing to see your baby born, but you also want to hear your baby cry.

SO LEAH named her second child **Simeon, which means** "God hears."

LEAH said, "Because the Lord has heard that I am unloved, He has given me this child!"

TELL somebody, "GOD hears my cries!"

"YOU may not have heard when I woke up at three o'clock in the morning, crying out to Jesus on behalf of my children, BUT God heard my cries!

"YOU may not have heard me crying through sleepless nights.

"YOU may not have heard me crying and begging the police to grant mercy for my son's behavior.

"BUT God heard my cries!"

TELL somebody else, "YOU may not have heard me crying when my daughter got pregnant out of wedlock.

"YOU may not have heard me crying out to Jesus for the money to pay the school fees and to keep food on the table, BUT God heard my cries!

"AND he has blessed me and is blessing me spiritually!"

High five three people and tell them, "I am blessed, and I am ready for an overdose of God's blessings!"

IT WASN'T long after that Leah began feeling a need to be connected.

YOU see, a person who is unloved has a constant need to be intimate!

LEAH felt unloved, and she longed for real intimacy!

TELL somebody, "Having sex with somebody who doesn't love you isn't intimacy! That's lust!"

INTIMACY has to do with a true connection—a closeness with someone that loves you.

LEAH wanted real intimacy, SO she named her third child **Levi!**

THE name Levi means "attachment—to be joined."

DO WE have anybody here this morning who is ready for true intimacy with God?

ANYBODY here ready to get lost in God's presence?

For in His presence, there is fullness of joy.

And at His right hand, there are pleasures forevermore!

ANYBODY here ready to fast and pray until a change comes?

For the prayers of a righteous man availeth much!

ANYBODY here ready to be drawn closer to God?

For who shall separate us from the love of God?

Shall tribulation or distress or persecution or famine or nakedness or peril or sword?

Nothing shall be able to separate us from the love of God!

LEAH wanted intimacy, so God gave her Levi!

GOD loves intimacy. He wants to be close to us.

MOTHERS! When you put God first in your life, He will put your concerns first.

IF YOU want your children saved, draw closer to God. Get attached to HIM.

IF YOU want generational curses to be broken off your families, become a friend of God and use the authority that He has given you.

For greater is He that is in you than he that is within the world!

IF YOU want to know the secrets of God's heart, come under His covering and know that "He that dwelleth in the secret place of the Most High shall abide under the shadows of the Almighty" (Ps. 91:1).

I am talking about the desire to be loved!

IF YOU feel unloved, draw close. Get attached to God who loves you unconditionally!

LEAH represents the type of people who we ought to be in GOD. SHE was never satisfied!

ONE OF the problems that I find among the people of God is that they are satisfied with very little.

They settle for less than they should have!

LEAH was unloved, and so she had a hunger and thirsting for love.

JUST like many here this morning, LEAH wanted to know what it felt like to be loved by her husband.

She wanted to know what it felt like to be appreciated as a mother.

AND SO she decided, "I am going to have a **fourth** child!"

TELL somebody, "I want to give birth again—spiritual birth!"

LEAH's quest for love reminds me of some women when in their search for love.

They keep having children for the same man or for different men.

And they do so with the hope that having children will make men love them.

SOME find love, but more often than not, most don't find love.

AND SO eventually, they are forced to turn their attention away from themselves.

And hopefully they turn their attention to God.

THIS was the case of Leah.

IF you recall, the birth of her first three sons had to do *with* her.

SON no. 1 was "God sees my affliction."

SON no. 2 was "God hears my cries."

SON no. 3 was "attachment, a need to feel attached/close to the man that she loved, who was not loving her back."

LEAH realized that putting all the attention on herself was not causing a change in her circumstance.

AND so she decided to turn her attention away from herself and toward God.

SO Leah named her fourth child **Judah**, which means **"praise."**

FOR she said, "This time, I will Praise the Lord!"

LEAH said, "This time, I am giving birth to my praise!"

TURN to two people and say to them, "Excuse me, but this morning, I am going to give birth to my praise."

TELL someone else, "Placing the attention on myself has not provided the results that I desire. SO this morning, I am taking the attention from off myself. And I am putting my attention on God. AND I AM giving birth to my praise!"

I AM NOT through preaching.

BUT I feel like pausing to allow somebody to give birth to their praise!

IF you feel unloved, IF you are a mother rejected by your family, rejected by your friends, rejected by even some church folks, THEN THIS is the time to give birth to your praise!

IF you have been dealing with feelings of unacceptance, IF people constantly criticize you and persecute you because you don't seem to fit into their status quo, THIS is the time to give birth to your praise!

Ask your neighbor kindly to give you pass, make you praise God.

ASK your neighbor to move out of your way and to give you some space because you are about to give birth to your praise!

MOTHERS!

We know what it is like to give birth in the natural.

BEFORE birth takes place, we have to deal with the labor pains.

SO IF pain is rocking your bodies right now, that is okay.

It is only labor pain!

IF you feel pressure weighing down on you, that is all right.

It is only labor pain!

TELL your neighbor, "Don't be alarmed. IT IS the labor pains that you are feeling!"

YOU see, pain precedes birth!

Discomfort precedes birth!

Contractions precedes birth!

SO give yourselves some room, because the doctor says...

Dr. Jesus says, "EVERYTIME that you feel the contraction, every time that you feel the pain, just PUSH!"

PUSH and give birth to your praise!

PUSH! PUSH! PUSH your praise OUT! PUSH!

YOU may have to hold on to somebody's hands for extra support.

BUT PUSH!

YOU may not feel like you have the strength to give birth, but PUSH!

YOU may be weary from your struggles, but PUSH!

FOR THE Lord inhabits the praises of His people!

GIVE birth to your praise AND praise God in advance.

FOR when the praises go up, the blessings will come down!

PRAISE God in advance for your child that will be saved.

Praise God in advance for your bills that will be paid.

Praise God in advance for a change in your situation.

TOO many people have gone weary in the church.

Too many are settling for less.

Too many are not reaping the harvest that God has for them.

SO OFFER a sacrifice of praise this morning and PRAISE HIM!

WE ARE in a delivery room.

IT IS time for another spiritual birth to take place.

Prayer warriors!

Find some people who need help with their delivery.

BECAUSE everybody in here must give birth to their praise today!

HOLD on to somebody's hands and tell them, "I am helping you through this. So PUSH!"

THE devil is a liar.

You have what it takes to give God all the praise!

WHEN DAVID wanted to confound his enemies, he began praising God in a crazy way.

He began dancing like he was a madman!

HE wanted to escape his enemies.

He wanted to get out alive!

DO we have any crazy praisers in the house this morning?

DO WE have anybody willing to dance like you are crazy and mess up the enemies plans?

WHERE are the crazy praisers?

LET'S have a dance of crazy praise.

YOUR dance of crazy praise is your dance to celebrate Mother's Day!

LET's have some music so that you can DANCE your frustrations away!

DO the celebration dance!

SEND up a PRAISE against your troubles!

SEND up a praise against your sickness!

LET this be the moment that you give birth to your praise!

SIT DOWN IF you can. I have to finish this message.

THE Bible says that Leah stopped having children after she gave birth to Judah.

After she gave birth to praise, she stopped having children.

YOU see, Leah was satisfied with the results of her praise!

She no longer depended on the love of a man, not when she had the love of God.

LEAH no longer allowed her circumstances to dictate how she felt and how she lived.

BUT instead, she allowed her faith in God to dictate her feelings.

BUT don't you know that the devil never gives up?

THE devil hates to see a good thing going.

The devil hates to know that you have gotten the victory.

The devil hates to know that you have gotten past your past.

SO he will try again to steal your joy.

LEAH allowed her faith to be weakened by her sister Rachel's ungodly/deceitful actions.

BECAUSE Rachel was barren and jealous of Leah's ability to have children, Rachel persuaded Jacob to lie with her maidservant and to allow her maidservant to bear him a child.

AND you know how some men are.

They never seem to be able to say no to sex!

SO Jacob quickly agreed.

And Rachel's maidservant bore him a child.

LEAH then became jealous.

She was jealous because Rachel now had a child for Jacob through her maidservant.

AND what do you think Leah did?

LEAH went and persuaded Jacob to lie with *her* maidservant and to bear him not just one child but two children.

Him having gone in to her on *two* separate occasions, JACOB was certainly having the time of his life!

MEN can't seem to say no to sex, even at the expense of it destroying their families.

AND IF that wasn't enough, Leah agreed to a barter arrangement with Rachel.

THAT agreement happened when Reuben found some fruits that seemingly enhanced a woman's fertility and brought it to his mother, Leah.

Rachel saw the fruits and asked Leah for them.

LEAH then did an even more disappointing thing.

LEAH, in remembering how for years Rachel had enjoyed the love of Jacob whilst she longed for it, agreed to give Rachel the fruits, but only if Rachel allowed her to lie with Jacob and bear another child.

MY God, this reminds me of an almost similar deception which took place earlier in scripture when Jacob had robbed Esau of his birthright!

LEAH had obviously descended from her original trust in the Lord.

YOU see, she was drawn by jealousy into imitating her sister's godless practices.

AND she had ascribed her children to luck and good fortune rather than to the Sovereign Lord.

LEAH no longer honored God in the names that she gave to her surrogate sons.

SHE named one of her surrogate sons **Gad,** which means "luck."

AND the other was named **Ashner**, which means "happiness."

AND then her fifth son with Jacob was named **Issachar**, which means "there is a reward."

AND that is **disappointment!**

HOW can someone go from acknowledging God as the Covenant-Keeper TO allowing these her new sons to be born as a reward that she had earned by her "selfless" gift?

THAT is disappointment!

TELL somebody, "If you no longer desire the move of God in your life, YOU are sure to meet up with disappointment."

LEAH was initially in a place of desire, a place of yearning and wanting the ultimate gifts of love and appreciation, so much so that she depended on God.

SO much so that she called out to GOD, and He saw her affliction. He heard her cries.

He understood her need for attachment, for intimacy.

AND He accepted her birth of praise.

BUT NOW LEAH had moved from that place of desire and had found herself in a place of disappointment.

WHISPER to somebody, "Don't lose your desire, or else you will find yourself in a place of disappointment."

PEOPLE OF God, no matter what the enemy throws at you, don't lose your desire for God.

NO matter the circumstance, don't lose your desire for God.

YES! You have been carrying the burden for a long time.

YES! You thought that when you praised God, everything would have been smooth sailing from thereon.

BUT God never said that the road would be easy.

He only promised to help you along the way.

"Don't lose your desire for God!" NEVER stop praising him!

BECAUSE if you stop praising God, you will meet disappointment!

IF you stop praising God, that problem that had ceased to exist will recur.

IF you stop praising God, that child that God had delivered from drug addiction may well find his/her way back to a life of drugs and prostitution.

IF you stop praising God, the financial breakthrough that you were beginning to experience will dry up.

NEVER stop praising God!

KEEP the praise going.

Regardless of what's happening around you, keep the praise going!

BUT YOU might say, "What if I am already in a place of disappointment?"

WHEN others were giving birth to their praise just now, you could not give birth because you weren't pregnant to begin with.

YOU might be wondering what to do if you are at the place where you are disappointed with yourself.

YOU are disappointed with your behavior.

YOU are disappointed with your short-sightedness.

YOU are disappointed with your sinfulness.

SO much so that your sinfulness has caused a spiritual abortion.

AND because of the spiritual abortion, you could not give birth to your praise?

WHAT do you do if you are already at your place of disappointment?

IF YOU are already at your place of disappointment, DO what the woman did at the banquet held at Simon the Pharisee's house.

WHILST weeping, she fell at Jesus's feet, and she proceeded to wash His feet with her tears and to wipe His feet with her hair.

THE woman was a sinner!

But she got the compassion of Jesus.

FOR He saw that she was not ashamed of her tears.

She was ashamed of her sins.

AND I believe that THIS woman wept not only for herself, but she wept for all women who fell from their highest and purest dreams.

YOU see, a woman's tears have the power to move the heart of God!

IF you find yourself in a place of disappointment, just weep like Mary of Bethany, who cried when her brother Lazarus had died.

HER tears caused Jesus Himself to weep.

AND then it moved Him to raise Lazarus from the dead.

YOU see, a woman's tears have the power to change the outcome of life's sorrows!

IF YOU find yourself in a place of disappointment, just weep like Mary of Magdalene, who had watched as they crucified her Lord.

AND thinking that He was still dead, when she could not find His body, SHE wept. Because for her, if Jesus is dead, life isn't worth living!

IF Jesus is not in your life, life isn't worth living!

IT IS not hard to see that Jesus had preempted the tears of persons such as Mary of Magdalene.

He had determined that He would raise from the dead in three days so that in His resurrection, we have new life.

YOU see, a woman's tears have the power to make Jesus bring the dead to Christ back to life!

WOMEN and MEN alike, IF you are already in a place of disappointment, just weep!

WEEP because tears are a language that God understands!

WEEP over your sins!

WEEP over your failures.

WEEP over your shortcomings.

YOUR tears will move God to action!

DO WE have any weeping mothers in the house today?

MOTHERS who were unable to give birth to their praise because they were not pregnant to begin with.

DO we have any weeping mothers in the house today?

YES! You gave birth to your praise.

BUT it was out of a heart of concern for those who have lost their desire.

And are now in a place of disappointment, YOU feel the need to weep for them.

ARE THERE any weeping mothers in the house today?

MOTHERS who are willing to weep over this backslidden nation?

WHERE are the weeping mothers?

THE mothers who know and understand the power of their tears?

MOTHERS who know the influence of their tears in the presence of Jesus?

WHEN women weep, Jesus identifies the intensity of our feelings.

THIS IS not just about your breakthrough or about your family's breakthrough.

THIS is also about the breakthrough of those outside of your circle of family and friends, persons who are in need of desperate help and don't even realize it.

PERSONS who have condemned themselves to a life of crime and violence.

Persons who have condemned themselves to Satan's hellish plans.

DO WE have mothers in the house, mothers who are willing to stand in the gap against child abuse?

MOTHERS who are willing to stand in the gap against rape and incest?

MOTHERS who are willing to stand in the gap against the complacency of our men?

WHERE are the weeping mothers?

Mothers who are willing to shed their tears at the altar on behalf of the many who are lost and dying?

WHERE are the weeping mothers? LET me see your hands!

AS mothers, it is time to bawl out before God!

LEAH'S place of disappointment only brought her continuous sorrow and grief.

And as such, IT forced her to make the decision to return to the One who loved her the best.

LEAH named her sixth child Zebulun, which means "honor."

Because she said, "Now my husband will honour me and glorify me."

LEAH even had a seventh child, a daughter this time whom she named **Dinah**, which means "judgment."

SEVEN IS God's perfect number.

SO THE TABLES were once again in her favor because God once again intervened in her situation.

And all it took was Leah's decision to put God first!

LEAH's third son, Levi, formed the family through whom Israel's priesthood comes.

AND her fourth son, Judah, is the father of the royal family, the one through which the Messiah, the Anointed Deliverer, comes.

BY God's design, LEAH was buried among the greatest of biblical prophets.

Her grave is with Abraham, Sarah, Isaac, and Rebekah!

TELL somebody, "That's what the right decision does!"

IT causes God to place His mark upon you.

IT gets God's attention.

And it facilitates the move of God in your life.

Desire, disappointment, decision!

Make the right decision today!

GOD bless you!

CHAPTER 4

Something Big Is Coming Out of This

The birth of my son and only child on May 4, 1994, is God's best gift to me.

Jordan Davion Samuels is not only a great son. He is a great born-again child of God. At the age of nine years, without any prompting from his grandmother or from me, he asked to be baptized. It was unplanned. During a baptismal service at our church, he simply walked over to me and said, "Mom, I want to be baptized." And without hesitation, I walked with him to the room where other males were being prepared for baptism. The feeling that came over me was unexplainable. The only way that I can state it is to say that I literally felt my womb like it gave birth all over again.

My son was raised without the presence of his biological father who chose to not be active in his life after our marriage ended. My son was almost three years of age at the time. God, who always makes a way, used my brother and father to serve as the male figures in his life while his grandmother and I steered him to Christ.

Jordan grew up being very active in our church. He was a member of the choir, the sign language ministry, and yes, he also preached the Word.

Many prophecies of him excelling were spoken over his life from a tender age, which left us amazed, because by society's stan-

dard, children with absentee fathers were not expected to do well...
but God.

When Jordan graduated from kindergarten, he wanted to be a
police officer. But by the time he got to high school, we noticed a
great change. Instead of watching shows that teenagers yearned for,
he was watching documentaries on aviation. He had a keen interest
in flying, designing, and repairing airplanes. It became his passion.

By the time he graduated from high school, there was only one
thing that he wanted to do—he wanted to become a commercial
airline pilot.

It is known throughout the world that it is extremely expensive
to undertake the requisite training and flight hours to become a commercial airline pilot. Plus, in addition to this, we wanted to ensure
that he also had a bachelor's degree to enhance his qualification when
there came a time that he was unable to fly.

My mom and I pondered our next move. We discussed it with a
friend who told us of a school in Jamaica that offered aviation training. He would be able to pursue a bachelor's in aircraft maintenance
and delay obtaining flight training. It was costly, but by faith, we
decided to enroll him in the school, and he became a part of the second cohort of students pursuing studies at the school.

After a year of pursuing studies at the school, we decided that
we had to find another way, as the school was still dealing with the
teething effects of being in its embryonic stage. He was not finding
the experience fulfilling, as the lecturers were increasingly becoming
absent from classes, plus his real passion was to fly airplanes. Added
to that, there were no other similar programs available to him locally.

I had discussed my frustrations with another friend who told
me of Florida Institute of Technology. He knew of someone who
had attended the school and had a great learning experience. We did
our research and found that they were listed among the best aviation
training institutions. He applied and he got accepted. Our family
was excited! There was only one drawback. Although he had also
won and was awarded a part of a scholarship from the school, the tui-
tion and housing fees were still extremely high. He was only nineteen
years of age at the time, and based on the immigration laws regarding

international students pursuing studies overseas, he had to live on campus until he attained at least the age of twenty-one years.

My mother and I prayed about it like we had nothing else to pray about. I remember I had nights when I would just wake up pondering our next move and asking God to make it clear to us what we should do. One night, as I lay awake talking to the Lord about it, He reminded me of the many sermons that I had preached about crazy faith. When I asked Him what He meant in reminding me of the sermons, He said, "You have often preached about persons having crazy faith. It is time that you live what you preach." That was all that I needed to hear. I knew that once God was with us in the process, it would be all right.

We gathered all the little money that we had, which included selling the house that I had owned after I had paid my ex-husband for his portion in the house, which is another story and testimony altogether.

In December 2012, my mom, Jordan, and I journeyed to Florida to get him settled in. He was scheduled to begin his studies on January 2013. After we had completed his orientation and had him fully settled, my mom and I started our preparations to return to Jamaica when Jordon broke down crying. He didn't want to stay.

I remember saying to him that night, "Jordan, that's all right. You don't have to stay. We can cancel your registration at the school, pack back up your things, and we can return to Jamaica together and figure something else out." I meant it because I totally understood how he had felt as we were a tight-knit family. We were never apart. This would have been the very first time. Over the years, when we took vacations together, we always returned home together. Except this time, it was not a vacation. The reality of him being left on his own in a foreign country had come home to him forcefully.

After he had cried some more and we held hands and prayed in our little hotel room, he kept silent for a while and then said, "Mom, I want to stay." His grandmother asked him if he was sure, and he said yes. It was at that time that God spoke to me and reminded me that Jordan pursuing a career in aviation was prophesied upon his life some three years prior. I shared with Mom and Jordan God's reminder to me of the prophecy, and we just broke out in praise to God.

The following morning, we had one last matter to finalize with the university's office, and when we went there, we met one of their elderly managers who just happened to be a Christian of similar beliefs. When he learned that we were from Jamaica and that Jordan was being left on his own, without us asking, he volunteered to pick Jordan up from his dormitory every Sunday and take him to church with him. He even gave us his personal contact details to include where he and his wife lived, and then he held hands with us and prayed. God used a stranger to be a blessing to us, as he lived up to his weekly commitment until Jordan was in the second year of his studies. He was only unable to continue his commitment because he retired and moved away.

The journey of putting my son through university in Florida was extremely rough financially. But we had one agreement with him. He was to remain focused and excel in his studies, which he did, and leave the rest to God and his grandmother and me. It was during this season that we learned firsthand that just because God is with you does not mean that the journey would be easy. Our financial resources were stretched to nothing, as not only were we paying for him to pursue his bachelor's degree, but we were also paying for him to pursue his pilot's training at the same time. It made us literally walk by faith and not by sight.

It was also during this season that we also experienced some of our greatest miracles, to include the many persons who God used to pour into our lives and support the vision. Our relationship with God grew to unimaginable levels as we had experienced His daily provisions.

Within Jordan's first year of university, he cofounded with a friend who was also from Jamaica the youth group Live to Inspire, which was featured internationally and locally through the various media platforms to include television and the print media. It also earned him an additional scholarship award from his school.

Live to Inspire was geared at motiving young people to excel despite the challenges that they had faced financially, racially, emotionally, and physically. The group of about twenty students traveled to churches and throughout the university, giving motivational speeches.

Then toward the end of Jordan's third year in university, he saw his father for the first time in over sixteen years. His interaction with his father prior to that was at the age of about six years. His father had called the home once when Jordan was about seven years, and he had apologized for how he had treated us during and after the marriage. He had also related that he had been having nightmares and visions with God instructing him to call us and to apologize to us. And if he hadn't done so, he had felt that he would have died. He had also promised to amend his ways by starting to financially support Jordan. He sent financial support twice after that, and then he stopped. We had surmised that the convictions of the Holy Spirit had worn off, and as such, he had simply returned to his old ways.

It was therefore a shocker when toward the end of Jordan's third year in university, his father called and advised that he wanted to reconnect with Jordan. He thereafter made plans and flew in to visit with Jordan on campus.

Jordan's only recollection of his father at that time was from photographs that he had seen. He advised that when he went to pick up his father from the airport, he kept staring at him, wondering if he had picked up the right person. He kept trying to match his father's face with the photographs that he had seen of him.

His father's visit had lasted a week, but the connection just did not unfold as his father had somehow anticipated. As to Jordan, his father was a complete stranger that he had grown to live without. One week of visit could not have immediately erased the years of neglect. His father did not quite understand this and did not take the lack of open-arm reception very well. However, there are no animosities, but there are still no relations outside of that which is biological. Casual and far and in between communications are what prevail.

Jordan graduated in December 2016 after his scheduled four years of study with a bachelor's degree in aeronautical science, and he is also a licensed commercial airline pilot. He was twenty-two years old. My mother wept literally as he took his walk for his degree and license. Whilst his uncle (my bother) and other family friends were cheering him on, I was in awe wondering if what was happening was for real. He was also one of the few black males who graduated in his field that day.

All that I can say is to God be all the glory! Something big came out of this and will continue to come out of this! This being our experience, our journey, our faith!

The Sermon

The **book of Ruth, chapter 1:3–9** reads thus:

> And Elimelech Naomi's husband died; and she was left, and her two sons.
>
> And they took them wives of the women of Moab; the name of the one was Orpah, and the name of the other Ruth: and they dwelled there about ten years.
>
> And Mahlon and Chilion died also both of them; and the woman was left of her two sons and her husband.
>
> Then she arose with her daughters in law, that she might return from the country of Moab: for she had heard in the country of Moab how that the LORD had visited his people in giving them bread.
>
> Wherefore she went forth out of the place where she was, and her two daughters in law with her; and they went on the way to return unto the land of Judah.
>
> And Naomi said unto her two daughters in law, Go, return each to her mother's house: the LORD deal kindly with you, as ye have dealt with the dead, and with me.

The L ORD grant you that ye may find rest,
each of you in the house of her husband. Then
she kissed them; and they lifted up their voice,
and wept.

I USE for a theme this morning the words **something big is
coming out of this!**

TURN to your neighbor and say, "Neighbor, you may not be
able to see it right now, but something big is coming out of this!"

SAY, "Neighbor, stop the crying. Stop the complaining, because
something big is coming out of this!"

THE story of Ruth is one of God's providential care.

In other words, it is a story of God's predestined care.

YOU see, God knows all things.

He knows our beginning and our ending.

He knows the good things and the bad things that we will have
to face.

And what He does is simply work it out in our favour.

He works it out for our good.

AND that is what makes the story of Ruth so powerful!

TELL your neighbor, "God knows all things, and He is orches-
trating. He is arranging and rearranging your life for your good."

THE story of Ruth took place during the period of the rule of
the judges.

Those were the dark days for Israel.

The people pretty much did whatever seemed right in their own
eyes.

YET during those dark and evil times, there were still some who
followed God.

SIMILAR to now, regardless of what is happening around us,
many still choose to follow God.

RUTH was one of the bravest women in the Bible, yet she was
a Moabite, which means she was from Moab, a carnal place.

MOAB was one of the nations that oppressed Israel during the
period of the judges.

SO there was hostility between the two nations.

HOWEVER, we find that during a severe famine in Israel, Elimelech, an Israelite, took his wife, Naomi, and their two sons to go live in Moab.

And that was how Ruth and Naomi met.

THE Bible tells us that sometime after taking up residence in Moab, Elimelech died, and Naomi was left with her two sons.

THE two sons had married Moabite women, one named Orpah and the other named Ruth.

BOTH Orpah and Ruth had converted to the Jewish faith.

They believed in the true and living God and were undoubtedly converted by heart through influences of their husbands and the daily testimony of their mother-in-law, Naomi.

BUT just when they thought that things could not get any worst with the loss of Elimelech, tragedy struck again.

Tragedy struck, leaving Naomi's two sons dead.

And Naomi was now left without a husband and without sons.

IT sure doesn't take much to imagine the grief that Naomi must have had to bear and the grief that both Orpah and Ruth had to contend with.

TELL your neighbor, "It may be rough right now, but hang on in there."

FOR Naomi, Orpah, and Ruth, being without husbands was a vulnerable position to be in.

As in those times, widows were often taken advantage of *or* ignored, and they were almost always poverty-stricken.

IT IS therefore not surprising that God's law provided that the nearest relative of the dead husband should care for the widow.

However, Naomi was in a spot. She had no relatives in Moab.

And she did not know if any of her relatives were alive in her homeland.

AND SO IT was at this juncture that we found Naomi being forced by her circumstance to make the decision to return to her homeland.

AND as I said that, I feel like pausing right here to say that what you are going through is a process to take you to where you are going.

EVEN during your most difficult times, God is at work.

ALL three women took to making the trip to Naomi's home-land. However, along the way, NAOMI decided that she should make the trip alone.

As to her, it seemed unfair.

NAOMI thought it unfair to require Orpah and Ruth to leave their homeland to go to hers, especially since she could not make them any promises of experiencing a brighter future there.

NAOMI was clearly nervous about her future.

It is obvious that she got worried.

It is obvious that she was concerned, not just for herself but also for her daughters-in-law.

THE tragedy of losing all the men of the family had left the three women sorrowful.

But the sorrow increased even more, especially for Ruth, when she realized that Naomi did not want them accompanying her.

I FEEL like telling somebody that when we come to the end of ourselves, it is in order to find the beginning of God.

THIS tragedy of loss had brought Naomi, Orpah, and Ruth to the end of themselves.

But God was up to something!

I DON'T know who this message is for, but God sent me to tell you that He is up to something!

NAOMI said to her daughters-in-law, "Don't come with me. Go back to your mother's homes."

BUT SQUEEZE somebody's hand and tell them, "Don't go back!" Keep moving forward.

Because once you have Jesus, you can't go back.

TELL somebody else, "Don't go back."

The blessing is ahead.

You may not be able to see it right now, but eventually you will. Just keep moving forward. Don't go back!

IT didn't take much for Orpah to give in to Naomi's request.

ORPAH, who had become a believer in Naomi's house, fool-ishly yielded to Naomi's request.

She decided to go back, which was a clear indication of her backsliding life.

Because surely, she could not stand alone as a believer in God in the midst of the idolatrous people of Moab.

SOME people here today are like Orpah.

You panic easily. You easily get frustrated.

BUT a move in the wrong direction could cost you dearly.

A move in the wrong direction can cause you to miss out, because whether you believe it or not, the best is yet to come!

ORPAH decided to remain in Moab.

She decided to return to her mother's home.

But Ruth refused Naomi's request.

RUTH basically said, "Naomi, I love you too much to leave you now. We have survived too many storms for me to abandon you now."

RUTH said, "Naomi, entreat me not to leave you."

IN other words, "Naomi, I am begging you, I am beseeching you, don't make me leave you. Don't make me go back."

"I DON'T want to go back to what I had already turned my back on.

"I DON'T want to go back to what God had already delivered me from.

"I DON'T want to go back to the life I had before.

"WE have come too far for me to go back now.

"WE have overcome too many hurts and pain for me not to be able to ride out this one with you."

RUTH said, "I will go wherever you go. I will live wherever you live. YOUR people will be my people. And your God will be my God."

SLAP somebody and say, "I am riding out this storm!"

RUTH was determined to not let the circumstances destroy her future.

SHE saw that although Naomi was a mighty woman of God, it was out of frustration that Naomi was admonishing her to leave.

Ruth saw that Naomi needed some encouragement.

TELL your neighbor, "Everybody needs encouragement sometimes."

TURN to somebody else and say, "Be encouraged."

ALTHOUGH Naomi was too discouraged to see ahead, RUTH must have had a vision of a future which showed her that being by Naomi's side was the only best place to be.

YOU see, Naomi had been good to her.

Naomi was the one who had led her to God.

Naomi had taught her the scriptures.

Naomi had taught her how to pray.

AND Ruth undoubtedly fell in love with the God that was in Naomi.

AND leaving Naomi would be like turning her back on God.

AND SO I can just imagine hearing Ruth encourage Naomi by saying, "NAOMI, we survived the storm of losing *your* husband and *my* father-in-law, so things will get better. IF we can just get through the storm of losing your sons."

RUTH must have said, "Naomi, remember you told me that God will never leave us nor forsake us. And that He is a *present* help in times of trouble. Trouble is now on every side. So God *must* be with us."

RUTH must have said, "Naomi, remember you told me to praise God in the good times and in the bad times. So now is a good time to praise God."

LISTEN, people.

Every time that the devil attacks you or your family, hit back with a praise!

THE devil attacks you to discourage you.

But when you praise God, it discourages the devil.

I WONDER if I can get twenty people in the house right now to make the devil mad by breaking out in praise.

TAKE ten seconds and just praise God.

Give God the highest praise!

I LOVE Ruth! You see, she strikes me as a dreamer.

AND You must be able to dream.

IF you don't have the ability to dream, then you don't have the ability to hope.

Because hope is dreaming.

ANYTIME you are a dreamer, you can be in one place. Yet see yourself in another place.

DREAMERS aren't bothered by how rough things get right now because they know that where they are is not where they will remain.

IF you know what I am talking about, TELL your neighbor, "I am a dreamer."

AS A dreamer, you may be relying on public transportation to move around right now, yet you see yourself driving a Mercedes Benz one day.

AS A dreamer, you may be single right now, but you see a honeymoon.

AS A dreamer, you may be living in a small one-bedroom house right now, but you see yourself living in a big house with many rooms one day.

AS A dreamer, although they got you fired, you see yourself in a better paying job.

DREAMERS see stuff changing.

They have active imaginations.

AND that is why, as dreamers, you can't let the devil get ahold of your minds.

EVERYTIME the devil speaks into your mind, rebuke him in the name of Jesus.

IF the devil, through his antics, takes your money, don't worry, because that is temporary.

You will get *more* money later.

BUT *never* let the devil have your mind.

KEEP your minds covered under the blood of Jesus.

WHEN your minds are covered under the blood, it keeps you dreaming. AND dreamers are hopeful.

Dreamers expect the unexpected to happen.

TELL three people, "Keep your minds under the blood!"

NOW say, "Jesus, cover my mind under your blood!"

RUTH encouraged and convinced Naomi to let her take the trip with her to her homeland.

AND when they got to her homeland, the whole town was shocked by their arrival.

IN FACT, someone was heard to be asking, "Is this really Naomi?"

LISTEN. Some people will be shocked that you made it out alive!

FOR all the hell that you went through, they expected you to die. BUT God!

LOOK at your neighbor and say, "You are *not* seeing doubles. It is really me."

YOU were limping last week, but you are still alive.

SOMETIMES you had to cry yourself to sleep, but you are still alive.

JUST yesterday, you thought that you would not have made it through the night, but look at you now.

You are still alive.

HIGH-FIVE three people and say, "It is really me. I am still alive!" (**Repeat 3x.**)

WHEN Naomi heard them ask if it was really her, NAOMI, who was still hurting from her loss, said, "Don't call me Naomi. Call me Mara. Because the Lord has made life very bitter for me."

BUT I feel like telling somebody, "You don't have to be ugly because things are ugly."

IN FACT, when the devil does things to make you frown, smile!

When the devil does things to make you cry, laugh!

AND maybe we should just pause for two seconds and laugh at the devil. COME on, laugh!

NAOMI said, "I went away full. But the Lord brought me back home empty."

BUT GOD sent me to tell somebody that when adversity empties you, He will fill you up.

GOD said, "What you are going through is just a test. It is a test to see if when it is all said and done, you will still stand."

IT is a test to see if when your back is against the wall, you will still trust Him.

IT is a test to see if when life backs you in a corner, you will still call Him Lord.

GOD said it is a test to see if after the devil huffs and puffs, you will still remain on a firm foundation.

IN FACT, as long as God's hands are on you, the devil's huffs and puffs will not destroy you.

IT IS just like the story of the three little pigs.

You remember it?

THE devil, who is like a roaring lion, seeks whom he may devour.

THE devil, like a roaring lion, will check us out to see how much stamina we have.

He will check us out to see how much character we have. He will check us out to see how much joy we have, how much wisdom we have, how anointed we are.

SO He goes to the first little pig's house.

You know the story!

THE first little pig built his house out of straw.

AND the big bad wolf (the devil) huffed and puffed and blew the first little pig's house down.

THEN the big bad wolf (the devil) went to the second little pig's house. It was built out of wood.

And the big bad wolf (the devil) huffed and puffed and blew the second little pig's house down.

BUT when the big bad wolf (the devil) went to the child of God's house, he found that our house was built out of rock.

Because God said, "Upon this rock, I will build my church, and the gates of hell shall not prevail against it" (Matt. 16:18).

SHAKE somebody and say, "My foundation is sure, because the rock is Christ Jesus."

WHEN the devil went to the child of God's house, he said, "I am going to huff and puff and blow your house down."

BUT high-five three people and tell them, "The devil has been huffing and puffing, but I am still standing. I am still solid as a rock."

NAOMI returned to her homeland, and she said, "The Lord has caused me to suffer. Because the Lord has allowed me to go through such tragedy."

BUT little did Naomi know that through it all, God was with her.

And God had caused her to return home for a purpose.

YOU may not understand why you are where you are at.

YOU may not understand your struggles.

BUT GOD said, "It is for a purpose."

So don't get bitter because it is going to get better!

GOD is getting ready to turn things around.

SO don't get bitter. It is going to get better.

GOD is getting set to take you to the next level.

Don't get bitter. It is going to get better!

NUDGE somebody and say, "I am going to the next level."

I SEE a cloud the size of a man's hand.

And God is getting ready to soak His church with a fresh anointing.

AN anointing that will drip with you all the way home.

THE BIBLE says that on the day of Pentecost, the Holy Ghost *sat* on them.

TELL somebody, "I want the Holy Ghost to sit on me so that I will always do right."

IN FACT, SAY, "Holy Ghost, sit on me!"

"Sit on me when my flesh is acting up.

"HOLY Ghost, sit on me!

"Sit on me until I learn how to control myself.

"HOLY Ghost, sit on me!

"Sit on me until Your will becomes my will.

"HOLY Ghost, sit on me!

"Sit on me when I am tempted to do wrong.

"And *don't* let me up until I change my mind.

"DON'T let me move, Lord. Hold me until I decide that come what may, You are too good to give up.

"HOLY Ghost, hold me!

"Hold me because I don't want to lose my focus.

"Hold me because I don't want to lose my strength.

"Hold me because I don't want to lose my mind.

"HOLY Ghost, hold me because I don't want to lose my anointing."

TELL your neighbor, "The Lord knows your heart, and he is sending a double-portion anointing your way. A double-portion anointing that will cause you to overcome."

TELL somebody, "This is your time for victory.

"This is your time for release.

"This is your time to return home.

"COME back to the basics.

"COME back to your roots.

"COME back to the place where you first met God.

"COME back to the place of revelations."

TELL somebody else, "I need God's help!

"I need a double-portion of His anointing!

"So sit on me, Holy Ghost!"

BECAUSE Israel's climate was quite moderate, there were two harvests each year, in the spring and in the fall.

THE Barley harvest took place in the spring, and it was during that time of hope and plenty that Ruth and Naomi had returned to the homeland of Bethlehem.

BETHLEHEM was a farming community.

And because it was the time of the harvest, there was plenty of leftover grain in the fields.

THIS grain could be collected or gleaned and then made into food.

AND it should be noted that when the wheat and the barley were ready to be harvested, harvesters were hired to cut down the stalks and tie them into bundles.

AND in keeping with Israel's laws, any grain that was dropped was to be left for poor people who would pick them up.

And that process was called gleaning.

THE purpose of that law was to feed the poor and to prevent the owners from hoarding.

It was kind of a welfare programme.

RUTH and Naomi, who was now aging, had returned home empty-handed and needed to be provided for.

AND so Ruth decided to go into the fields to glean the grain so that they could get food to eat.

IT wouldn't have been much, but at least it was better than nothing.

IN Ruth chapter 2, we see that as Ruth went out to gather grain behind the harvesters, she found herself working in a field that just happened to belong to a man named Boaz.

And Boaz just happened to be the relative of Ruth's deceased father-in-law, Elimelech.

AND while Ruth was there gathering grains, Boaz just happened to arrive on the scene.

And he greeted the harvesters.

BUT after he greeted the harvesters, the first question that he asked was "Who is this girl?"

ASK your neighbor, "Who are you?"

NOW tell them, "I am a chosen generation.

"I am a royal priesthood.

"I am a peculiar person. I am a holy nation."

ASK somebody else, "Who are you?"

TELL them, "I am the apple of His eyes.

"I am the head and not the tail.

"I am above and not beneath.

"I am a success and not a failure."

ASK one more person, "Who are you?"

Tell them, "I am His righteousness.

"I am blessed and not cursed.

"I am rich and not poor.

"I am free and not bound!"

NOW tell somebody, "Something *big* is coming out of this!"

YOU see, you have got to understand that the meeting of Ruth and Boaz was not a coincidence.

WHEN Ruth and Naomi had embarked on their journey to the homeland, neither of them knew what they would face.

Neither of them knew what their fate would be.

Neither of them knew how they would survive.

It was a step of *faith*.

BUT God had a plan. God always has a plan.

WHEN we think we are left on our own, when we feel like God has forsaken us, when we think that God will never come through for us, right in the nick of time, God will show up in a way that blows our minds.

YOU see, God is always working out His purpose through our adversities.

AND WHAT Naomi had not yet known was that the pull that she had to return to her homeland was the pull of God.

WHAT Ruth had not yet known was that the determination that she had to return with Naomi to her homeland was a determination instilled by God.

YOU have been getting some pulls.

AND YOU have been feeling determined to press on.

AND you have been possibly thinking that it is just your mind pulling at you.

BUT I am here to tell you that this has nothing to do with you.

It is God nudging you into the right direction.

IT IS God ensuring that you are at the right place at the right time for the right reason.

TELL your neighbor, "You must be glad now that you held on, because something big is coming out of this!"

SAY, "Neighbor, don't focus on what you left behind because it is nothing to be compared with what you are coming into."

YOUR life may have been going through a lot of ups and downs, but in the end, your life will be up and NOT down!

RUTH caught the eyes of Boaz, and he immediately favored her.

THE foreman of the field told Boaz who Ruth was, AND Boaz immediately told Ruth to stay with them and to not go to any other fields.

BOAZ told Ruth, "I have already warned the young men not to bother you."

Which meant that he had seen her from afar and had already set up an edge of protection around her, even before he was formally introduced to her.

I FEEL like telling somebody, "God sees you. It may seem like He is far away, but He sees you. He sees your faithfulness.

"He has been watching you, and warnings are going out to all possible enemies."

PEOPLE who the devil is setting up to come after you, people who the devil is setting up to envy you for your breakthrough, they didn't seek to help you when you were struggling.

But now that God is bringing you into something BIG, into a new place, new blessings, new health, new wealth, they want to fight against you.

BUT God will fight against those who fight against you, and He will bless those who will bless you.

FOR the Lord is your shepherd. You shall not want.

He makes you to lie down in green pastures.

He leads you beside still waters. He restores your souls.

TELL somebody, "The enemy has been warned!"

Touch not the Lord's anointed and do his servant no harm!

BOAZ told Ruth, "When you are thirsty, help yourself to the water that the young men have drawn from the well."

IN fact, Boaz had even gone on to set up arrangements for Ruth to get longer hours at gleaning, so much so that Ruth ended up having more than enough.

WHEN God gets through with you, you shall have more than enough!

OTHER gleaners were there working, but only Ruth got the attention of the boss.

OTHER gleaners were possibly there working weeks before Ruth came along, BUT only Ruth found Boaz making special arrangements for her.

UNDOUBTEDLY, the other gleaners must have been thinking, *But this isn't fair.*

But can I remind you that God's favor ain't fair!

GOD doesn't play by our rules. He is a Creator. He will create roads in the wilderness and rivers in the desert places.

SAY, "Neighbor, this is a good time to thank God for your struggles, because your struggles created favor for you."

FAVOR gives you privileges that you never worked for.

FAVOR moves you to the front of the line.

LIKE Ruth, YOU were the last one to come in.

You are at the back.

But God's favor will move you to the front.

BECAUSE you are at the back, it doesn't mean that you were the least.

YOU are at the back because you are a secret weapon getting ready to be revealed. You are going to be a force to be reckoned with.

WHEN God's favor is upon your life, people see that the race is not for the swift but for those who endure to the end.

WHEN God's favor is upon your life, people see that the last shall be first.

THIS is also a good time to thank God for your enemies.

IN fact, send them a thank you note. For God prepareth a table before you in the presence of your enemies.

THANK God for your enemies. Thank God for your crisis.

Because they got you blessed!

RUTH was astonished at the kindness of Boaz toward her. And when she inquired, Boaz told her that he had *also* heard about the love and kindness that she had showed to her mother-in-law, especially after her husband's death.

LISTEN. If you treat people good, you will get treated well.

"IF you do good to others, others will do good to you."

WE must love our neighbors as ourselves.

For whatsoever a man soweth, that he shall also reap.

WHEN last have you stood in the gap for somebody?

WHEN last have you prayed for somebody other than your family?

WHEN last have you told somebody you loved them?

WHEN You know that a brother or sister is in need, do you run to help them, knowing very well that you can?

Or do you just sit by and watch them suffer?

DON'T forget that the scripture tells us that "Blessed are the merciful for they shall obtain mercy" (Matt. 5:7). "Blessed are the peacemakers, for they shall be called the children of God" (Matt. 5:9).

WHEN last have you hugged somebody other than your friend?

WHEN last have you fed the hungry?

WHEN last have you visited with the sick?

NO MAN is an island. No man stands alone.

Each man's joy should be joy to you.

And each man's grief should be your own.

DO unto others as you would have them do unto you!

Today for me, but tomorrow for you!

THERE should be a song entitled "Today for Me, Tomorrow."

WHEN Naomi heard the news of the sequence of events regarding Boaz's kindness toward Ruth, her hope for the future was renewed.

AND TYPICAL of her character, she thought first of Ruth, encouraging her to put herself in the position for Boaz to be the family redeemer.

A family redeemer was a relative who volunteered to take responsibility for the extended family.

WHEN a woman's husband died, the law provided that she could marry a brother of her dead husband.

BUT Naomi had no more sons for Ruth to marry.

AND even in such a case, the nearest relative did not have to marry the widow.

And if he chose not to, the next nearest relative could take his place.

NAOMI had her eyes set on Boaz marrying Ruth.

And it was clear from the onset that Boaz had a distinct liking for Ruth.

SO NAOMI gave Ruth some instructions to set things in motion.

NAOMI basically said, "Ruth, it is clear that Boaz likes you. AND he has what it takes to redeem the family."

IN other words, "There is no way that someone can be so open in revealing their love for you. And you do not reciprocate. You do not love them back."

JESUS is our redeemer.

And there is no way that He can be so open in revealing His love for us.

And we do not reciprocate…we do not love Him back.

NAOMI said, "Ruth, wait until Boaz goes to lie down beside the threshing floor."

THE threshing floor is where the grain is separated from the wheat.

AND in spiritual terms, the threshing floor is where the qualified is separated from the unqualified.

I FEEL like telling somebody, "IT is separation time!"

God is separating the accused from their accusers.

IT is separation time.

"God is separating the oppressed from their oppressors."

YOU see, the Bible tells us that the wheat and tares shall grow together until the day of harvest.

AND FOR Ruth and Naomi, it was harvest time.

FOR us today, it is harvest time.

GOD had handpicked Ruth and Naomi.

He had set them up and qualified them to be blessed.

TELL YOUR neighbor, "It is harvest time."

It is your time to be blessed. It is your time for overflow.

AND something BIG is coming out of your trials.

Something BIG is coming out of your crises.

Something BIG is coming out of your heartaches.

GOD is going to use your setback for a comeback!

NAOMI said, "Ruth, in keeping with the custom of the day, lie at the feet of Boaz and share a part of his covering. As this will signal to Boaz that you want him to redeem you for an inheritance. So that our future is secure."

I WONDER how many here today know that Jesus is our redeemer.

AND as our redeemer, we are guaranteed an eternal inheritance.

We are guaranteed His covering, His protection.

NAOMI and Ruth had been through some tough times.

And this was their opportunity to secure a brighter future.

BUT IF they were to inherit a secured future, they had to be positioned for it.

AND you can only position yourself for the future by recognizing that you *don't* live for the present.

But you live for the future.

WHAT you don't have *now*, you will soon get!

AND that is why you must never say you don't have it.

You must always say you don't have it YET!

SO when somebody asks you, "Do you have a fifteen-million-dollar house?"

TELL them, "I don't have it YET!"

WHEN somebody asks you, "Do you have a six-million-dollar car?"

TELL them, "I don't have it YET!"

ASK your neighbor, "Have you received your promotion NOW?"

TELL them, "I have not received it YET."

BECAUSE what you don't have now, you will soon get!

NAOMI understood the importance of positioning herself for the future.

And so Ruth, on the advice of Naomi, positioned herself for the blessing.

AND sure enough, Boaz was ready to bless her.

Boaz was ready to redeem her.

BUT they still had a hurdle to cross.

JESUS has positioned you to bless you. And you are at the edge of your breakthrough.

But Satan has placed a hurdle in your way.

BUT in the name of Jesus Christ of Nazareth, every hurdle is coming down today! You shall cross over.

IN the name of Jesus Christ of Nazareth, every obstacle shall be removed. You shall overcome!

IN the name of Jesus Christ of Nazareth, every weapon formed against you shall *not* prosper.

TELL your neighbor, "Something BIG is on the horizon for you, AND you shall receive it in Jesus's name!"

THE hurdle to cross was that Boaz wasn't the closest relative to Ruth.

And so he couldn't automatically marry Ruth without the closest relative first declining to do so.

AND SO BOAZ went in search of the relative.

And he made him an offer. And because of the relative's greed, the relative took up the offer, which instantly eliminated him from marrying Ruth.

And it immediately paved the way for Boaz to marry Ruth.

THERE is going to be a wedding in this place today!

It is celebration time!

Celebrate the defeat of the enemy.

Celebrate the victories won and the victories to be won.

Devil, you think we're done, BUT we have just come!

IT is party time! Where are the dancers? Where are the shakers and movers?

FIND seven people as a sign of God's perfection and tell them, "Something big is coming out of this!"

BECAUSE whatever God ordains must come to pass.

GOD had set it in time for Boaz to marry Ruth and then for Ruth to go on to conceive and to bring forth a son named Obed.

AND Obed became the father of Jesse.

And Jesse the father of David.

And Jesus came through the lineage of David.

BOAZ had redeemed Ruth.

And their son Obed, whose name means "worship," continued the family line that ushered in the presence of the Promised Messiah, thereby proving that God is *always* in control.

TELL your neighbor, "That's what worship does."

It ushers in God's presence.

God is spirit, and those who worship Him
must worship in spirit and truth. (John 4:24)

WORSHIP gives strength to the believer.

Oh, magnify the Lord with me, and let us
exalt His name together. (Ps. 34:3)

WORSHIP dismantles spiritual warfare.

> For He that keepeth Israel shall not slumber nor sleep.
> For the Lord is our keeper. The Lord is the shade upon thy right hand. And He shall preserve thee from all evil. (Ps. 121:4–7)

IF YOU believe that something big is coming out of what you are going through, worship God!

SAY, "LORD, I worship you."

"For in my distress I cried unto you and you heard me and you delivered my soul."

LORD, I magnify you.

"Worthy are you Lord to receive glory and honor and power for you, Almighty, all powerful. You are wonderful."

LORD, you have been good to me, much more than I deserve.

> FOR a day in your courts is better than a thousand elsewhere. (Ps. 84:10)

WORSHIP God until you feel the breakthrough.

WORSHIP Him like you know He is pulling you through.

WORSHIP Him like you know that had it not been for God on your side, you would not be here!

WORSHIP Him for the reassurance of His love.

WORSHIP HIM, AND in all things, give Him thanks!

CHAPTER 5

Jesus Has Need of You

I love my father dearly, although I was always closest to my mother. One of the things that held me close to my mother was that she was always there, and we were both Christians whilst my father was not.

My father was not perfect. He used to smoke, and he would drink and get drunk at times, but we never went to bed hungry. He could be relied on to take my brother and I to school daily. And as youngsters, we looked forward to him coming home every Sunday evening with ice cream for us.

When I became a mother, he also played a role in my son's life in continuing the tradition of taking him to school some mornings.

He is quiet-natured and hardly gets angry, unless he is discussing politics, which was rare, but salvation was never his plan. He had a weakness for women, which interfered with his marriage to my mom and limited his interactions with us as his children.

My mother prayed ceaselessly for the salvation of my father, even when he was not good to her. She also honored him for allowing her the freedom to not only serve God but to use our home as a place of refuge for many persons from our church and otherwise who, at one point or the other, needed a temporary shelter.

When I assumed responsibility for my parents, I told my father that his style of living had to change because it was negatively affecting the welfare of my mother and our home. When he did not seem committed to change, I arranged in 2011 for him to live away from us, and then he eventually returned to his hometown.

It was during the first year of him being away from us and in his hometown that the reality of him being separated from his family hit him. In his moments of loneliness, he surrendered his heart to the Lord, he was baptized, and he now serves as a deacon in his church.

When I asked my father why it had to take him being away from us for him to change his lifestyle and to surrender to God, he said, "I took things for granted. Something had to wake me up to the reality that I was lost and have a need for God."

My mother and father remained friends and married up to her death in 2017. In fact, whenever he came into Kingston, he would visit her at home, and she would cook him a meal, and they would chat and reminisce. They became great at being friends.

One thing that I take away from my experience with my father is that the Lord has need of us, and He will always find a way to bring us to Himself. All that we need to do is to keep praying for our loved ones. The Lord has need of them.

The Sermon

Scripture: St. Matthew 21:1–6
I HAVE read this story many times before.
And I have often wondered, Why an ass? Why a donkey?
I KNOW it was prophesied by the ancient prophet Zechariah many years before that Jesus would ride into Jerusalem on a donkey.
But still, why a donkey?
I REMEMBER as a youngster going to primary school.
I stopped to watch a game on the outskirts of a playing field.
And before I knew it, I was knocked to the ground by a donkey.
A man had been rounding up his donkeys to take them home.
And I had not seen them coming.
And one knocked me to the ground flat and almost trampled me.
BUT outside of the fact that my experience with a donkey wasn't good, why did Jesus choose to send for a donkey?

Why not a horse, which is a better and more sophisticated breed of animal?

ESPECIALLY when on the surface of things, donkeys really aren't that great!

They are stubborn.

They are dull.

They are smelly.

And they are small in comparison to the horse.

BUT Jesus sent His disciples to get Him a donkey.

I BELIEVE that Jesus was deliberate in His request because there are some important lessons for us to learn from this passage.

AND the main one is that **Jesus has need of you.**

THE LORD sent me to encourage somebody today.

He sent me to tell you that He has need of you.

AND that is what I want to briefly speak to you on this morning the fact that **Jesus has need of you.**

TELL somebody, "On the surface of things, you may not be too bright. You may not even look too good. You probably can't even speak well. But **Jesus has need of you!**"

YOU see, research has actually showed that although donkeys are a little rough on the outside, on the inside, donkeys are actually very gentle and patient.

They don't even seem angry when they have a very heavy load to carry.

AND although they seem dull, they love their master and will sometimes find him out and run to their master even when he is in a crowd.

SO it is no coincidence then that it was prophesied *and* that Jesus would speak of a donkey in this passage.

NOW let's observe Jesus's words to His disciples.

THE first thing He said to them was **in verse 2:** "Go into the village over against you and straightway ye shall find an ass."

NOW this tells me that the ass—the donkey—was selected.

He was selected, handpicked by God.

He never had a say in the matter.

He never volunteered.

He was simply selected by God to be a part of His plan.

THE donkey was selected.

Because as we've read, Jesus was specific in the directions that He gave to His disciples.

HE didn't just say, "Go and look around the place and see if you can find a donkey."

But He told them specifically where to look.

CAN I just tell somebody today that you have been selected?

You have been selected, handpicked by God.

You are a part of God's plan.

GOD sent me to tell you it is time to stop running from your calling.

It is time to submit completely to Him.

Because whether you like it or not, you have been selected!

"You have been chosen, marked by God for His purpose!"

JESUS says in JOHN 15:16, "You did not choose me, but I chose you and appointed you to go and bear fruit—fruit that will last."

TELL someone else, "IF you don't come to Jesus, Jesus will send to get you."

IN this passage, Jesus sent His disciples for the donkey.

I DON'T know who or what Jesus will send to get you.

But I believe if He has to speak to you in your dreams, He is going to do it.

If he has to use an earthquake to shake you out of your slumber, He will do it.

If He has to use a storm to bring you closer to Him, He will do it.

Ephesians 2:10 tells us, "We are God's workmanship, created in Christ Jesus to do good works, which God prepared in advance for us to do."

You have been selected, chosen by God!

TELL two persons, "I am here to stay because I have been chosen by God!"

THE mark of God is upon me!

SECONDLY, verse 2 goes on to read, "Ye shall find an ass tied, and a colt with her: loose them and bring them unto me."

THE donkey was **available but bound.**

The donkey was not out grazing in the field.

The donkey was not being used.

Instead the donkey was tied up.

The donkey was bound.

JESUS instructed His disciples that upon finding the donkey, they should set it loose.

IN OTHER words, they should untie the donkey.

And once it is untied, they should bring the donkey to Him.

AND when I read this, the Lord spoke into my spirit and told me that THERE would be some persons here today who are **available but bound.**

Some have been bound by witchcraft.

Some have been bound by negative words spoken over their lives.

Some have been bound by sins and pleasures.

BUT Jesus is here today to set you free.

JESUS told me to tell you that He would be untying some people today.

He will be freeing people from bondage today.

YES, you are available. There is life in you.

But something or someone has bound you.

WELL, today is your day for deliverance.

Today is your day for breakthrough.

IT is time to get loosed.

SHAKE yourselves and say, "Loose me, Jesus!"

Loose me from sin.

Loose me from depression.

Loose me from poverty.

Loose me from complacency.

Loose me from demonic forces.

Loose me, Jesus. Loose me!

Great things are happening in this place even now because there is no point to you being available if you are still bound!

CRY out, "Loose me, Jesus! I want to be completely free today!"
FINALLY, the donkey was **useful but unused**.

THE donkey was useful because it could serve the purpose of being ridden.

NO wonder Jesus told His disciples to not just loose the donkey but to also bring the donkey to Him.

Jesus wanted to use the donkey for the purpose for which it was created.

JESUS wants to use you for the purpose for which you were created.

UNDOUBTEDLY, the donkey was strong enough and healthy enough to bear Jesus's body weight.

It must have had good eyesight.

It must have had a good body structure.

It must have been well-fed and not weak and half-dead looking.

Yet still the donkey was unused!

THERE are too many persons sitting in church doing nothing.

YOU are strong enough and healthy enough, but you are unused!

You are useful but unused.

YOU have been sitting on your talent, hiding it, saying that you've only got one while others have many.

But if you keep your talent unused, God will do to you as He did to the servant who was given one talent.

GOD will take your talent away from you and give it to those who are wise enough to use their talents.

> - You can sing, but you refuse to sing for God.
> - You can play an instrument, but you refuse to play one for God.
> - You have good planning and administrative skills, but you refuse to use them for God.

Whatever the gifting that you have been sitting idly on, whatever the talent that you have allowed to remain unutilized or underutilized, God is calling on you today to use your talent for His glory.

God said the following:

> ➢ I have already equipped you with the requisite skills.
> ➢ I have called you to this ministry.
> ➢ I have chosen you as a worker in this ministry.

But you have been sitting down idle.
You have been idle while souls are dying.
You have been idle while people are perishing.
THIS is a call to recommit to doing the work of God.
WHAT is your talent?
What is your gift?
What is your ministry?
Jesus has need of you.
He needs to use you to raise the dead.
He needs to use you to cast out demons.
He needs to use you to heal the sick.
TELL somebody, "Jesus has need of you!"
HE needs you just as he needed **Peter** to say to the crippled man, "Silver and gold have I none, but in the name of Jesus Christ of Nazareth, rise up and walk."
GOD needs you just as he needed **Moses**, who stretched out his rod for the deliverance of the people.
HE needs you just as he needed **David**, who, with five stones and great faith, defeated Goliath.
GOD needs you just as he needed **Gideon**, a man of valor.
HE needs you just as He needed **Deborah**, who took on the challenge of the battle when others like Barack were afraid to.
JESUS needs you just as He needed **John the Baptist**, the voice of one crying in the wilderness, "Repent and be baptized!"
TOUCH two persons and tell them, "Jesus has need of you!"
IF YOU believe that Jesus has need of you, TELL someone else, "I am chosen, available, and useful."

CHAPTER 6

It Should Have Killed You, But!

It was late in the night, and we were on our way back home from a National Youth Convention that was held out of town. At the time, I was the youth director for our local church, and I had asked one of our youth board members to use my car to drive us to and from the convention. Jordan, who was seven years of age, and the youth board member's wife were also with us. Other members of our team were traveling behind us as we made the journey back together.

The youth convention was a powerful expression of God's glory, and so as we were journeying back to our hometown, we made outbursts of singing and praises to God for having met with us in such a powerful way. I had closed the convention with a prayer directed at tearing down Satan's kingdom and making positive declarations over our lives, which had resulted in an outpouring of the anointing to the point that it had even become difficult to have ended the service.

We were a little bit more than half of our journey back home and had found ourselves trailing behind a huge truck when suddenly, the youth board member drove the car around the truck in an attempt to overtake it, only for us to see another vehicle heading directly toward us for an unavoidable head-on collision. It all happened so quickly that all I remember was bowing my head and quietly praying one word: "Jesus."

As I said, "Jesus," I felt like a cool wind took the vehicle, lifted it up out of the way, and placed it safely before the truck, allowing us to continue our journey without impact. There was perfect silence in our car and an unexplainable peace that left us speechless. None of us said a word about what had just happened until about ten minutes after when the youth board member's cell phone rang. It was another member of our group that had called. He and others who were traveling behind us had seen what had almost happened, and they, too, were left speechless, as they were bracing to see the collision and were still puzzled by how our car had escaped it. It was clear that the devil had been angered by what had transpired through our lives as we ministered during the convention that day, and so he had attempted to fight back at us, but he had forgotten that God's angels encampeth round them that fear Him. It should have killed us, but!

Over a two-week period, I had noticed that I would dream seeing bats, and they would be flying around until suddenly, one would come charging at me to the point that it frightened me out of my sleep. Whenever this happened, I would always see a bat on the wall of our verandah as I left for work.

I did not understand it, but I remember praying for the Lord to cancel and destroy every evil plan of the enemy concerning my life.

One morning, as I was frightened out of my sleep after seeing the bat coming at me, my cell phone rang. It was a woman that God had used powerfully in my life on more than one occasion. When I answered the cell phone, she was speaking in tongues, and she did so for about five minutes. In between tongues, you could hear her tearing down and destroying the wiles of the devil, then she began to prophesy over my life. She said, "The principalities and powers that were coming against you have been destroyed. No weapon formed against you shall prosper. The evil that you saw coming at you has been rendered powerless. You are covered and protected by the blood of Jesus, covered and protected by the blood of Jesus, covered and protected by the blood of Jesus, for you are mine! Thus saith the Lord of Host." That was the last time that I had those dreams, which were always followed by the presence of a bat on our verandah. All that I can say is, it should have killed me, but!

The Sermon

And said unto them, Sirs, I perceive that this voyage will be with hurt and much damage, not only of the lading and ship, but also of our lives.

Nevertheless the centurion believed the master and the owner of the ship, more than those things which were spoken by Paul. (Acts 27:10–11)

And we being exceedingly tossed with a tempest, the next day they lightened the ship;

And the third day we cast out with our own hands the tackling of the ship. (Acts 27:18–19)

And the rest, some on boards, and some on broken pieces of the ship. And so it came to pass, that they escaped all safe to land. (Acts 27:44)

And when they were escaped, then they knew that the island was called Melita.

And the barbarous people shewed us no little kindness: for they kindled a fire, and received us every one, because of the present rain, and because of the cold.

And when Paul had gathered a bundle of sticks, and laid them on the fire, there came a viper out of the heat, and fastened on his hand.

And when the barbarians saw the venomous beast hang on his hand, they said among themselves, No doubt this man is a murderer, whom, though he hath escaped the sea, yet vengeance suffereth not to live.

And he shook off the beast into the fire, and felt no harm.

Howbeit they looked when he should have swollen, or fallen down dead suddenly: but after they had looked a great while, and saw no harm come to him, they changed their minds, and said that he was a god. (Acts 28:1–6)

I USE for a theme **"It Should Have Killed You, But!"**

SQUEEZE two persons' hands and tell them, "You may not have yet realized it, but it should have killed you!"

HOW many of us here tonight are willing to look back at our lives and are willing to be honest enough to admit that had it not been for the grace of God, we would have been dead and gone a long time ago?

CAR wrecks, drug abuse, domestic violence, sickness and disease, and so many other ills have taken the lives of some of those we have been acquainted with.

Yet we are still here!

AND IT WASN'T because we did anything out of the ordinary.

IT WASN'T because we were perfect and always did everything right.

IN FACT, The truth is, we actually deserved to die.

FOR all the wrong things that we have done.

FOR all the shortcomings.

FOR all the disobedience.

WE really didn't deserve all the mercies that we had received.

AND IF YOU really wish to be honest, some of you here, right now, CAN recall the fact that you should have died in a car accident some time ago.

You should have been the one spending your life behind prison walls.

You should have been the one who died of cancer.

SO many things should have killed you.

Yet you are still here.

THERE were even times when persons numbered your days because you came so close to death.

DOCTORS at one point gave some of you over to die because they couldn't help you anymore.

YES! The enemy had set numerous traps to cut short your life.

They worked obeah on you.

They prayed against you.

They created mischief for you.

They set poison for you to eat.

AND it should have killed you!

But God's faithfulness, His mercies, kept you alive!

HIGH-FIVE three persons and tell them, "It should have killed me, but I am still alive!"

THERE are two events recorded in the passages of scripture that we have just read.

AND BOTH events note how God miraculously protected His people.

THE FIRST event that we read came to us from Acts 27, where we found that the people had a journey to make.

And the apostle Paul had cautioned them not to sail.

PAUL cautioned them not to take the journey because there were signs that the weather would have been extremely bad.

AND AS IT was then, SO it is now, because how many of you know that we don't always listen to wise counsel?

IN THIS life, we could have saved ourselves a lot of grief and pain if we had just listened to those who tried to instruct us.

THE PEOPLE in Paul's time didn't listen to Paul's counsel.

And as such, they ended up sailing directly into the storm of their lives.

AND THE storm got really bad, just as Paul had predicted.

And as such, the people had to lighten the ship.

BUT YOU know, lightening the ship may *not* have been such a bad thing.

Because a bad storm becomes a good storm when it helps us to realign our priorities.

YOU SEE, storms can serve a great purpose in a Christian's life.

It can help us to refocus.

It can bring us to a place of consciousness.

It can help us to quickly identify what we should really accommodate in our lives as against what is excess baggage.

THE ship that Paul and the others had sailed in was completely destroyed by the storm.

But because of God's faithfulness, because of His grace and mercy, the passengers who were on board the ship made it to dry land on boards and on broken pieces.

IF you know that you serve a faithful God, SOMEBODY ought to lift up their hands right now and say, "I may be in a storm right now, but I'm going to make it to dry ground!

"I am broken, but I know that I am going to make it.

"I am wounded, but I'm still going to make it, even if I have to hop on one foot.

"I AM struggling, but I am still pressing on.

"I AM confused, but I am still pushing ahead.

"I HAVE been rejected, but I am not giving up. I am going to make it!"

IN FACT, touch two people and tell them, "I KNOW that I am not everything that I should be. I am still struggling with some habits and hang-ups. I am still wrestling with some anger and un-forgiveness issues. I still slip up every once in a while. And I still say some things that I shouldn't have said."

TELL somebody, "I KNOW that I am not where I should have been by now. But I know that I am moving in the right direction. I KNOW that I am chopping up the water all around me. But it's just because I don't want to drown. THE storm was designed to kill me. But I know that it didn't. Because I am still here."

SAY, "Neighbor, "Look at me! I am still here!"

ACTS 28:1–6 reconfirms that Paul and the crew made it through the storm safely.

But now they had found themselves on a strange island.

A STORM has a way of doing that to you.

It has a way of taking you to a place where you have never been before.

Simply because God is about to do something extraordinary in your life!

TELL your neighbor, "The fact that you made it through the storm means God is about to do the extraordinary in your life!"

THE fact that you have made it thus far is a clear indication that God is up to something significant!

FORTUNATELY for Paul and the crew, the people on the island were hospitable.

THE people of the island saw how cold Paul and the crew were and how they were shivering.

And so they decided to build a fire to make them warm.

TELL somebody, "Fire can be a good thing!"

AND Paul, being the obvious gentleman that he was, began assisting with the building of the fire by gathering sticks and laying them in the fire.

BUT AS PAUL laid the sticks in the fire, a viper, a snake which was hiding itself among the stick, fastened itself to Paul's hand.

I FEEL like asking somebody, "WHAT demon has fastened itself to you?"

WHAT crisis has attached itself to your life?

WHAT fleshly desires have you been struggling with?

DON'T lose hope. There is a way of escape!

DON'T lose hope. God will make a way!

BECAUSE the passage goes on to say, "Howbeit they looked."

IN other words, the people of the island began to watch.

They anticipated, they waited to see what would have now happened to Paul.

YOU see, a venomous snake had bitten him.

And if a venomous snake bites you, the result ought to be that your body becomes poisoned, possibly swollen with eventual death.

LISTEN. THERE are people that are watching you who do not want you to make it.

THEY are anxiously waiting and anticipating your downfall.

THEY rejoice when they see you going through hardships and trials.

THEY are watching and waiting to celebrate your downfall.

To celebrate your breakdown.

To celebrate your defeat.

BUT God is your keeper!

PAUL should have been swollen or fallen down dead suddenly.

Medical science says he should have died. Every legal advisor would have agreed that he should have died. Every natural circumstance suggests that he should not have made it.

It should have killed him. Yet it didn't!

YOU are here tonight.

Yet the circumstances of your life should have killed you.

FOR all the mistreatment that came your way, you should have ended up in a mental institution.

FOR all the aches and pain that have attacked your body, you should have been laid up in a hospital, mad at God and mad at the world.

BUT God sent me to tell you that not only are you going to make it, but you are not even going to look like you have been through what you've been through.

WHEN the children of Israel went through the Red Sea, God didn't just part the waters.

He dried the ground that they walked on.

WHEN the children of Israel reached the other side, there wasn't even mud between their toes.

FOR a little while, it had looked like the enemy was closing in on them and was going to overtake them.

BUT they just kept on walking.

AND while they were walking, God was taking care of their enemies.

WHILE they were walking, their enemies were being drowned.

I WANT to tell somebody tonight, "Just keep on walking!"

IT doesn't matter what people say about you.

It doesn't matter what they do to you.

It doesn't matter what the doctors say.

It doesn't matter what the rebellious child does.

IT doesn't matter what the financial report says.

THIS is not the time to sit and cry. Just keep walking!

AND when God gets through blessing you, you won't even look like you've been through what you've been through.

AND the only evidence of you going through what you went through WILL be a greater faith, a greater love, a greater confidence, a greater commitment, and a greater testimony.

I KNOW tonight that some of you are going through the greatest fire of your life.

And it's the kind that hurts.

And it's the kind that makes you cry.

AND I know it's going to sound crazy, but what you ought to be doing right now is praising God that you made it *to* the fire!

PAUL made it *to* the fire!

HE had been in a storm.

HE survived the storm, and then he made it *to* the fire.

THERE are other people that never made it *to* the fire.

And there are other people that died at the door.

DO YOU understand what I'm saying?

REMEMBER THE story about the three Hebrew boys.

They made it to the fire, and then they walked through the fire.

And when they came out on the other side, the only evidence that they had been through the fire was that they were liberated from their bondage.

THE enemy had bound the three Hebrew boys before casting them into the fire.

But when they walked through the fire that which was used to bound them, it got burned off by the fire.

THE three Hebrew boys came out on the other side with no hurt.

Their clothes were not burnt.

Their hair was not singed.

And there was not even the smell of smoke on them.

WELL, THE fire should have killed them, but it didn't.

BUT somebody may be saying that God just took the heat out of the fire.

BUT God didn't take the heat out of the fire because the fire had actually killed the men who threw the three Hebrew boys into the fire.

And it destroyed that which bound them in the fire.

THE king's three most mighty men in his army died at the door!

IT IS A miracle that you have made it this far.

By all rights, you shouldn't be here.

YOU shouldn't have lived through that depression.

YOU shouldn't have lived through the abuse.

YOU shouldn't have lived through the heart attack.

SOMEBODY else that I am talking to, you shouldn't have lived through the stab wounds.

You shouldn't have survived the cancerous disease.

YOU shouldn't have made it.

Other people didn't make it. But you are still here.

THE king's three mighty men could have very well represented the three greatest athletes, the three most popular people, the three voted most likely to succeed.

THEY had everything going for them.

IF anybody should have made it, it should have been them.

BUT they died at the door!

ON THE OTHER hand, nobody expected you to make it.

But here you are. Still alive!

YOU are in your right mind, serving God filled with the Holy Ghost and power.

AND you want to complain because you are going *through* the fire?

WHAT YOU ought to be doing is praising God that you made it *to* the fire.

SOMEBODY shout out, "Thank God I made it to the fire."

YOU COULD have died at the door.

YOU COULD have died when the gunmen invaded your community.

YOU COULD have died when they worked witchcraft against you.

YOU COULD have been serving a life sentence in prison.

YOU COULD have lost your mind and walked the streets like a vagabond.

BUT God had His hands on you!

YOU DIDN'T even know Him, yet He was watching over you.

YOU WEREN'T serving Him, yet He was keeping his hands on you. He sent His angels to deliver you.

I DON'T know about you, but I wasn't the strongest one.

I wasn't the smartest one.

I wasn't the most popular one. I wasn't the one expected to make it.

BUT I made it, and there's no other explanation but God.

SOMEBODY shout it out again: "Thank God I made it to the fire!"

NOW you are going to get out of the fire.

But God just wanted to remind somebody that He was with you before you ever got into the fire.

And He is *not* going to leave you now.

AS a matter of fact, if you are in the middle of the fiery furnace tonight, it is positive proof that you are coming out.

BECAUSE the miracle started at the door.

AND if God wasn't going to bring you out, you would have died at the door.

You wouldn't have made it *to* the fire.

TOUCH your neighbor and tell them, "Now I know I'm coming out!"

IT IS a miracle that I have made it this far.

And God wouldn't have brought me to the middle if He wasn't going to bring me out.

I KNOW THAT I am talking to some people right now.

Some people are going through the fire.

And I know that you are feeling the heat.

AND I didn't come to tell you that the fire isn't real or that it doesn't hurt.

I KNOW some of you are going through the greatest fire of your life.

And for some of you, it's a financial fire.

For somebody else, it is a fire of sickness and a battle for your health.

Somebody else may be going through the fire of divorce or marital problems.

Still somebody else is going through the fire, dealing with rebellious children.

BUT I came to tell you that something good is going to come out of this.

I KNOW right now that sounds like insanity.

Because there is no visible, tangible, physical evidence of anything good in this fire.

BUT I came to prophesy to you and to declare to you on the authority of God's Word that if it didn't kill you before, it's not going to kill you now!

YOU are going to make it.

You are not going to burn up in the fire.

You are coming out.

And I don't mean you are going to come crawling out on your hands and on your knees, all beaten up, broke, and busted with no clothes, no money, no peace, no joy. With your eyebrows burned off, smelling like smoke.

THE devil is a liar!

It should have killed you, but it didn't.

Because you are coming out blessed.

It should have killed you, but it didn't.

Because you are coming out healed and delivered.

It should have killed you, but it didn't.

Because you are coming out with money.

You are coming out with joy.

You are coming out with peace.

THE KING CHOSE his three most mighty men.

IN other words, he chose his best, his strongest, his meanest, his best trained soldiers in his army.

SOMEBODY may say, "Preacher, I don't understand it. BECAUSE IT just feels like I am fighting on a different level. IT feels like the enemy is stronger than before and even smarter than before."

WELL, that ought to tell you something.

THE devil wouldn't be bringing out his best if you weren't a threat to him.

THE fact that the devil is bringing out the big dawgs tells me that you must be a threat to him and that you are getting close to your destiny and close to walking in your purpose.

YOU are getting ready to step into a greater anointing—an anointing that you have never experienced before.

AND the devil is trying to intimidate you and to make you back down.

BUT don't be dismayed. Stand firm in God!

TOUCH three people and tell them, "The fire should have killed me, but it didn't."

IF THE devil had his way, you would have been strung out on drugs.

IF THE devil had his way, you would not have recovered after you had fallen into sin.

IF THE devil had his way, your messed-up life would have been the end of you.

IF THE devil had his way, you would not have survived the shame and disgrace of your circumstance.

AND THAT'S why I am here to tell you that the fire is a good thing!

IT purifies you.

IT strengthens you.

IT destroys the yokes of bondage.

AND IT sets you free.

IT sets you FREE TO worship! FREE TO be who God has destined you to be.

TELL SOMEBODY, "I'm working on my testimony. I MAY BE in the middle of my test. But that only means that I am halfway through to a testimony. I am working on my testimony!"

THE BIBLE says that "Paul shook off the beast."

AND this wasn't' a little wimpy wave of the hand with Paul saying, "Oh, come on, mister snake. This is not nice. Please get off me. Please remove your fangs from my skin."

THAT viper had actually attached itself to Paul.

SO much so that Paul had to become violent and aggressive against it.

THERE ARE some things that you can pray about and ask God to take away.

And then there are some things that make you become violent and aggressive.

THERE are some things that you will have to shake loose.

You will have to shake like your life depends on it, because it does!

IN FACT, if I were you, I would begin right now to SHAKE that fear loose.

SHAKE that depression loose.

SHAKE that addiction loose.

SHAKE that spirit of hopelessness and suicide loose.

SHAKE that spirit of lust and perversion loose.

SHAKE that spirit of poverty and lack loose.

SHAKE that spirit of sickness loose.

SHAKE that dead and powerless religious spirit loose.

SHAKE off the beast!

YOU will have to shake for your family, shake for your health, shake for your mind, shake for your ministry, shake for your finances.

Shake, shake, shake, shake.

SAMSON SAID, "I will go out as at other times and shake myself."

And this tells us that there was some physical action on Samson's part.

Some physical action that was designed to signal the anointing—the anointing came upon Samson as he shook himself.

THERE IS something about shaking that activates the anointing.

BUT shaking is not all there is to it.

You also need to be close to the fire, because the fire is good.

THERE ARE a lot of people who shake.

That is, you go through the motions of being a Christian.

But not that many really have the fire.

IN FACT, I believe that we have reached the place where we are considered old-fashioned and outdated if we talk too much about the Holy Ghost and fire.

BUT I still believe that the only thing that can destroy the devil's power IS the fire of God.

WE STIL serve a faithful God who answers by fire!

PAUL shook the viper off into the fire.

YOU need to ask yourself if you are living close enough to the fire.

DO you have the fire in your life?

DO you have the fire in your home?

THE VENOMOUS snake should have killed Paul.

The people around had fully expected him to die.

But he shook it off into the fire.

It was the fire that destroyed the thing that was trying to kill Paul.

SOMEBODY listening to me, the devil has unleashed some things against you to try to destroy you.

But it's not going to kill you. ALL you need to do is to turn up the heat.

TELL your neighbor, "Excuse me, but I've got to turn up the thermostat."

YOU might want to move to the other side of the room and get ready to praise God like you have never praised Him before.

GET ready to shout! Get ready to worship!

IF you are close to the fire OR IF you are going through the fire, you don't have any time to try to be cute.

You don't have the time to try and fit in.

BECAUSE that which has been trying to destroy you, God is getting ready to destroy it by the fire.

SO start praising God for your life.

Start praising God for your destiny.

Start praising God for your ministry.

Praise Him for your children. Praise Him for your health.

TELL somebody, "I know that I don't deserve His mercies, but I'm Grateful for it. I know that I don't deserve His forgiveness, but I'm thankful for it. I know that I don't deserve His favor, but God's favor ain't fair. I know that the devil meant it for evil. But God is turning it around for my good."

I KNOW what it feels like to be shipwrecked.

And I know what it feels like to be bitten by the serpent.

BUT I also know what it feels like to shake that snake off into the fire.

SOMEBODY listening to this message right now, you know you should have died.

You know if some people had been able to carry out their intentions, you would have been dead.

BUT touch three people and tell them, "God is with me, and that's why I'm still here. I am still here because God has a plan for my life and a destiny that I am going to fulfill."

FOR there is no God like Jehovah!

Jehovah fights for me!

Jehovah protects me!

Jehovah watches over me!

> Whither shall I go from His spirit? or whither shall I flee from His presence?
>
> If I ascend up into heaven, Jehovah is there: if I make my bed in hell, behold, Jehovah is there.
>
> If I take the wings of the morning, and dwell in the uttermost parts of the sea;
>
> Even there shall Jehovah's hand lead me, and His right hand shall hold me.
>
> If I say, Surely the darkness shall cover me—Even the night shall be light about me. (Ps. 139:7–12)

AND that's why…

> I will praise God; for I am fearfully and wonderfully made: marvellous are His works; and that my soul knoweth right well.
>
> My substance was not hid from Him, when I was made in secret, and curiously wrought in the lowest parts of the earth.
>
> His eyes did see my substance, yet being unperfect; and in His book all my members were written…

How precious also are God's thoughts unto me, O God! how great is the sum of them!

If I should count them, they are more in number than the sand: when I awake, I am still with God. (Ps. 139:14–18)

GOD is my keeper.
GOD is my shield and hiding place.
GOD is my refuge and strength.
GOD is my present help in times of trouble.
THERE is no God like Jehovah! (Repeat.)
Praise Him for His faithfulness.
Praise Him for His grace and mercies.
Praise Him for His loving kindness.
THERE is no God like Jehovah!
AND THAT'S why it should have killed you, but it couldn't.
GOD is on your side.

For the Lord is our light and our salvation—whom shall we fear?

The Lord is the strength of our lives—of whom shall we be afraid?

WHEN the wicked—even our enemies—came upon us to eat up our flesh, they stumbled and fell.

THOUGH war should rise against us, our hearts shall not fear! (Ps. 27:1–3)

THERE is no God like Jehovah.
HE is our rock.
He is our peace.
He is our guide.

Fret not thyselves because of evildoers, neither be thou envious against the workers of iniquity.

For they shall soon be cut down like the grass, and wither as the green herb.

TRUST in the Lord and do good.

Delight thyself also in the Lord and He shall give thee the desires of Thine heart.

Commit thy way unto the Lord. Trust also in Him and He shall bring it to pass. (Ps. 371–5)

Rest in the Lord and wait patiently for Him.

Cease from anger and forsake wrath. (Ps. 37:7–8)

FOR The Lord knoweth the days of the upright and their inheritance shall be forever.

THEY shall not be ashamed in the evil time. And in the days of famine—they shall be satisfied. (Ps. 37:18–19)

FOR the steps of a good man are ordered by the Lord.

And He delighteth in his way.

Though he fall—he shall not be utterly cast down.

For the Lord upholdeth him with his hand. (Ps. 37:23–24)

BUT the wicked shall perish and the enemies of the Lord shall be as the fat of lambs. THEY shall consume into smoke—shall they consume away. (Ps. 37:20)

BECAUSE AS David said:

I have seen the wicked in great power and spreading himself like a green bay tree.

Yet he passed away and lo, he was not. Yea, I sought for him, but he could not be found. (Ps. 37:35–36)

IT should have killed you, but it couldn't.
Because God is on your side!
PRAISE HIM! GIVE HIM THANKS FOR KEEPING YOU
ALIVE AND WELL!

CHAPTER 7

Fight Like a Girl!

One of the things that I have learned throughout the years of my Christian journey is that although Christ has paid the ultimate sacrifice and has already made a way of escape for us, we have to be prepared to fight for what is rightfully ours.

About two months after being separated from my husband, I was made redundant from a company that I had worked with for over nine years and had begun the process of finding a new job, which did not come quickly. During the process of sending out job applications, attending interviews that did not result in a job offering, fasting, praying, and trusting God, my funds dried up to the point where I could barely maintain myself and my son. It was not until eight months after being made redundant that a door had opened and I was invited for an interview that ended up paving the way for my next job.

Within a week of being on the job, my car that was in need of repairs got worse. The power steering wheel pump needed to be replaced as it would leak out the power steering fluid almost as fast as I would pour it in, and the front-end needed to be repaired as it made a loud sound with no promise of stopping when I applied brakes or when I attempted to go around corners. What made it even worse was that at the end of the first week of being on the job, my gas level became so low that the gaslight came on, and I had no funds to purchase gas as I was on a monthly pay cycle.

I remember going to church the Sunday evening before the start of my second week on the job with my gaslight on. I took the chance to drive with my gaslight on empty, as I had mustered up the faith to believe that God would have spoken to someone at church about my need and have them give me some money that would at least purchase gas for my car. I kept praying during the service. I lingered a while after the service, looking around to see if anyone was coming to me, but no one did. With my heart a bit broken, I drove back home with my car on empty.

The use of my car was critical in getting me to work and back and in taking my son to kindergarten and back, because in those days, the public transportation service was extremely poor. I had prayed that night, "Lord, you promised to supply my needs according to your riches in glory. I just do not understand why no one came to me, but I am still trusting You to make a way. Amen."

On Monday morning, I got up and got dressed for work. I had just a little money left in the bank—two thousand Jamaican dollars to be exact. And so I thought to myself that after reporting for work that morning, I would ask for some time to go to the bank to get the money to purchase some gas and to purchase power steering fluid. My thought was that hopefully the purchase would get me through a portion of the week. I did not have a plan for after that.

After reporting to work that morning, I was walking toward my car to leave for the bank when I heard the voice of the chairman of the company that I was employed in. "Which way are you going?"

I turned around with a smile on my face and said, "I am going to Half Way Tree." It was a major town in Jamaica.

He then asked, "Can I get a lift with you?"

I almost froze, but without wanting to seem like I was thinking about it for too long, I responded, "Sure."

The truth is, I did not understand why the chairman of the company would have wanted me to give him a lift, because not only did he own and drive and expensive car, he also had a personal driver who was standing right there in the car park. Added to that, I did not want him nor anyone driving in my vehicle because I was extremely embarrassed by the loud sounds coming from the front-end of my car and now from the power steering as the fluid had ran out.

I went in my car, and he quickly joined me by sitting in the passenger seat next to me. As I drove out and onto the main road, he asked, "All is well?"

I was not sure what he meant because I was new to the company, and I had only briefly met him before during orientation, and so the only response that came to me was "Yes, all is well." It was a faith response geared at dismissing my fears, because not all was well.

As we drove, I observed that whenever I applied brake, which resulted in a loud sound, he would hold on to the handle above his seat. And through the corners of my eyes, I saw that his feet were applying brakes too. About the third time of him doing so, he clearly could not take what must have seemed to him like risking his life, and so he asked, "Oh my god! What is wrong with your car?"

With the greatest feelings of embarrassment, I said, "The front end needs repairing." Just then, I turned to go around a corner, and a loud sound came from the power steering.

He asked, "What is that?"

Again, feeling even more embarrassed, I said, "The power steering needs fluid, and so I am going to get some money to buy power steering fluid and to buy some gas."

He immediately responded by saying, "No, Ms. Samuels. You cannot drive a vehicle like this. The minute that you get back to the office, please take it to the mechanic shop [the company had its own mechanic shop that repaired and serviced its fleet of vehicles] and tell them that I have given permission for them to repair whatever is wrong with your car at no cost to you. They will then call me." He then asked me to leave him at a building that we were approaching.

I wanted to scream, "Hallelujah! Thank you, Jesus!" However, I controlled myself, as I was still wondering if I had heard him correctly, and so all that I said was "Okay, sir. I will. Thank you."

As he had instructed, I did. The condition of my car was so bad that it took one full week for them to complete the repairs. And when the repairs were complete, my car was equipped with brand-new front-end parts, a brand-new power steering system, four brand-new tires, and a full tank of gas! In addition, if that was not enough, during the week that they were repairing my car, the chairman arranged for the company driver to take me to and from work each day!

God is simply amazing! He works in unusual ways. I had initially anticipated God using someone at church to give me gas money, but God had something better in store for me. I had not initially understood why the chairman—a total stranger to me—would have wanted to travel in my car, but God wanted him in my car so that He could use him to bless me. I remember asking the chairman months later what made him ask me for a lift that morning, and he said, "I really don't know. I saw you heading to leave, and I just felt like asking you for a lift." We serve that kind of God. That was the victory of the first fight regarding this car.

The second victory occurred almost a year after my divorce. Funds were low because my ex-husband had stopped maintaining our son from the time of our separation two years prior to our divorce, and I still had to contend with legal fees and added mortgage payments, which had resulted as I had to go through the courts to preserve my ownership rights in a housing property that we had both owned.

Although divine intervention gave me victory in the first fight three years prior, I was not able to maintain my car thereafter as I had to prioritize the use of my salary. I had no savings.

The same car was once again in need of front-end repairs, albeit to a lesser extent this time, which also resulted in it making a loud noise. And not only that, I now had another challenge of making payment for insurance coverage renewal.

I remember being at work the day. The insurance coverage was set to expire at midnight, and when I looked in my purse, the money that I had was insufficient to pay the premiums that were due. However, I decided to take a step of faith.

With permission granted for me to briefly leave office, I started my journey to the insurance company. I had no clue how God was going to work things out, but I remember thinking to myself, *God is able.*

What also made this move one of great faith was the fact that it was the policy of the insurance company to not renew insurance coverage on a defective vehicle. You first had to ensure that the vehicle was in good running order for them to provide coverage. Nonetheless, something inside me had refused to simply watch the day go by. I had to do something, and so I made my way to the insurance company.

As I journeyed to the company, I heard the noise in the front end. Upon entering the premises of the insurance company, I heard the noise in the front-end, and I remember pausing as I watched the insurance assessors test-drive other customers' vehicles to determine if they were fit to secure coverage, and I thought, *What am I doing?*

However, as soon as an assessor was available, I drove and parked my vehicle in the marked area. I then got out of the vehicle and handed my keys to the assessor. Whilst I stood waiting on the side, the assessor drove off with my vehicle in a reckless manner, twisting and turning it in all sorts of ways as he test-drove it, and all the while I was praying, "Jesus, Jesus, help me, Lord."

Within minutes, the assessor was back with my vehicle, and he remained in the vehicle whilst he filled out my vehicle assessment form. When he was through, he got out, handed me the form and my keys with a big smile on his face, and said, "Wow! Your vehicle is in excellent condition! You can proceed to go into the office to have your vehicle insurance coverage renewed."

I was shocked, to say the least. I prayed that he did not see the surprised look on my face, but as I walked away, I remember saying, "Thank you, Jesus! One down, one to go!"

When I got into the office, I had a little wait, and then it was my time to meet with the customer service representative. She took my form, read it, and then said, "Your vehicle is in an excellent condition, and because your vehicle is in an excellent condition, you qualify for a discount." When she applied the discount that I had qualified for, the sum that I was required to pay was the exact amount that I had in my purse—down to the last cent, with a few coins to spare. God did it again!

I had my insurance coverage renewed, and to prove that it was a miracle, when I was driving off the premises, I heard the sound in my front end. God had clearly deafened the assessor's ears to the sounds and his feel to the damaged front end. One week later, my brother heard of a place that was closing down and selling out dirt cheap the front-end parts that I needed. I was able to purchase the parts, and my brother, who has mechanical skills, replaced the parts in my front end for me. God did it again! That was two victories in one for the second fight regarding this car!

The next victory occurred after my fifth year of employment with the company and two years after the victory of my second fight. I was promoted to a managerial position, and the promoted position provided me with a company car. My brother was in need of a car at the time, and I decided to be a blessing to him by giving him the car.

Almost three months after giving him the car, I was on my way from work and heading to church to attend our Wednesday evening service. For some reason, I felt troubled in my spirit, and so as I traveled, I found myself praying for the protection of my family, and that was when my brother called.

He sounded frightened. He said, "Denise, I was just held up, and I had to run, leaving the car behind to save my life." I asked him where he was, and after he told me, I diverted from going to church and drove to go get him instead.

When I arrived to pick him up, you could still see the fright on his face. He had explained that he had dropped off a friend at his home, and whilst he was waiting for the friend to go inside his house, he heard his back door open. And before he realized what was happening, a man held a knife to his neck and what felt like a gun was held to his side, and the man said, "Turn the car around and drive." He said that he knew that if he had driven off with the man, he would have probably been killed, and so he decided to fight his way out.

He said that he held on to the hand with the knife and wrestled it away from his neck, which resulted in his hand being slightly cut. He said he then quickly opened his door and ran for his life. He said that the street had others on it, and he felt that the man did not want to raise any undue alarm, which was why he had not fired the gun at him. It was also clear that his getting away from the man was nothing short of a miracle!

We drove to the police station and reported the incident. The policeman who took our report showed us a lengthy list of stolen vehicle reports and advised that none of the vehicles were ever recovered. He told my brother that he should just be thankful that he got away safely but that he should not be hopeful about finding the vehicle. I immediately found myself saying out aloud, "The devil is a liar!"

You see, as far as I was concerned, God had performed too many miracles regarding this car for someone to simply steal it. As far as I was concerned, this story had to end differently from all the others!

After we left the police station, my brother borrowed my phone and called two of his friends to meet him by our house. He wanted them to assist him in driving through the area where the vehicle got stolen, just to see if by chance he would see the vehicle. Whilst they left to do that, I called up some of my prayer warriors, and then my mother, son (as young as he was), and I joined our hands in our living room. We started storming the gates of hell to release that which was stolen! By the time we got through praying, we knew that something had happened in the spiritual realm, as the glory of God came down, and so we left the matter in God's hands.

Exactly two days after the vehicle was stolen, my brother got a call from the police advising that the vehicle was found abandoned in a plaza. He said that the police had advised that they observed that the vehicle had been parked in the plaza from the day before. And when they observed that it still was not being attended to on the second day, they decided to do a check on the license plate number and realized that the vehicle had been reported stolen. And so they had it towed to the police station and also dusted it for fingerprints.

I took my brother to retrieve the vehicle, and that was when we became aware of yet another miracle.

The night that the vehicle was stolen, my brother had ran leaving his wallet in the vehicle. It was his habit to remove his wallet from his back pocket whenever he sat to drive. Well, not only was the vehicle found intact, but his wallet was also found intact in the vehicle. It had contained his driver's license and other pertinent cards. The only thing that was missing from his wallet was the four hundred

Jamaican dollars that he also had in it. God did it again! This was another case of a two-in-one victory—all because I chose to fight like a girl!

The Sermon

Judges 4:1–9

THE Bible is certainly a male-dominated book that reflects a male-dominated culture.

AND EVEN if we separate the history in the Bible from world history, we see that human history is full of tales of testosterone-driven leaders, using the force of military might, personal strength, and personal charisma to cause change.

YET we know that the involvement of women in history has been critical. AND surprisingly enough, we know that the involvement of women in the male-dominated narratives of the Bible was absolutely vital.

AND the more that I thought about this truth, the more I felt the need to remind women that we are not just cheerleaders.

We are not just figureheads.

But we have been chosen—handpicked by God—to do His work here on earth.

If you love being a woman, SAY, "Neighbor, "I am a woman, and I am loving it!"

PLESE TURN YOUR Bibles to **Judges 4:1–9**.

AND it reads thus…

> And the children of Israel again did evil in the sight of the LORD, when Ehud was dead.
>
> And the LORD sold them into the hand of Jabin king of Canaan, that reigned in Hazor; the captain of whose host was Sisera, which dwelt in Harosheth of the Gentiles.
>
> And the children of Israel cried unto the LORD: for he had nine hundred chariots of iron;

and twenty years he mightily oppressed the children of Israel.

And Deborah, a prophetess, the wife of Lapidoth, she judged Israel at that time.

And she dwelt under the palm tree of Deborah between Ramah and Bethel in mount Ephraim: and the children of Israel came up to her for judgment.

And she sent and called Barak the son of Abinoam out of Kedesh naphtali, and said unto him, Hath not the LORD God of Israel commanded, saying, Go and draw toward mount Tabor, and take with thee ten thousand men of the children of Naphtali and of the children of Zebulun?

And I will draw unto thee to the river Kishon Sisera, the captain of Jabin's army, with his chariots and his multitude; and I will deliver him into thine hand.

And Barak said unto her, If thou wilt go with me, then I will go: but if thou wilt not go with me, then I will not go.

And she said, I will surely go with thee: notwithstanding the journey that thou takest shall not be for thine honour; for the LORD shall sell Sisera into the hand of a woman. And Deborah arose, and went with Barak to Kedesh.

THE truth is, the term "fight like a girl" is usually used as an insult on playgrounds across the globe.

LITTLE boys, when testing their strength and skillfulness against each another, revert to this well-known slap in the face by throwing down the gauntlet of this time-proven stab.

THEY try to hurt each other by telling each other, "You fight like a girl" or "You run like a girl" or "You throw a ball like a girl."

AND the truth is, especially for men, if this statement was arbitrarily made to you, it would have been as if your world came to a screeching stop. And all that was holy had been profaned.

And for you, revenge must be quick as your reputation was at stake!

HOWEVER, I want us to reevaluate this insult.

I want us to take a new look at this concept of doing some things like a girl.

And I submit to you that rather than it being an insult, it may in fact be a great challenge to us all.

YOU SEE, if you have ever seen girls fight, you would know that there are two ways that girls fight.

THE first way is the slapping—play fight.

That really doesn't amount to much.

HOWEVER, the second type of girl fight is a totally different ballgame.

VISUALIZE with me if you will a mother grizzly defending her cub.

THAT mental picture is the fight that I am referring to.

SOME of the most vicious fights ever are two girls literally going at it tooth and nail.

Eye gouging, hair pulling, shrieking girl fight!

This is the fight that I want to spur you toward.

I WANT TO spur you towards this type of fight, because in the passage that we just read, it speaks about a girl, a woman named Deborah.

And she had a unique character in the Bible.

DEBORAH was a prophetess and the only woman to have been a judge of Israel.

HOW she had come to be chosen for that position is not recorded. But it is evident in her story that her leadership was honored.

AS judge, Deborah was also leader of the army of Israel, and her story took place during a time when the Israelites had their third falling away from God.

YOU SEE, after God had delivered the Israelites from Egypt into Israel, they went through seven apostasies, or seven falling aways from God.

IN OTHER words, on at least seven occasions, they went from serving God *to* backsliding, *to* being chastened by God *to* crying out to God, *to* God delivering them and then back *to* serving God.

The cycle repeating itself again for at least seven times.

AND EACH time that they had fallen away from God, they would suffer oppression and wars.

And yet with each falling away, God raised up a deliverer to rescue the them from their oppression.

IN THIS instance, Deborah was one such person.

GOD chose a woman in a particularly male-dominated time.

YOU SEE, I need you to understand that gender is never a problem with God.

YOU SEE, whilst man looks at the outward appearance, God looks at the heart. He looks at the soul.

AND THERE is no such thing as a masculine soul.

And there is no such thing as a feminine soul.

A soul is just a soul, and some are housed by males.

And some are housed by females.

SO what God focuses on is the condition of the soul.

He focuses on the readiness and on the willingness of the soul to do what needs to be done.

THE soul is the mind (which includes the conscience).

It is the will. It is the emotions of a person.

AND whilst there are some traits about the soul that transcends both male and female, our souls, our minds, our will, our emotions, are also conditioned by culture and determines our actions.

WOMEN have been cultured to be protectors.

We will do anything in our power to safeguard those we love.

WOMEN have been cultured to be domesticated.

We will spend our last energy on cleaning the house and on preparing meals.

WOMEN have been cultured to look attractive.

We will do all that is required to ensure that we are at our physical and intellectual best.

WOMEN have been cultured to serve.

We are selfless. We will wait on you.

We will do without so you can have.

We have a servant's heart.

WOMEN have been cultured to submit.

Someone who submits honors authority.

So we are worshippers in nature.

SO WHEN I say, "Fight like a girl," I am saying girls have what it takes to get the job done.

DON'T judge us negatively because we are feminine.

DON'T judge us negatively because we are cultured to wear a dress. We are more equipped than you think.

DON'T forget, when God gave us dominion over the earth as male and female, we were naked.

So our cultured clothes don't make us who we are.

We are not limited by outward appearance.

There is something inside of us spiritually driving us.

We are more than what meets the eye!

ISRAEL was in trouble.

And God needed somebody who was equipped to get the job done. And when He looked throughout Israel, He found that the best person to get the job done was a woman named Deborah.

AND her name says it all.

Because Deborah means "bee," and in spiritual terms, a bee is a "wise spiritual messenger."

VERY little is known about Deborah in terms of where she came from, BUT isn't it just like God to take somebody from obscurity and put them in a place of prominence?

DEBORAH wasn't chosen by man. She was chosen by God.

High-five somebody and tell them, "I am chosen."

YOU may not have come from royalty.

YOU may not have the best of everything.

Yet God chose you.

AND ISN'T it wonderful to know that God chose you regardless!

TELL your neighbor, "God chose me."

It didn't make sense in the natural.

But it made every sense in the spiritual. God chose me!

A MAN may not have chosen you because outwardly, you weren't beautiful enough.

Outwardly, you were not the right shape.

Outwardly, you were not the right size.

A MAN may not have chosen you because he didn't think that you were educated enough or talented enough.

A MAN may not have chosen you because he didn't think that you would fit in.

BUT thank God for looking beyond the natural into the supernatural. And He chose you.

SLAP somebody and tell them one more time, "I am chosen!"

ONE of the things that we do know about Deborah is that she was married to a man named Lapidoth.

AND Lapidoth means "torch" or "fire spark."

AND what I think God was saying was "Whomever I choose, whomever I put my anointing on, if you are in their space, you must be their fire spark."

You must be their encourager.

MEN should know that if their wives can handle money better than they can, then they shouldn't be handling it.

They should be encouraging her.

IF their wives are better businesspersons, then they shouldn't be putting her down.

They should be the fire behind her in business.

OUR men must know that they don't have to show the boys that they are the men of the house by competing with their wives.

AS they would have already proven that they are the man of the house because they chose the right woman.

SO GOD chose Deborah to get the job done.

And not only that, but in so doing, He placed her in an unusual place.

He placed her to do ministry under a palm tree.

There weren't many palm trees in Israel at the time.

SO we can safely say that God placed her in a rare and unusual place where anybody who had to go to see her had to go to a place that was not common in the land.

WHEN God chooses you, He places you in an usual place.

Where by His power, you display unusual gifts.

Where by His power, you perform unusual miracles.

Where by His power, you bless people in unusual situations.

THE place where God has you may not always be comfortable.

But it is what He requires to accomplish His will.

TOUCH somebody and tell them, "I am not like everybody else."

GOD has placed you in an unusual place because you have an unusual anointing.

To do an unusual job, AND because of that, you are not like everybody else!

WE have no record of Deborah having children.

But in the capacity of her calling, she was the mother of the nation of Israel.

And added to that, she was a judge. She called the shots.

AND the truth is that women who are that powerful can be intimidating to men.

BUT there is no need for a man to be intimidated by the calling and the anointing upon a woman's life.

Unless he is not man enough.

PEOPLE may even think that the strength of a woman is sometimes a reflection of the weakness of her spouse.

BUT Lapidoth, by virtue of the meaning of his name, understood that women of strength remain strong because of the spark that is provided to keep the fire burning in her.

COME ON, WOMEN. Turn to a woman seated near to you and ask her, "Are you a woman of strength?"

NOW, men, ask yourselves, "Do I have what it takes?"

LISTEN, WOMEN. YOU may have had people in your life who did not give you a spark.

But rather, they sought to put out your fire.

AND you know that you have a problem when you have to fight the person closest to you in order to get to the next level.

AND that is why you have to be careful of the people you hook up with, lest they tear you down rather than enhance you.

AND, MEN, you are not weak because you have a strong woman.

Because it takes a strong man to deal with a strong woman.

YOU shouldn't want to be with somebody you can just walk over.

YOU shouldn't want to be with somebody whose ideas you don't respect.

And you don't respect their opinions.

BUT rather, you should want to be with somebody who can match you on your level and at the same time facilitate you both advancing to the next level.

PAIRING yourselves up with someone weak does not help your cause.

PSALM 34 says, "Oh magnify the Lord with me."

It didn't say, "Oh, magnify the Lord above me."

Nor did it say, "Oh, magnify the Lord below me."

You need to magnify the Lord together.

LISTEN. If you are with somebody and you can't see eye to eye, you are still alone.

IF you are with somebody and you are not on the same level of persuasion, you are still alone.

AND, women, whilst men must not be intimidated by your strength, you must not challenge their priesthood.

YOU may be strong enough to be boss to a hundred men outside the home, but inside the home, you must be strong enough to submit to your husband in his capacity as priest.

AND I say in his capacity as priest because men don't expect women to submit.

When you stop being a priest and start being a hippo.

BECAUSE Ephesians 5:22 says, "Wives, submit yourselves to your own husbands—as you do to the Lord."

AND that is the part that most men forget—the part that says "as you do to the Lord."

NO strong godly woman is going to submit to a hippo, because when a woman submits to God, God doesn't abuse her.

God doesn't disrespect her.

God doesn't abandon her in times of need.

EVERY woman who submits to God gets treated like royalty.

God advances her.

God provides for her.

God is there for her in the good times and in the bad.

SO if you want a woman to submit to you as a priest, you have to behave like a priest.

High-five three persons and tell them, "Argument done!"

SO GOD handpicked a woman named Deborah.

AND He placed her under a palm tree.

Known by her name, it was called "the palm tree of Deborah."

YOU see, if you associate with something long enough, you are known by it.

YOU can become known *by what you do.*

You may not know the person's name, but if you say you know the sister who is always worshipping and dancing in the spirit, people will know exactly who you are talking about.

YOU can become known *by who you are married to.*

You know the lady's husband who always holds her hand while they are walking into church? Yes, that one.

YOU can become known by where you worship and by who you worship.

DEBORAH was known by her place of worship and the ministering service that she provided.

GOD placed Deborah under a palm tree.

And as unusual as it was, it was a place that allowed her to hear His voice.

IN THE stillness of the breeze, God could speak to Deborah.

And He could use her to be His mouthpiece.

She was a prophetess.

AND SO IN verse 5 of the chapter that we read, it said, "And the children of Israel came up to her for judgement."

THE children of Israel were being punished for turning against God again.

But in a moment of mercy, God wanted them delivered.

And He brought them up before Deborah.

And He revealed to her that he had spoken to Barak about the matter.

AND so we see in verse 6 that Deborah called Barak.

And she said to him, and I am somewhat paraphrasing, "Hath not the Lord God of Israel commanded you to go to Mount Tabor and prepare for battle? Didn't God tell you to take ten thousand men with you? And that He would make you win the battle against Sisera?"

AND you know what Barak's response was?

"If thou wilt go with me, then I will go. But if thou wilt not go with me, then I will not go."

NOW Barak, whose name means "lightning," was a warrior. He was an army general.

Yet at a time when he was most needed to shine, as lightning does, he basically said to a woman, "I have the power to command the ten thousand men. But I don't have what it takes to win the war. I am not anointed for that."

WHICH position are you holding that you are not anointed for?

GOD says, "It is not enough to be in the post without the anointing."

YOU SEE, power does not equate to anointing.

YOU have a lot of powerful people.

Powerful because of their position—their job title.

Powerful because of their wealth.

Powerful because of their status—their KSA.

Powerful because of who they associate with.

But their power can be easily overthrown by the anointing.

BECAUSE power is no match for God's anointing.

THE anointing makes the ordinary man able to do extraordinary things.

BARAK had power. But Deborah had the anointing.

YOU can't have victory without the anointing.

YOU may be the head of your household, but you need the anointing to keep the family together.

YOU may be a leader in your own right, but you need the anointing to steer the people right.

I DON'T care how smart you are.

It takes the anointing to destroy the yoke.

I DON'T care how powerful you are.

It takes the anointing to break the chains.

BARAK said to Deborah, "If thou wilt go with me, then I will go. But if thou wilt not go with me, then I will not go."

BARAK recognized his limitations.

BARAK recognized that he was in the position, but he couldn't fulfil the purpose.

BARAK recognized that it was pointless fighting with power alone.

He needed the anointing to do the supernatural.

BECAUSE the weapons of our warfare are not carnal but mighty through the pulling down of strongholds.

OUR battles are fought in the spiritual realm and materialized in the physical realm.

YOUR life depends on the anointing.

YOUR ministry depends on the anointing.

YOUR abilities depend on the anointing.

You can't overcome without the anointing.

AND SO what Barak was in fact saying to Deborah was "I have got the power. But I need the anointing. I NEED the anointing that makes you ferocious despite the fact that you are a girl. I NEED the anointing that makes you bold and fearless although you are a girl."

WHAT BARAK was saying to Deborah was "I NEED the anointing to make me committed like you. I NEED the anointing to make me determined like you.

BARAK was saying Deborah, "I NEED the anointing to remove my focus from gender and ego to realize that God can and will use anybody who makes themselves available to do His will."

SO DEBORAH, who knew her God-given mandate, said to Barak, and I am paraphrasing, "Of course, I will go with you. But understand that because you fail to be in a state of readiness when you should have been, there will be no glory in it for you. Because God will use a woman's hand to win the fight against Sisera."

IN OTHER words, "God will use a girl to fight."

TELL your neighbor, "Fight like a girl!"

EVERY woman has a Deborah inside of her.

And every man should seek to have the critical characteristics of a Deborah inside of him.

TELL somebody else, "Fight like a girl!"

GOD told Deborah what to do and when to do what.

AND as He instructed her, she directed Barak and his ten thousand men until all of Sisera's men were defeated.

AND when Sisera fled and thought that he had escaped, God got the help of another woman named Jael.

(Read the full story in Judges 4.)

When Barak arrived in pursuit of Sisera, Jael had already finished off Sisera once and for all.

SLAP somebody and tell them, "Fight like a girl."

BOTH Deborah and Jael were anointed for the task.

They were ready when God was ready.

AND despite the fact that Barak played a role in the fight, I AM SO glad that he refused to go without the anointing.

THE fight could not have been won without the anointing.

WE NEED some Deborahs and Jaels to rise up and to storm the gates of hell.

AS inadequate as you may feel or perceive yourself to be, you must stand up and fight! Get involved.

Reexamine who you are. You are a warrior.

You are armed and dangerous. You are positioned.

TOO many of our men are in prison.

The yoke must be destroyed by the anointing.

TOO many of our men are perpetrators.

And an almost equal amount have become victims of crime and violence.

The yoke must be destroyed by the anointing.

TOO many of our children are more and more becoming wayward.

The yoke must be destroyed by the anointing.

DEBORAH and JAEL, arise.

You are anointed to travail even when the men won't do it.

DEBORAH and JAEL, arise.

You are anointed to warfare for the family.

I DON'T know who I'm talking to right now.

BUT somebody here today IS desperately in need of the anointing.

To walk in victory over their circumstance.

JACK HANDEY wrote in his book *Fuzzy Moments* that "There used to be a bully who would demand his lunch money every day. And since he was smaller, he would give it to him. BUT then he decided to fight back by taking karate lessons. But the instructor wanted five dollars a lesson. And that was a lot of money for him. And so at that point he realized that it was cheaper to pay the bully so he gave up karate."

TOO MANY times we find it easier to pay the bully than learn how to defeat him.

IT IS amazing how many people want something for nothing.

THEY want a great church, but they want the pastor to build it.

THEY want a great marriage, but they don't want to take time to cultivate and to nurture the relationship.

THEY want a big ministry, but they don't want to take the time to lay the foundation through prayer and fasting and studying the Word.

BUT victory comes after you win the fight.

YES, the fight is fixed.

But you will never experience the outcome if you never get in the fighting ring.

NUDGE your neighbor and say, "Get off the sidelines and get in the ring!"

THERE is somebody listening to me right now.

Somebody who is in a dry place.

Somebody who is willing to say like Barak did: "I will not go without the anointing."

GOD says to tell you if you are desperate enough, in the same place where the enemy said it is over, He will cause you to tap into a fresh anointing.

IN the same place where the enemy said that he would destroy you, God will cause you to rise up with boldness and renewed faith.

THERE is a drought-breaking anointing in this place right now!

SOMETHING is stirring in my spirit.

Something is moving in this place.

THERE are too many people in the church who are moving without the anointing.

TOO many people are just going through the motions, keeping up appearances.

THEY shout when it's time to shout.

THEY clap when it's time to clap, BUT no anointing.

I WISH somebody would lift their hands toward heaven right now AND say, "Lord–, I want the anointing. I want a fresh anointing!"

SAY, "LORD, I want to sing with the choir, but I am not going without the anointing. LORD, I want to do ministry with the missions team, but I am not going without the anointing. LORD, I want to serve on the evangelism group, but I am not going without the anointing."

SAY, "LORD, I need to win this battle with the flesh, but I can't do it without the anointing."

THE anointing is a good thing.

IT will make you break out of prison like Paul and Silas.

IT will cause hungry lions to lose their appetite as it did for Daniel.

THE anointing will cause a cripple like the man at the pool of Bethesda to get up and walk.

THE anointing will cause the blind like Bartimeus to gain back sight.

THE anointing is moving in this place!

THERE is a restoration anointing flowing right now!

BECAUSE some Christians are living like they are on the playground. But they are really on a battlefield.

GOD wants you restored. He wants you revived.

GOD wants to change some things in your life.

To push you over the victory line.

WE NEED to join forces and plunder what needs to be plundered.

WE NEED to join forces and build what needs to be built.

BUT we cannot do it without the anointing.

TO always be on the side of victory, we need to be spiritually hungry.

SPIRITUAL HUNGER is a magnet.

SPIRITUAL HUNGER will draw the anointing.

SPIRITUAL hunger will open the door for the manifestation of the power of God.

AM I TALKING to anybody who is hungry for the presence and the anointing of God?

AM I TALKING to anyone who wants the reality of the tangible manifestation of the anointing and the power of God?

AM I TALKING to anybody who is not satisfied with religion and tradition?

AM I TALKING to anyone who wants the power of Pentecost in their life?

I BELIEVE there are some hungry and thirsty people listening to me right now.

PEOPLE who refuse to be satisfied or pacified with anything less than a personal encounter with the true fire—the anointing of God.

SOMEBODY is going to catch on fire today.

SOMEBODY is going to get hit by the power of God today.

THE anointing of God is going to seize your life.
THE anointing of God is going to take hold on your life.
THE anointing of God is going to set your life on fire.
OUR God is a consuming fire.
There is a consuming anointing in this house right now.
JUST as the fire of God fell on Mt. Carmel and consumed everything, so also is the consuming fire of God falling on your life.
I FEEL something happening right now.
I FEEL an anointing falling in this house.
I FEEL the fire of God falling in this house.
YES, the God that we serve still answers by fire.
WHEREVER there is an altar, He answers by fire.
WHEREVER there is a sacrifice, He answers by fire.
WHEREVER there is prevailing prayer, He answers by fire.
WHEREVER there are hungry hearts, WHEREVER there is a desperation for him, He answers by fire.
AND the God who answers by fire is here right now, just like He was in the fight to defeat Sisera.
And He will deliver the children of Israel.
GOD is here to save you. HE is here to deliver you. HE is here to restore your marriages.
HE is here to heal your broken heart.
HE is here to revive you, to Resurrect you, to put his fire back in you.
THE God who answers by fire is here to give you a fresh anointing, to set your heart and your life on fire.
HOLY GHOST fire, fall on us.
LIFT YOUR hands and ask Him to fall on you.
ASK Him to send the fire, to send the anointing.
ANOINTING, fall on us today.
FALL on our hearts.
FALL on our lives.
FALL on relationships.
HOLY GHOST FIRE, FALL on our ministries.
FALL on our visions and dreams.
FALL on our attitudes.

FALL on our families.
FALL on our finances.
FIRE OF God, FALL on us. Consume us.
Burn up dead religion. Burn up carnality.
Burn up dead traditions.
Burn up everything that is not of you.
AND anoint us afresh for your glory.
SOMEBODY is going to get a revelation that is going to shift them into a greater anointing than they have ever had.
SOMETHING is getting ready to change in your life.
And if you believe it, if you know that you are **positioned to soar**, if you want to **finish strong,** you must get in the ring with the anointing to fight.
And fight like a girl.
IN FACT, encourage seven persons by telling them, "Fight like a girl. Fight like a girl." (Repeat.)

CHAPTER 8

Break Up with the Flesh

I have been blessed to have a brother. And not just a brother but an older brother whom I love and who I know loves me.

Growing up was not without its sibling rivalries, but we recognized very early that what was most important was having each other's back.

We attended the same basic and primary schools together, and what I found most comforting was that if anyone bullied me, they had to also contend with my brother, as he would show up to defend me—no questions asked.

My brother played a pivotal role in assuming the male role model position in my son's life when his father (my ex-husband) had abandoned the role. To this day, my brother and my son are inseparable. In fact, when my son was younger and my brother would take him out, persons would think that he was his son.

It was my brother who had taught my son how to ride a bicycle. He gave him his first set of driving lessons. He taught him how to change car tires. He was the one who had some of the first conversations with him about the birds and the bees. He is one of his greatest cheerleaders. He taught him how to toughen up and be a man.

I will forever be grateful to my brother for the time that he had spent being that father figure that I was not created to be. And he didn't do it simply because he had no biological children (not yet anyway). He did it because we were cultured by a mother who had made us understand that above everything else, family matters.

An indoctrination that was also passed onto us by our mother was the importance of putting God first. We had to wake up early mornings on weekdays for prayer. And every Saturday morning was family devotion time, when we had to recite scriptures and pray out loud. We had to attend Sunday school. We had to attend Sunday and weekday services. We had to save from our lunch money to give our weekly offerings. We had to pray before going to our beds at nights. We had to learn to trust God to provide for us. All these were part of our childhood upbringing, but as we grew, I found that I was growing in the Lord whilst my brother chose not to, and it clearly was not because he was denied the teachings and trainings that I had received. It was because he had somehow opted to not break up with the flesh.

We still have plenty to celebrate. However, because he was not a drinker, a smoker, a gambler, nor a drug user, he has never gotten into trouble with the law. In fact, the worst thing that my brother has ever done is to not say, "Lord, I surrender" and actually stick to it.

I have often counselled my brother about his soul—not that our mother did not do her fair share. His response has always been and continues to be "Soon. Keep praying for me."

Yet often I remember his acts of courage. I will never forget the night that a car had overturned on our road during the middle of the night, and without thought that the vehicle could explode, my brother quickly got a sledgehammer and took the door apart to release the injured man from the vehicle. I keep praying for my brother.

I will never forget the times he struggled financially to make ends meet, and yet not once did he resort to a life of crime. Instead, he tried different business initiatives, and he would always say, "Denise, you remembered to pray for me?" I keep praying for my brother.

How can I forget that as grown as he is, when I was going through the initial separation from my now ex-husband, he wept. Years ago, when he was migrating, leaving our little family behind, he wept. When Mom had passed, he wept before, during, and after her celebration service. He wept openly like a baby as he repeated the sinner's prayers. I keep praying for my brother.

I just know that one day, my brother will break up with the flesh. You see, I have learned that it is not enough to be good and to do good things. More than anything else, God requires from us a life totally surrendered to His will.

The Sermon

Judges 16:1–6 and 16–17

> Then went Samson to Gaza, and saw there an harlot, and went in unto her.
>
> And it was told the Gazites, saying, Samson is come hither. And they compassed him in, and laid wait for him all night in the gate of the city, and were quiet all the night, saying, In the morning, when it is day, we shall kill him.
>
> And Samson lay till midnight, and arose at midnight, and took the doors of the gate of the city, and the two posts, and went away with them, bar and all, and put them upon his shoulders, and carried them up to the top of an hill that is before Hebron.
>
> And it came to pass afterward, that he loved a woman in the valley of Sorek, whose name was Delilah.
>
> And the lords of the Philistines came up unto her, and said unto her, Entice him, and see wherein his great strength lieth, and by what means we may prevail against him, that we may bind him to afflict him; and we will give thee every one of us eleven hundred pieces of silver.
>
> And Delilah said to Samson, Tell me, I pray thee, wherein thy great strength lieth, and where-

with thou mightest be bound to afflict thee. (Judg. 16:1–6)

And it came to pass, when she pressed him daily with her words, and urged him, so that his soul was vexed unto death;

That he told her all his heart, and said unto her, There hath not come a razor upon mine head; for I have been a Nazarite unto God from my mother's womb: if I be shaven, then my strength will go from me, and I shall become weak, and be like any other man. (Judg. 16:16–17)

IN keeping with our focus on the family and also our focus on the need for us.

To exercise dominion—authority—as children of God in these trying and testing times, IT got me thinking that there is no way we can successfully play our individual roles within the family.

There is no way we can truly exercise dominion—the authority given to us by our Lord and Savior Jesus Christ—without us first dealing with ourselves.

AND the Lord led me to the story of Samson and Delilah as recorded in the passage of scripture that we just read.

AND the Lord said, "Tell My people it is time to break up with the flesh."

AND so I use for a theme today the words **"break up with the flesh!"**

TURN to your neighbor and say, "Neighbor, breaking up is often hard to do. But God wants you to break up with the flesh."

LOOK at somebody else and say, "It is breaking up time!"

AS a refresher, let me remind you that Samson should have been the purest of human beings. He was ordained by God to be a Nazarite, a person consecrated unto God.

IN FACT, when he was conceived, God, through an angel, told his mother that SAMSON should not cut his hair.

HE told her that Samson should not drink wine or any fermented drink.

AND THIRDLY, that Samson should not have any contact with a dead body.

SAMSON was therefore *not* just a Nazarite from birth. Rather, he was a Nazarite from conception.

As undoubtedly, his mother would have started to refrain from consuming the things that God had instructed her not to feed him.

SAMSON was chosen by God.

He was anointed from the womb.

HE didn't get the Holy Ghost when he was twenty years old like some of you did.

God had His hands on Samson from his mother's womb.

Yet Samson had a problem.

He had a problem with the flesh.

SAMSON'S weakness was that he was a playboy.

IN three different chapters in Judges, Samson had three different women.

HE kept running in and out of relationships.

HIS problems with the flesh even led to the point where he allowed himself to hook up with a known enemy.

Judges 14 tells us of a time when Samson went down to a place called Timnath. And there he saw a young Philistine woman. And his flesh caught fire for the woman.

JUST like some men today, when they see some women, they can't keep their heels.

Their flesh goes into overdrive.

And it doesn't even matter if they are married or not.

They find a way to satisfy the flesh.

SAMSON's flesh caught fire for the Philistine woman to the point where he told his father to go get her for him, as he saw her as being right in his eyes.

YOU see, that is the problem with the flesh.

It always wants to satisfy itself.

SAMSON'S parents even questioned his choice.

But Samson had an intense relationship with the flesh.

He allowed his flesh to control his actions.

He allowed his flesh to control his desires.

He allowed his flesh to control his intentions.

Samson was consumed by the desires of the flesh.

BUT THE flesh is the gateway to the demonic.

MANY times, unless it is generational, it is through the flesh that demons gain entrance into a person's life.

WE are first tempted by the devil—by demons—because they seek to gain entrance into our lives or to carry out a plan to kill, steal, or to destroy us.

AND if we give in, they become welcome into our lives.

And once they enter, they will serve as bad friends who will constantly seek to negatively influence us.

THIS was clearly the case with Samson.

He was chosen by God, yet he allowed the flesh to open the door to lust.

SAMSON needed a family. He needed a wife.

But he went searching for her in all the wrong places.

AND CAN I just pause here to talk to some people who, like Samson, are searching for a spouse—a wife or a husband—but are looking in the wrong places.

FIRST and foremost, the Bible says in Genesis 2:18, "It is not good that the man should be alone—I will make him an help-meet for him."

GOD was there.

Yet God said it is not good for man to be alone.

I KNOW that some people like to say that God is my husband or God is my wife.

And if in saying that, you simply mean that God keeps you. Then that is okay.

BUT let me remind you that God's relationship with us is spiritual.

HIS love for us is that of the agape love and not of the erotic love.

SO yes, God keeps you.

But He does not function in the physical realm.

He functions in the spiritual realm.

SO He can never truly be your husband.

GOD said, "It is not good for man to be alone."

Yet the animals were there.

TELL your neighbor, "A pet won't do."

NO pet can substitute for what God intended when He said it is not good for man to be alone.

GOD said, "I will make for man a help-meet."

AND a help-meet in simple terms is one who is divinely suitable for the other.

BECAUSE in Genesis 2:21–22, the Lord caused a deep sleep to fall upon Adam.

And he took one of his ribs and closed up the flesh.

And the Lord used the rib that He took from Adam to make Eve and brought Eve to him.

SO Eve wasn't made from Adam's flesh.

So your reason for hooking up with somebody should not be about the flesh.

EVE was made from Adam's rib.

And a rib is a strengthening or supporting material.

AND Genesis 2:23 tells us that when Adam awoke, he said, "She is now bone of my bones and flesh of my flesh and she shall be called woman."

Because she was taken out of man.

AND this is remarkable because Adam was asleep when God took the rib out to make Eve.

And there is nowhere in scripture that tells us that God told Adam what He had done.

Yet the very moment that Adam saw Eve, he knew that she came from him.

THERE was something about Eve that made Adam know that he knew her before he saw her.

Eve was made for him.

YOU have no business being with somebody who God didn't make for you.

YOU have no business going from woman to woman or from man to man and say you are testing the waters.

IT WAS God who saw that Adam needed an Eve.

And at the right time, when God saw that Adam was ready, He presented Eve to Adam.

YOU need to learn to wait on God and not be like Samson.

RATHER than to wait on God, Samson continually compromised his commitment for convenience.

He played with the flesh.

AND THE Bible tells us that Samson eventually fell in love with a woman named Delilah.

AND his love or lust for Delilah kept luring him back to her, although it was clear that her feelings for him wasn't mutual.

IT is a terrible thing to love somebody and not have them love you back.

DELILAH was his enemy.

And Samson kept sleeping with the enemy.

WHEN you sleep with the enemy, you allow yourself to become vulnerable to the evil devices of the enemy.

YOU see, sleep puts you in a subconscious state.

It takes away your ability to be alert.

It leaves you defenseless to the enemy's attacks.

DELILAH'S only intention was to know the secret to Samson's strength.

SHE wanted to know the secret of his anointing so that she could have him destroyed.

DELILAH knew that Samson was no ordinary man.

He had power and might.

DELILAH knew that Samson was special.

He had the interest of many.

The Philistines were willing to pay her in exchange for him.

DELILAH knew Samson's weakness.

Samson loved satisfying the yearnings of the flesh.

He loved being with Delilah.

He loved how she made him feel.

HE was after a wife, but Delilah was after *his* life.

AND maybe I just need to pause and tell somebody that the enemy is after your life.

He is after your anointing.

The enemy is after your strength.

DON'T believe the lies of the enemy.

YES! The enemy may have told you that you are the sweetest thing since sliced bread.

The enemy may have told you that you have the best Coca-Cola-shaped body.

The enemy may have told you that you are a knight in shining armor.

BUT the enemy is only playing with your mind.

The enemy is trying to wear you down so that you will give up more.

DELILAH kept asking Samson for the secret to his strength—the secret to his anointing.

AND SAMSON kept entertaining Delilah because he wanted to please Delilah.

He wanted Delilah to like him just as much as he liked her.

BUT as a child of God, you have no business trying to make somebody like you.

YOU have got to understand that a Delilah will never like you no matter what you do.

A Delilah will never like you because the spirit in her is not going to receive the spirit in you.

THE spirit in her is of the devil.

And the spirit in you is of God.

AND so there will always be a fight for first place.

SOME of you listening to me right now know what I am talking about.

EVERYTIME you go to the place that you know you shouldn't be going, a fight begins in your spirit.

EVERYTIME you go to bed with the person that you have no business sleeping with, a fight begins in your spirit.

EVERYTIME you make that phone call that you have no business making, a fight begins in your spirit.

SAMSON left the sanctity of where God would have him be and entered the darkness of a sinful bed.

SAMSON wanted a woman more than he wanted God.

Some of you want a man more than you want God.

SAMSON wanted to be in a relationship with Delilah more than she wanted to be in a relationship with him.

SOME of you want to be needed.

You want to be in a relationship where you are needed because you think if you are needed, the man or the woman that you are with won't leave you.

BUT you don't need to be needed.

You need to be *appreciated.*

YOU SEE, people can hate who they need.

PEOPLE can despise who they need.

BUT they can't despise who they *appreciate.*

AND THAT is why you need to trust God to supply all your needs.

STOP looking to a man or to a woman to supply your needs because they will get tired of doing so and resent you for it.

LOOK to God to supply your needs.

Because when God handles your needs, He takes the edge off your desperation.

AND when you get desperation out of your life, you can stand up and say, "Not you. Not you. Keep going. Keep going."

WHEN God takes the edge off your desperation, it gives you the power to wait until you can be appreciated.

TELL your neighbor, "I am not desperate for nobody but God."

YOU see, when you are appreciated, you can look somebody squarely in the face and say, "I didn't enter this relationship to be your slave. I entered this relationship on your level."

BECAUSE you are not looking to them to supply your needs.

You are looking to God to supply your needs.

WHEN you trust God to supply your needs, you don't have to sneak into somebody's bed in exchange for anything.

BUT rather, you can tell them, "You see my TV? A Jesus gave it to me.

"You see my car? A Jesus gave it to me.

"You see the clothes that I wear? A Jesus gave it to me."

DON'T sell yourselves short.

No man or woman can provide for you like Jesus can.

If Jesus won't do it, then it can't be done.

SOME people get hurt when their relationships don't work out.

But you should give God praise.

For every man or woman who rejected you in the past, THEY rejected you because you refused to put up with their foolishness.

THEY rejected you because they didn't want to buy a puss in a bag.

BUT you are not a puss.

You are a child of God.

You are a royal priesthood. You are a holy nation.

You are a peculiar person, a special person.

YOU see, when you are rejected by a Godless person, it is a blessing.

DON'T worry when a Godless person puts you down.

Because one day soon, God will send somebody who will make you feel like a million dollars.

LISTEN. The Bible is clear that all that the world has to offer is the lust of the eye, the lust of the flesh, and the pride of life.

A NUMBER of you are seeking to be validated.

You are seeking to be approved by the opposite sex.

BUT validation is subjective.

SAMSON was seeking to be validated by Delilah.

So he kept giving in to her whims and fantasies.

ONE of the mistakes that people make is to they believe that it is how good they are that makes people choose them.

AND because they think that they are the reason that they got chosen, the minute the person starts to lose interest in them, they think it is their fault.

AND because they think it is their fault, they begin to intensify their drive to keep the person interested in them.

BUT those of us who are wise enough know that you can do everything for somebody, and they will still leave you.

SOME of you have been good to people.

You have made many sacrifices in your relationship.

You have done all you possibly can to make the relationship work.

And yet the person still walked out on you.

SOME of you have become bitter.

You have become bitter because you were used and abused.

You were mistreated and forsaken.

YOU have become bitter because no matter what you did, THE person just wouldn't love you.

The person kept being unfaithful to you.

The person still left you.

AND when you see who they left you for, **smile.**

Lord, have mercy!

WHEN you see who they went and shacked up with, WHEN you see who they are now hanging out with, your temper will boil the more.

BUT I am here to tell you, "Don't be bitter. Things are going to get better."

GOD sent me to tell you that they walked out on you because they can't go where God is taking you.

When people come into your life, it is not about where you are.

It is about where you are going.

YOU SEE, somebody who doesn't have the heart for you can take everything that you give to them and still leave you.

AND GOD doesn't want you losing sleep at night crying over people who don't know how to appreciate you.

GOD doesn't want you having a nervous breakdown, worrying over somebody who couldn't care less about you. IT IS time to break up with the flesh!

TELL your neighbor, "Break up with the flesh!"

YOU are too gifted to be wasted.

YOU are too gifted to be ignored.

YOU are special in God's sight.

Don't let the flesh abort your purpose.

THREE times Delilah begged Samson to tell her the secret to his strength. And he lied.

HE lied because he knew the consequences of telling the truth.

BECAUSE after all, how could he tell the woman that he had been sleeping with that he was a Christian?

HOW could he tell the woman that he had been sleeping with that he sang in the choir?

HOW can you tell the man that you have been sleeping with that you are an active member in the church?

SAMSON knew better, but he failed to do better.

AND on top of that, Delilah was persistent. She wouldn't let up.

And so she kept asking Samson to reveal his secret.

THE devil is persistent.

He will not let up. And if you lay yourselves careless, he will rob you of your strength, your dignity, and your identity!

SAMSON knew that Delilah was out to get him.

He knew that Delilah was out to trap him because she kept calling the Philistines, the enemies, upon him.

Yet Samson kept sleeping with her.

JESUS! Who am I talking to?

YOU know that the relationship that you are in is killing you spiritually, but you still stay with the person.

WHO am I talking to?

You know that the relationship that you are in is destroying someone else's family.

But you still stay with the person.

WHO am I talking to?

You know that the relationship that you are in will destroy your family.

But you still stay with the person.

You still entertain the person.

GOD is calling you to break up with the flesh!

I KNOW that I am talking to somebody today.

As I would be one crazy woman to think that nobody in this sanctuary and nobody viewing by livestream has problems abstaining from sex outside of marriage.

I WOULD be one crazy woman to think that nobody under the sound of my voice has problems with the flesh.

AND MAY I just hasten to say that whilst your struggle with the flesh may not be related to sex, what about the fact that you struggle with telling the truth?

WHAT about the fact that you struggle with taking what does not belong to you?

What about the fact that you are backstabber?

The fact that you are a malice-keeper?

Galatians 5:19–21 reminds us that the works of the flesh are adultery, fornication, uncleanness, lasciviousness, idolatry, witchcraft, hatred, variance, emulations, wrath, strife, seditions, heresies, envyings, murders, drunkenness, revelings, and such.

AND that "they which do such things shall not inherit the kingdom of God."

IT doesn't matter how long you have been saved or how anointed you are.

We still fight certain things.

We still have some real struggles.

AND we will never be who we are destined to be until we recognize that our fight is against principalities, against powers, against the rulers of the darkness of this world, against spiritual wickedness in high places.

GOD is calling you to break up with the flesh!

TELL somebody, "It is breaking-up time."

SAMSON knew that Delilah was out to get him.

But the gratification—the pleasure of sex—kept him spiraling out of control.

LISTEN. CAN I be real with you?

EVERYBODY in here who is celibate, EVERYBODY in here who chooses to obey God and to abstain from sex outside of marriage proves that God is sure enough a mighty God.

BECAUSE sometimes the stuff that you have to go through to remain celibate, you couldn't have gone through it without God.

IF GOD allowed me, I would have asked all the celibate people and the unmarried people who have been keeping themselves for God to shout out a praise.

BUT I don't want to cause any embarrassments.

SO everybody, just shout out a praise!

SOMEONE who truly loves God finds it easy to obey God.

YOU see, you can't obey God unless you love Him.

YOU HAVE to love God so much that you are willing to deny flesh for more of Him.

CHARACTER and emotions can split you down the middle.

ON the one hand, your character based on the principles and teachings of God is standing up.

AND on the other hand, your emotions, your desire to be loved, your yearnings of the flesh are standing up.

AND character and emotions are at war.

BUT you have got to understand that God often requires us to do things that we don't feel like doing.

And not giving in to your emotions is not always easy.

But it is possible.

A LOT of people are single today because the roles of God's design have been overturned.

YOU see, God provided for the man way before the woman got here.

ADAM had everything he needed to provide for a woman before God gave him a woman.

BUT today, a lot of people are single because God had to provide for the woman, as the man was not in his rightful place.

MEN have been failing to assume their rightful place.

Some men no longer want to provide for a woman.

They are instead looking for women to provide for them.

AND that is why some women are still single, especially if you are like me, because I don't want no man who can't assume his rightful position.

WOMEN must understand their value and worth.

Not any and every man can be with you.

CAN I give you a joke?

ONE time, somebody told me that someone they knew liked me.

But that he was intimidated by my strength.

AND I said, "Good. He isn't the one. If he is intimidated from afar, he is going to be even more intimidated up near."

WOMEN of strength don't need no weakling.

WOMEN must have standards.

And don't settle for less than what God designed for you.

A LOT of women are single because men are not in their rightful place.

IN FACT, the right order is God leading with man following God.

And woman following the man who is following God.

BUT when Eve got Adam to eat of the forbidden tree, the roles overturned.

WHEN Delilah kept luring Samson back to her, the roles overturned.

AND what ended up happening was...

WOMAN leading with man following woman.

AND we know that God does not follow ANYBODY!

FLESH and God cannot walk together.

You can't entertain the flesh, or else it will destroy you.

SAMSON kept sleeping with the enemy until the enemy wore him down.

DELILAH said in Judges 16:15, "How can you say, you love me, when your heart is not with me? You have mocked me these three times and have not told me where your great strength lies."

AND with those words, Samson gave in and He told her the truth.

HE said in Judges 16:17, "My hair has never been cut, because I was dedicated to God as a Nazirite. And if my head were shaved, my strength would leave me."

IN OTHER WORDS, Samson said, "I am supposed to be a Christian. I was water baptized and Holy Ghost filled. AND if I keep sleeping with the enemy, if I fail to obey God's instructions to break up with the flesh, my anointing is going to leave me."

AND that was all that Delilah needed to hear to be able to hand him over to the enemy.

AND SO when Samson went to sleep with Delilah again, in complete disregard for the instructions of God, "Delilah had his hair shaved and then she began to hit him but she could see that his strength was leaving him."

THE woman that Samson had loved, THE woman that once satisfied the desires of his flesh, began to physically abuse him.

I MUST pause to say that anyone that you are with that was not divinely made for you will eventually abuse you.

BECAUSE IF they were not divinely made for you, they cannot make you better.

They cannot be the wind beneath your wings.

They will only pull you down and abuse you.

SAMSON used to mock Delilah by telling her lies about the secret of his strength.

But now she was mocking him.

DELILAH called out, "Samson, the Philistines are upon you."

And the Bible says that he shook himself as at other times but found his strength was gone.

His anointing was gone.

IT IS a terrible thing to lose your anointing.

IT IS a terrible thing to lose your God-given power.

IT IS a terrible thing to lose your God-given authority.

BUT there is no way that you can play with fire and not get burned.

THERE is no way that you can play with sin and not pay the price. Sin is expensive.

THERE is no way you can entertain the desires of the flesh and not experience the consequences.

SAMSON ended up losing not only his anointing but also his vision.

YOU see, the fall to the ground is sequential.

It comes in stages.

The enemy will strip you level by level.

AND Judges 16:23–24 tells us that the Philistine leaders declared a great festival to celebrate the capture of Samson.

THE people made sacrifices to their god Dagon and excitedly praised him for delivering Samson to them.

THEY gloated as they saw Samson in chains.

They even demanded that Samson be brought out to them so that they could make fun of him.

SAMSON had hit rock bottom.

And he possibly thought, *This is it! I messed up big time, and God has forsaken me. I will never be able to fulfill my purpose of beginning the deliverance of the Israelites out of the hands of the Philistines.*

BUT EVEN when we are down and out, aren't you glad that God still isn't through with us?

SAMSON must have known that although he had greatly disappointed the Lord, although he was disobedient, although he had failed God, God is a God of mercy and of love.

AND Samson decided to use his setback as a comeback.

YOU see, when you hit rock bottom, it means you are at the perfect place to bounce back up again.

AND that is why nobody has the right to write you off.

NOBODY has the right to condemn you.

NOBODY has the right to look down on you.

Because being at the bottom doesn't mean it is over for you.

IN FACT, a bounce can push you past your criticizers.

A bounce can push you past your accusers.

A bounce can push you to the front of the line.

FOR the last shall be first.

ALL you have to do is break up with the flesh.

SIX of you come down here.

You are at the back of the line because of your relationship with the flesh.

BUT the minute that you break up with the flesh…

(Everybody turn around.)

GOD causes you to be at the front of the line.

Because the last shall be first.

TELL your neighbor, "If you want to be first in line, break up with the flesh."

HIGH-FIVE three people and tell them, "I don't know about you, but I am breaking up with the flesh!"

SAMSON made the decision to break up with the flesh.

The enemy had robbed him of his natural vision.

But he still had insight and foresight.

YOU see, man can kill the body, but he can't kill the soul.

SO while his accusers were drinking and dancing and making fun of him, he asked a little boy to lead him to the pillars that held the building up.

HE asked a little boy to lead him to the pillars that facilitated the works of the flesh.

HE asked a little boy to lead him to the pillars that kept the roof of the building in place.

And he said, "Place my hands against the two pillars."

IN OTHER words, "Place my hands against the pillars of flesh. Place my hands against the pillars that, if removed, will destroy the flesh."

AND the little boy did as Samson had asked.

And then Samson cried out to God.

SAMSON said in Judges 16:28, "Oh Lord Jehovah. Remember me again."

IN OTHER words, "Oh Lord Jehovah, I know that I failed you. But today I am breaking up with the flesh."

OH Lord Jehovah, I know that I took advantage of your mercy.

But today I am breaking up with the flesh.

OH Lord Jehovah, I know I transgressed your ways.

But today I am breaking up with the flesh.

SAMSON cried out to the Lord, "Oh Lord, remember me again."

Remember when I used to fast and pray.

Remember when I hungered and thirsted for your righteousness.

Remember when I hardly missed a church service.

OH Lord, remember me again.

Remember when I used to feed the hungry.

Remember when I used to clothe the naked.

OH Lord, remember me again.

Remember when I used to lay hands on the sick and see them recover.

OH Lord, remember me again.

Remember when I used to operate in the gifts of the spirit.

I used to prophesy.

I used to deliver words of knowledge.

I used to preach and teach your word.

I used to have faith for miracles.

I used to sing on the choir.

I used to dance and sing for your glory.

SAMSON cried out, "OH Lord, remember me again."

I used to love my neighbor as myself.

I used to visit the sick and shut-ins.

I used to witness to people and lead them to Christ.

SAMSON said, "Oh Lord, remember me again. Please strengthen me one more time."

IN OTHER words, Samson was saying, "LORD, restore my anointing one more time."

Give me back my praise one more time.

Give me back my joy one more time.

Give me back hope one more time.

Give me back peace one more time.

ONE more time, Lord. Anoint me again.

Set me on fire again. Use me for Your glory again.

Let me fulfil my purpose.

AND when Samson placed his left hand on one of the pillars of the flesh, HE must have said, "LUST, I bind you in the name of Jehovah God.

"DEPRESSION, I bind you in the name of Jehovah God.

"LOW SELF-ESTEEM, I bind you in the name of Jehovah God.

"FEAR, I bind you in the name of Jehovah God."

AND THEN as he placed his right hand on the other pillar of flesh, he must have said, "I lose victory in the name of Jehovah God.

"I lose a fresh anointing in the name of Jehovah God.

"I lose spiritual power in the name of Jehovah God.

"I lose power over the flesh in the name of Jehovah God."

AND AS he said so, Samson pushed against the two pillars.

And as he did so, he said, "Let my flesh die with every other flesh in the house."

IF YOU understand what I am talking about, put your hands on your body and say, "Flesh, die in the name of Jesus Christ of Nazareth."

SAMSON understood that flesh brings nothing but destruction.

Flesh brings nothing but shame and disgrace.

Flesh brings nothing but heartache and heartbreaks.

SO Samson was determined to kill the flesh.

AND AS the building crumbled and the flesh began to die all around him, I can just hear Samson saying in his spirit, "IT IS going to be all right. I am now doing what I was born to do.

"IT IS going to be all right. I feel a breakthrough coming. My strength has come back."

AS the flesh was being destroyed, Samson must have said, "I have been talked about, but it is going to be all right now."

I HAVE been ridiculed, but it is going to be all right.

SAMSON must have said, "I HAVE been through divorce.

"I HAVE been through broken relationships.

"I HAVE suffered great pain.

"But it is going to be all right."

AND ALL the enemies of the flesh were totally destroyed.

JESUS has given you power to conquer the flesh.

No weapon formed against you shall prosper.

JESUS has given you power to wait upon the Lord.

No weapon formed against you shall prosper.

JESUS has given you power to have a sound mind.

No weapon formed against you shall prosper.

JESUS has given you power to rise above your circumstance.

No weapon formed against you shall prosper.

JESUS has given you the power to be the wife or husband that He called you to be.

No weapon formed against you shall prosper.

JESUS has given you power to be all He has destined you to be.

No weapon formed against you shall prosper!

IF You believe it, SAY, "Thank you, Jesus, for the power!"

CHAPTER 9

Don't Let the Stone Stop You!

At the age of about nine years, my uncle, one of the youngest brothers of my father, came from the country to live with us. He was about twenty-two years at the time and was extremely naïve.

His parents (my grandparents) had sent him to live with us as things had become financially challenging for them, and they had feared that he was being possibly influenced by a Rastafarian group. The way that he spoke when he had initially arrived at our home had confirmed the possible influence, although he never outrightly admitted to it.

I still recall that just after my uncle had come to live with us, he gave us a story that had left our family laughing in stitches for days. He had told us how persons living in the country would know that some-one in Kingston had been electrocuted because the blood ran through the electrical power lines through to the country. To this day, we chuckle when we recall his story. It was a story that he actually believed before we told him know how impossible that would have been.

He was very contrasting too. He had told us from the start that he did not eat pork, yet he ate ham and would enjoy my mom's cooking of seasoned rice with pigtail. He had told us that he did not like salt, yet he would at times complain that the food was fresh. My uncle, the only uncle that I am close to, didn't speak much, but he had, and to this day he still has one of the most infectious laughter. You would be dead not to laugh when he does. So back then, to my brother and I as children, he had become the welcomed humour of the house.

It was not long after living with us, however, that I had found myself still at a very young age witnessing to my uncle, telling him about Jesus Christ and urging him to give his life to the Lord. He had oftentimes resisted my prodding, countering it with questions concerning the existence of God. But I would push back, defending my belief.

One of my mom's requirements for him living in our home was that he had to attend church, even though my father, his brother and her husband, never attended church at the time. It was within a matter of months of me witnessing to him and him going to church that he finally surrendered to the Lord, attributing his decision to my witness.

The decision to accept Christ thereafter radically changed his thought process and outlook on life. The country boy who had come to town with many stones of naivety and insufficiencies was no longer satisfied with moping around the house, but he had developed a zeal to achieve more than what life had initially seemed to offer.

He went back to school and had crafted and developed a skill that became his livelihood and made him one of the best in his field.

Although he met and married the love of his life with the union producing a son, he remained close to our family and had formed a bond with my mom that caused many to believe that he was her biological brother.

My uncle is a testament that stones, although are obstacles, are not meant to stop you. They are simply meant to challenge you to forge ahead and become the best version of yourself in Christ. To this day, he remains a Christian, actively serving as a deacon and ministry leader in our church.

The Sermon

Mark 16:1–4 says:

> And when the sabbath was past, Mary Magdalene, and Mary the mother of James, and

Salome, had bought sweet spices, that they might come and anoint him.

And very early in the morning the first day of the week, they came unto the sepulchre at the rising of the sun.

And they said among themselves, Who shall roll us away the stone from the door of the sepulchre?

And when they looked, they saw that the stone was rolled away: for it was very great.

The Sermon

Easter Monday means the memory of the death, burial, and resurrection of our Lord and Savior, Jesus Christ.

It is still fresh in our minds.

AND here in the passage of scripture that we have read, we find that women were on their way to the tomb where they had laid Jesus.

BECAUSE at least three days earlier, Jesus had been crucified and buried in a sepulcher.

IN FACT, the scripture tells us that a Roman governor named Joseph had asked Pilate if he could take the body of Jesus and put it in a tomb that he had reserved for his own burial.

AND UPON receiving permission, the body of Jesus was removed from the cross and placed into that borrowed tomb.

AND on top of that, the Bible tells us that Jewish leaders had requested and had received of Pilate permission to have a huge stone and armed guards placed in front of the tomb so that no one would have been able to steal the body and then claim that Christ was alive.

AND SO HERE we find these women on their way to anoint the body of Jesus.

AND perhaps they went because somebody had to. Because after all, that was the custom.

It was expected.

It was an act that was usually carried out by women.

BUT COULD IT have been a case where the women went because the men were too scared to come out of hiding?

I DON'T mean to beat down on the men.

But there was a reason the scriptures highlighted the fact that it was the women that went AND not the men.

YOU SEE, many of Jesus's friends and followers had retreated into hiding.

THEY had retreated out of fear.

Out of fear that they would have been made to suffer the same fate as Jesus.

And we are talking about the same fear that had caused Peter to deny Christ three times.

WE are talking about the same fear that made Pontius Pilate say, "I find no fault with Him" AND then turn around and hand Him over to be crucified.

THE men were fearful.

But the women refused to let fear stop them.

YES! There were reasons to be fearful.

YES! There were reasons to be hesitant.

Because Jesus had suffered a horrible death, and no one knew the next move of the Jewish leaders.

BUT the women must have remembered that fear was not of God.

And so they refused to let fear stop them.

TOUCH three persons and tell them, "Don't fear!"

Fear is of the devil.

There is a greater purpose ahead.

TOUCH three more persons and tell them, "Have no fear!"

I DON'T KNOW what you are going through right now, but have no fear!

THE devil may have told you that today marks the period leading up to your own death and burial.

But God says, "Have no fear!"

IN THE passage that we read, I see that there must have been some faith on the part of these women.

BECAUSE these women knew that the tomb was sealed up.

They knew that the tomb was sealed up with a stone, and that the stone was huge. As the scripture says, it was great.

THESE women knew that it would have been impossible for them to move the stone on their own.

THE women knew that it would have been impossible for the stone to be removed without getting the attention of the Jewish leaders.

YET that did not stop the women from making the journey!

IT IS ALSO clear that these women also had *no* idea as to how they were going to get past the stone to get to Jesus.

IN fact, they were already on their way to the tomb when they asked themselves the question, "Who shall roll away the stone?"

AND perhaps, just perhaps, there is something that we can learn from these women.

FOR ONE THING, these women did not let the stone stop them.

THEY did not let the stone stop them from taking the journey to be with Jesus.

THEY did not let she Stone stop them from preparing to anoint Jesus with their precious spices and oil.

THEY did not let the stone stop them from commencing the journey, which would have culminated in an act of worship.

AS these women's mission was to honor the One whom they had grown to love.

THEIR mission was to honor the One who had given His life so they could live.

THEIR mission was to honor their miracle worker.

THEIR mission was to honor their Lord and Savior.

THE women did not let the stone stop them.

Because they knew the importance of taking a stance and honoring their Lord!

NOW PLEASE note something with me.

THE stone was one of the many stones that appear in the Bible.

AND that is why, as we exegete this passage, we must understand that the stone is symbolic of a burden.

The hard places in our lives.

AND just as the stone was not easily removed, so it is that our burdens are not easily removed.

AND AS I prepared to deliver this message, the Lord showed me that there would be some persons here today who are weighed down by a stone that has been cast upon them.

SOME of you are bearing the stone of financial difficulty.

SOME of you are bearing the stone of depression.

SOME people are bearing the stone of guilt.

SOME persons are bearing the stone of a broken heart.

SOME are even bearing the stone of ill health.

WHILST some persons are bearing the stone of a broken marriage, a broken family.

Or they are just spiritually, morally, mentally, and physically broke.

YOU SEE, being broke is a heavy burden.

DO I have a witness this morning?

IN fact, PROVERBS 27:3 tells us that "A stone is heavy."

THE stone that is weighing down on you is huge.

IT is enormous. And if it should ever be removed from you, everybody would take notice.

Because there would be a significant change in you.

THERE would be a significant change in you.

Because the heavy stone that is on your back sometimes makes you unbearable to deal with.

AS A matter of fact, even for those of you who are rooted in the Word, THE stone that is weighing you down sometimes seems like it's just too much for you to even bear.

AND that is just how the enemy wants you to feel.

BUT GOD sent me to tell you, "Don't let the stone stop you!"

ISAIAH 8:14 says that a stone can be a stone of stumbling.

In other words, a stone can trip you up!

YOU may think you are doing okay.

YOU may think that you've got it going on.

YOU may think that you are walking the straight and the narrow.

YOU may even think that you are so close to Christ, that nothing can get next you.

BUT then all of a sudden, you trip because the devil put a well-placed stone of stumbling in your path.

BUT I came to tell you that IF you trip, don't fret.

Just try to catch your balance and keep on keeping on.

IF YOU trip, don't give up on what you set out to accomplish.

AND even if you stumble and fall, get back up on your feet.

Dust yourself off. Straighten out your clothes and walk.

BUT DON'T LET THE STONE STOP YOU!

ZECHARIAH 12:3 tells us that stones are burdensome.

THEY are not meant to be easy.

THEY are not meant to accommodate your lifestyle.

THEY are not meant to fit into YOUR scheme of things.

THEY are not meant to bring efficiency to your life.

BUT they *are* meant to alter the way that you do things.

STONES are meant to alter the way you see things.

They are meant to get in your way, to hinder you, and to even stop you from accomplishing anything that GOD wants you to do.

STONES are burdensome. But don't let the stone stop you!

GOD has given us a way out of no way.

Because I can hear the psalmist say in Psalm 55:22, "Cast thy burden upon the Lord and He shall sustain thee."

IF THERE is anybody here today, anybody who knows that GOD can and that GOD will sustain you...

YOU ought to tell your neighbor, "GIVE your burdens to the LORD, and DON'T LET THE STONE STOP YOU!"

BRETHREN, STONES are designed to break you!

STONES are immovable and capable of breaking most substances.

MATTHEW 21:44 goes as far as saying that "Whosoever shall fall on this stone shall be broken."

That's because stones are hard and difficult to overcome.

THEY can hurt and may even kill you if you are hit by one.

AND that is why in ancient days, stoning was the most common form of carrying out a sentence on someone who had been condemned to death.

STONES can kill you!

IF YOU don't believe me, just ask a little shepherd boy named David.

THE Bible tells us that David used three smooth stones to slay a Philistine giant called Goliath.

EVERYONE in the army of Israel was afraid of this giant.

EVERYONE was overcome by his size and his ferociousness.

Yet with three smooth stones, David overcame this great big giant, causing him to fall to his death.

David used small stones.

SO imagine what a great big stone can do to you!

PEOPLE OF God, don't be mistaken. Stones can kill you!

Don't let them stop you in your track.

Don't let them stop your experience for your testimony.

THE **stone of disobedience** can kill you.

I have found that one of the greatest challenges for most Christians is the challenge to be obedient to God!

WHEN God says fast, you eat!

WHEN God says pray, you sleep.

WHEN God says give, you take.

DISOBEDIENCE cost Saul his throne.

GOD told him to kill all the enemy—animals and all.

Yet because Saul was a man pleaser, Saul kept an enemy alive.

Plus some of the choicest animals.

IN THE end, we learned that disobedience is worse than witchcraft.

CHILDREN Of God, stones can kill you!

DON'T let the stone of disobedience kill you!

THE **stone of deception** can kill you.

DO you remember what happened to Jacob after he stole his brother Esau's birthright?

JACOB had to flee the country and live in fear of his brother's threats for most of his life.

THE spirit of deception has been attacking the church.

THE devil has been deceiving people.

He has been robbing people of their birthright.

ONCE you are a child of God, you have a birthright to live in freedom.

ONCE you are a child of God, you have a birthright to be blessed.

You have a birthright to be healed.

You have a birthright to be the head and not the tail.

A birthright to be above and not beneath.

SO don't let the stone of deception rob you of your birthright.

THE **stone of faithlessness and ungratefulness** can kill you.

DO you remember the children of Israel?

GOD had miraculously delivered them from Egypt and Pharaoh.

AND rather than trusting God to take them the rest of the journey, they spent the next forty years grumbling and complaining.

They made idols.

They rebelled, and they kept looking back.

TELL somebody, "Stay focused! Stop looking back!"

DON'T let the past distract you. You need to get past your past!

BECAUSE the end result for the children of Israel was that they never made it to the promised land, except the two who refused to look back.

TELL your neighbor, "I refuse to look back!"

"I am committing to be faithful.

"I am committing to stick it out.

"I am committing to pressing on.

"I refuse to look back!"

IT WOULD have been easy for these women in the passage that we read to *not* have even began their journey knowing that this huge stone was standing in their way.

YET they made the journey anyway!

WE NEED to be more like these women of faith.

They knew that the stone was blocking their destination.

Yet they would not let the stone stop them!

WHEN you find yourselves climbing up the rough side of the mountain, bills are many but dollars are few, don't let the stone stop you!

WHEN your name is scandalized and dragged through the miry clay, don't let the stone stop you!

WHEN you come across someone who knows not the LORD and their heart is cold, stony, and impenetrable, keep on giving them LOVE, and don't let the stone stop you!

WHEN your health is failing you and you are lying on your bed of affliction, you ought to look up to the hills from whence cometh your help, and don't let the stone stop you.

WHEN you don't know how you are going to finish your education because you don't have the necessary funds, don't let the stone stop you.

YOU SEE, the devil wants the stone to stop you.

THE devil wants the stone to stop your marriage from working.

THE devil wants the stone to stop your financial blessing.

THE devil wants the stone to stop you from knowing God's plan for your life.

THE devil wants your family to fail.

THE devil wants your job to be a burden to you.

THE devil wants to stop you from being a success.

That way, you are unable to help anybody.

THE devil wants to stop you from worshipping and praising GOD.

BUT IF there are any saints in this place today, persons who are willing to help bear the infirmities of the weak, YOU ought to tell your neighbor, "Don't let the stone stop you!"

YOU SEE, God has a plan!

GOD speaks and plans fall into place.

GOD speaks and systems are automatically created to serve His will.

GOD'S plan is to remove the barrier.

His plan is to remove the wall.

His plan is to remove the stone.

AND that is why in the scripture that we read, God rolled the stone away!

TELL somebody, "God will roll the stone away!"

BEFORE the women got to the tomb, the stone was already rolled away!

YOU may have asked the question, just like these women did, "Who will roll away the stone?"

WELL, we know who will. GOD will roll the stones away!

HE will roll away your stone of unforgiveness.

HE will roll away your stone of bitterness.

HE will roll away your stone of depression.

IN fact, GOD is rolling stones away right now.

FOR the scripture says, "And it shall come to pass, that before they call, I will answer, and while they are yet speaking, I will hear."

WHATEVER you are going through, whatever stone is in your way, KNOW that God is going to roll it away.

And something good is going to come out of your experience.

SOMETHING good came out of the experience of the women in the passage that we read.

They found that Jesus had risen from the dead.

Just as He said He would have been.

SOMETHING good is going to come out of your situation, so don't let the stone stop you!

I KNOW that some of you are going through the greatest storm of your life right now.

And it's the kind of storm that hurts.

It's the kind of storm that makes you cry.

AND I know that it is going to sound crazy, but what you should be doing right now is praising God in advance!

THE truth is, IT'S a miracle that you have made it this far.

By all rights, you shouldn't be here.

YOU shouldn't have lived through that car wreck.

The officers on scene had said it's a miracle, because no one should have come out of that car wreck alive.

BUT the stone didn't stop you!

SOMEBODY else that I am talking to, you shouldn't have lived through that drug overdose.

You shouldn't have lived through the poison that they set for you.

You had enough in your system to kill you.

YOU shouldn't have made it. Other people didn't make it.

Yet you are still here.

HIGH-FIVE three people and tell them, "I'm still here."

I didn't know that I would make it, but I am still here!

Many turned their backs on me, but I am still here!

YOU HAVE been wounded many times.

YOU HAVE been ridiculed and ostracized, but thank God you are still here!

YOU are still here because you didn't let the stone stop you!

I AM talking to somebody right now.

It is a miracle that you are not in prison.

IF you were to tell the truth, you know that you are just as guilty and guiltier than some people who are serving prison terms right now.

But God was merciful to you!

HUG two persons and tell them, "God's mercies kept me!"

TELL somebody, "JUSTICE demanded my life, but God's mercies kept me!"

THERE IS somebody listening to me right now.

You know it's a miracle that you are not in a mental institution somewhere.

Other people have gone through a lot less than what you went through.

And they lost their minds. They went off the deep end.

SO WHAT are you telling me, preacher?

I AM telling you that you ought to be praising God.

That you made it thus far.

NOBODY expected you to make it, but here you are, alive.

YOU are alive in your right mind, serving God, filled with the Holy Ghost and power.

And you want to complain because of a stone?

YOU need to praise God because the stone is what pulled you to Jesus even when others walked away.

REMEMBER, the women went to the tomb although others stayed away.

NUDGE your neighbor and say, "Let your stone pull you to Jesus."

I KNOW that I am talking to some people right now, people who are going through the fire of their life.

AND I know that you are feeling the heat.

AND I didn't come to tell you that the fire isn't real.

I didn't come to tell you that the stone isn't real.

BUT I came to tell you that something good is going to come out of your experience!

I KNOW that right now, what I am saying sounds like insanity, because there is no visible, tangible, physical evidence of anything good in your situation.

BUT I came to prophesy to you and to declare to you on the authority of God's Word that something good is going to come out of your situation!

SLAP your neighbor. High-five and tell them, "Something good is going to come out of your situation!"

YOU SEE, the rolling away of the stone wasn't for Jesus. It was for you!

Jesus could have spoken to the stone, and the stone would have moved.

Jesus could have touched the stone, and the stone would have moved.

OR better yet, Jesus could have just walked right through the stone and exit the tomb because Jesus has the power to do everything!

SO THE rolling away of the stone was for us, not Jesus!

I REMEMBER that JESUS rolled the stone away for a woman who had a spirit of infirmity for eighteen years.

For eighteen years, she was bowed together and could not lift herself up.

BUT SHE didn't let her stone stop her.

FOR eighteen years, she kept going to the temple.

SOMEBODY here needs to know that all that you need to do is to keep on going.

THE woman kept on going UNTIL one day, Jesus called her.

And He said unto her, "Woman, thou art loosed from thine infirmities."

GOD is setting you loose today!

He is setting you loose from selfishness, loose from stubbornness, loose from sickness and disease.

Hezekiah was terminally ill and was told that he was going to die.

Until he cried out to God, and God rolled the stone away by extending his life for fifteen more years.

HANNAH couldn't have children. She was barren.

But when she prayed, the Lord rolled her stone away by opening up her womb so that she could give birth to a great prophet.

SOMEBODY needs to place their hands on their abdomen and say, "I am going to give birth in Jesus's name.

"I am going to give birth because my Stone has been rolled away.

"I am going to give birth to my blessing.

"I am going to give birth to my breakthrough.

"I am going to give birth to my deliverance.

"I am going to give birth to my healing.

"I am going to give birth to my miracle."

WHO AM I talking to right now?

GOD says, "Somebody needs to give birth to their praise!"

I WANT to talk to some people who know that they have destiny over their lives.

PEOPLE who know that there is a reason and a purpose for their existence and for the stone.

I WANT to talk to the ones who want everything God has ordained for their lives.

And they refuse to let go. You refuse to give in. You refuse to give up!

I WANT to talk to some people who have a fight in their spirit.

The kind of fight that Caleb had when at the age of eighty-five years, he said, "Give me my mountain!"

In other words, give me my stone!

Because he knew that no stone—no devil from hell—was big enough to stop him from getting what God had promised!

ANYBODY here wants what God has promised you?

Anybody here refuses to settle for less than what God said you can have?

Anybody here with your minds made up that whatever it costs, you are going to get what God has promised you?

I WISH somebody would just shout out three times and make God glad and the devil mad.

"I'm not letting my stone stop me!"

NOW LISTEN.

If you are satisfied with where you are at, with what you have got, with seeing what you're seeing, and with doing what you're doing and experiencing what you're experiencing, THEN this message is probably not for you!

BUT if you happen to be one of those rare breeds of people called dreamers, and if something inside you is kicking, and if your spirit is divinely dissatisfied, and if you know God has destined you for more, THEN you are the one that I am talking to!

FIRST of all, I would be doing you a disservice if I didn't tell you that every promise comes with a price.

THERE is no victory without a fight.

And there is no testimony without a test.

THERE is no crown without a cross.

And there is no resurrection without a crucifixion.

THERE is no healing without a sickness.

THERE is no deliverance without a fire.

YOU have to go through something to get to your promise!

THE women we read about in the passage had to go through the pain of watching Jesus being wounded.

THEY had to go through the sorrow of watching Him die and buried.

THEY had to go through the thought of never having Him among them again before they realized that they got their promise.

YOU see, Jesus had promised to never leave them nor forsake them.

JESUS had promised that on the third day, He would rise from the dead.

YOU have to go through something to get your promise.

BEFORE Joseph went to the palace, he went to the pit and to the prison.

BEFORE the three Hebrew boys were promoted, they went through the fiery furnace.

BEFORE Jairus's daughter was raised from the dead, she had to die.

"DON'T let the stone stop you!"

THERE is a Jordan for every one of us.

THERE is a stone for every one of us.

Even Jesus had a stone!

But He didn't let it stop Him from going on to conquer death, hell, and the grave.

YOUR stone may be different from mine.

But what is the same is the fact that the stone stands between us and the promise.

And the only way that you or I can get to the promise is by faith!

YOU can't float over on feelings. Feelings won't get you across.

AND you can't get through on secondhand knowledge.

RELIGION won't get you through it.

THE only thing that can remove your stone is a *living* faith in a *living* God.

WHEN the women saw that the stone was rolled away, they didn't run away.

But rather, they stepped into Jesus's tomb.

THEY moved in the direction toward their promise.

IT was a miracle that the stone was removed from the opening of Jesus's tomb.

And so the women had essentially moved in the direction of a miracle.

GOD sent me to tell somebody to start moving in the direction of your promise.

YOU have got to have enough vision and enough faith in God to get moving.

TELL your neighbor, "I'm moving toward my miracle."

THE circumstances may be against you, and the odds may be against you.

BUT it really doesn't matter as long as God is for you.

Because if God is for you, who can be against you?

YOU SEE, you have got a word from God to empower you for your future.

And the word is "Don't let the stone stop you."

Move toward your promise. Move toward your miracle!

AND that's all that you need—a word!

WHEN you have a word from God, you can sleep like a baby in a den of lions.

WHEN you have a word from God, you can have your meal barrel full and your cruse of oil full in the middle of a famine.

ALL it takes is a word!

PETER got a word.

Jesus told him to "launch out into the deep and to let down his nets for a draught."

AND Peter said, "At thy word we will let down the net."

AND because Peter obeyed the word of the Lord, he went into overflow.

ONE word from God changed Peter's circumstances.

He went from nothing to too much in one step.

He went from emptiness to overflow in one step.

He went from broke, busted, and disgusted to being blessed, happy, and wealthy in one step.

PETER ended up with abundance of fish that it almost sank his boat.

He had to call others to come and help bring in the blessings.

AND even then, it was still such an abundance that it almost sank their boats too.

LISTEN, people of God. Though weeping may endure for the night, joy cometh in the morning.

PETER went from a night season of wearied, toilsome, and fruitless endeavor to a morning season of overflow and joy and blessings in one step.

LET me prophesy to somebody who has the faith to reach out and grab it.

SOMEBODY is one step away from your miracle.

One step away from your breakthrough.

One step away from too much blessings.

YOU are one step away from that which you have been believing God for.

NUMBERS 23:19 says, "God is not a man that he should lie, neither the son of man that he should repent, if he said it he will do it, if he hath spoken it he will make it good."

GOD told me to tell you that there are some things that have been chasing you.

In fact, that thing has been threatening to drown you and take you under.

BUT God said, "Don't let that thing stop you from receiving that which is yours!"

STAND on the promises of God. Obey His Word.

And watch poverty and lack run from you.

Watch sickness and disease run from you.

Watch hopelessness and discouragement run from you.

Watch worry and anxiety run from you.

Watch fear and confusion run from you.

Deuteronomy 28:7 says, "The Lord shall cause thine enemies that rise up against thee, to be smitten before thy face: They shall come out against thee one way but they shall flee before thee seven ways."

THE miracle is not in the knowing OR even the believing.

The miracle is in the doing.

WHEN Ezekiel obeyed the Lord and started prophesying over the bones, things started changing.

It was a process that continued until there was a full manifestation.

TELL your neighbor, "I'm in a process!"

NOW tell your other neighbor, "I am making progress!"

Keep moving.

Keep praying.

Keep sowing.

Keep coming to church.

Keep on confessing.

Keep tithing, and keep believing.

THE main thing is to keep moving and not let your stone stop you!

SOMEBODY is coming through on your praise.

SOMEBODY who wasn't going to make it is going to make it because you praised God in the middle of your situation.

ANYBODY can praise God after the fact, but there is something about a midway praise, a midnight praise, and an "in the middle" praise that gets God's attention and breaks things open.

YOU may be going through the worst trial of your life, but praise God anyway.

YOU may be going through hell in your finances, but praise God anyway.

YOU may be going through the valley of the shadow of death, but praise God anyway.

SOMEBODY is coming out of depression because of your praise.

SOMEBODY is being set free from a spirit of suicide because of your praise.

SOMEBODY'S prodigal son or daughter is coming home because of your praise.

AT MIDNIGHT, "Paul and Silas prayed and sang praises unto the Lord and the prisoners heard them."

IT didn't say that the prisoners joined them or even that they enjoyed their singing.

The Bible simply said that "the prisoners heard them."

AND suddenly, there was an earthquake that shook the foundations of the prison, and every door flew open.

And every prisoners' bands were loosened.

GOD IS causing a spiritual earthquake right now.

A spiritual earthquake to break loose every cord of bondage.

A spiritual earthquake to eradicate demon possession and demon oppression.

A spiritual earthquake to break loose blessings upon this congregation!

GOD is going to cause a spiritual earthquake to roll the stone away.

THE passage of scripture that we read said when the women looked, they saw that the stone was rolled away.

TELL somebody, "Look!"

SAY, "Lord, give me spiritual eyesight. Lord, help me to see!"

ASK two people, "Can you feel it?"

CAN YOU feel the spiritual earthquake right now?

The spiritual earthquake that is breaking you free.

Free to lift your hands.

Free to worship God.

Free to be who God purposed you to be!

DON'T let the stone stop you!

Because we have a stone that is on our side.

That stone is bigger than any stone that the devil can throw our way.

THE stone that I am talking about is bigger than any stumbling block that the devil can lay down before us.

OUR stone is just like a mountain, and we can hide behind the mountain of a stone when the going gets a little rough.

YES, we can!

Because I heard Jesus say to Peter, "On THIS ROCK"—or as some version say—"on THIS STONE, I will build my church. And the gates of hell shall not prevail against it!"

DO I have a witness in here?

I HEARD a songwriter say, "In times like these, we need a savior. In times like these, we need an anchor. Be very sure, be very sure, your anchor holds and grips the solid rock."

THIS rock is Jesus. Yes, he's the one.

THIS rock is Jesus, the only Son.

IF YOU keep your hands firmly attached to the gospel plough.

IF YOU stay anchored in the LORD of LORDS and the KING of KINGS and don't turn back from the almighty GOD.

THERE is another kind of stone that John says in the book of Revelation will be our inheritance.

IN Revelation 2:17, I can hear John saying, "He that hath an ear, let him hear what the Spirit saith unto the churches; To him that overcometh will I give to eat of the hidden manna, and will give him a white stone, and in the stone a new name written, which no man knoweth saving he that receiveth it."

AREN'T you glad about Jesus having your new name waiting inside a white stone?

YOUR new name will speak of victory.

YOUR new name will speak of the fact that you are more than conqueror through Christ Jesus.

DON'T let the stone stop you!

CHAPTER 10

If You Can Have It, God Can Heal It

When I was in my late twenties, I realized that there were times that I would be walking and either of my knees would quickly slip out and then go back in place, causing me to fall to the ground in excruciating pain. Overtime, I realized that the frequency of it happening began to increase, and so I took the matter to the Lord by fasting, praying, and believing the Lord would heal me.

As a result of my knees being easy to slip out of place, I had refrained from kneeling to pray. Doing so was uncomfortable as the weight of my body applied added pressure to the knees, causing them to feel like they would slip at any minute. Instead, I opted to sit at the edge of my bed and pray in the night.

One night, as I sat to pray, the Lord said to me, "Kneel." I proceeded to remind the Lord that kneeling was not an option, as it would have caused my knees to slip. Then I would return to saying my prayers.

The next night, I did the same thing as usual. I sat on the edge of my bed to pray. As soon as I opened my mouth to say my prayers, I heard the Lord said to me once again, "Kneel." This happened again on the third night, and as I proceeded once again to tell the Lord that I couldn't, I felt like His Spirit was about to leave me, and so I obeyed with some amount of hesitation, trying to keep the weight of my body off my knees and on to the bed instead. I prayed, albeit a shortened version, and quickly got up.

The next night, as I got ready to pray, the Lord told me to kneel again, and this time, I immediately obeyed. I continued kneeling to pray since then to the point where I don't know exactly when my full healing occurred. However, to this day, I am able to kneel and pray for however long I want, and I am able to walk without any fear of my knees slipping in and out as it no longer happens. I was totally healed, and all because irrespective of my fears, I obeyed the Word of the Lord.

Throughout my teenage years and up to my early twenties, I found that I would at times have irregular and long flowing periods. It got to the point that my mother, who had resided overseas at the time, would send me a large number of sanitary napkins so that I would never be without.

I began to seriously pray about it, as it was uncomfortable and at times a real inconvenience because of the duration of the flow, and so I had beseeched the Lord to heal me.

I was home one Saturday, and a housekeeper who had come in to perform domestic duties for the day came and told me that her menses had started, for which she was not prepared, and asked if I could give her a sanitary napkin to use until she got home. When I went to get a sanitary napkin for her, the Lord said, "Give her all the napkins that you have." I paused, wondering if I had heard the Lord correctly, because I had a huge bag with napkins that I had needed based on my own crisis. So of course, I proceeded to remind the Lord that I had need of the napkins, and then I proceeded to take two napkins from the bag to give to her when I heard the Lord say again, "Give her all the napkins that you have."

This time, His voice was so audible that I knew that I just had to do it. I gave her the huge bag of napkins, which even shocked her. I told her that I was doing so based on the Lord's instructions. She was elated! I then found out that she had none at home and was planning to buy a pack on her way home.

Initially, I had thought that meeting her needs was the miracle. It wasn't until a few days later when my menses had started and ended in normal time, and it has done so ever since that I realized that meeting her needs was only an aspect of the miracle. The other aspect is that I was totally healed from the condition, and all because I obeyed the voice of the Lord through an act of faith.

My son was only months old when he developed a fever that would not go away despite the medications that I gave to him. The Lord had told me to pray and stand in faith, but instead, I opted to go back to the doctor, only to be given more medication for him that just didn't work.

I remember lying in bed with my son next to me. He would fuss each time that I attempted to place him in his crib. His fever was so high that his body was hot to the touch, and no amount of bathing him in cold water or dousing him with medicine had worked.

As any praying mother would have done, I cried out unto the Lord for my son. In fact, I preceded my cries to the Lord with cries of repentance for having disobeyed His prodding to pray instead of revisiting the doctor. I remember saying, "Lord, I am so sorry for having disobeyed Your voice, but if You heal my son, I will obey You next time." I then kept repeating, "Heal my son, Jesus. Heal my son, Lord. Heal my son. And as the words "Heal my son" left my mouth the second time, instantly, I felt my son's body feel cool.

I immediately cried out to my mother, "Mommy, Jordan's fever gone. Jordan's fever gone." I also immediately ran to her with baby Jordan in my hand, and I said, "See him here. Feel him." And that she did, and she reconfirmed that the fever had indeed left him. God is a faithful healer!

These are just a few of my testimonies which confirms that if you can have it (whatever sickness or disease that it is, even COVID-19), God can heal it.

The Sermon

> The LORD is my shepherd; I shall not want.
> (Ps. 23:1)

I USE for a theme tonight the words **"if you can have it, God can heal it!"**

TURN to your neighbor and say, "Neighbor, I don't know what your problems are. But if you can have it, God can heal it!"

SAY, "Neighbor, there is nothing too hard for God to do. There is no sickness too great. There is no burden too heavy. There is no struggle too difficult for God to handle. If you can have it, God can heal it!"

SAY, "Neighbor, I don't care what the doctors say. I don't care what the world leaders say. The Lord is my shepherd, and I shall NOT want."

AND that is a direct Word from God!

LISTEN. The Word of God is the power of God.

Your healing is in the Word.

Your deliverance is in the Word.

Your joy is in the Word.

Your prosperity is in the Word.

Your anointing is in the Word.

Your destiny is in the Word.

IN the beginning was the Word, and the Word was with God.

And the Word was God.

The same was in the beginning with God.

All things were made by Him.

And without Him, the Word was not anything made that was made. (John 1:1–3)

EVERYTHING begins with the Word.

You can shout, dance, run, holler, talk in tongues, and jump pews, but you haven't even gotten started until you get in the Word.

I DON'T know what your situation or condition or problem is.

But I know what your answer and your solution is.

It is the Word of God.

GOD sent his Word and healed them.

And He delivered them from all their destructions.

FAITH is the hand that reaches out and takes hold of the blessings of God.

BUT it is the Word of God that quickens the hand of faith.

IN RECENT times, we have seen an upsurge of new viruses worldwide, and many people have been panicking, especially regarding the deadly called Ebola.

AND whilst we *must* take all necessary precautions to safeguard ourselves, God said to remind His people that He changed not.

IN biblical times, the people had to contend with leprosy, but that didn't limit God's power.

He healed many with leprosy.

IN generations before us and leading up to us, people had to contend with cholera.

People had to contend with malaria.

People had to contend with polio.

People had to contend with AIDS.

AND there are many stories of how God miraculously healed many.

SO just like the others, Ebola is no match for God.

AND if Ebola is no match for God, CHIKV certainly is no match for God.

WE don't know why God allows His people to have to contend with sickness and disease.

But one thing we know is that every sickness, every disease, is another opportunity for God to heal by His miraculous power.

HE may not heal in our timing.

HE may not heal in the manner we would want Him to heal.

But He will surely heal.

THE God who heals cancer, the God who heals heart conditions, the God who heals the lame, the God who heals diabetes and hypertension is the same God who can heal all other sickness and disease.

EVERY new disease is a test of the effectiveness, the usefulness, the value of the stripes that Jesus took for our healing.

SATAN is attempting to discredit the healing power of Jesus.

SATAN is attempting to discredit the scripture, which says, "He was wounded for our transgressions, He was bruised for our iniquities, and the chastisement of our peace was upon Him and by His stripes, we are healed."

SATAN is attempting to make us feel that healing and miracles are of the past. BUT the devil is a liar.

Jesus is the same yesterday, today, and forever.

THE SAME God who sent Naaman to wash in the Jordan River seven times to be healed from leprosy is still God today.

THE SAME God who opened Sarah's womb and Hannah's womb so that they could bear children is still God today.

THE SAME God who healed Hezekiah from terminal illness and extended his life is still God today.

TELL your neighbor, "God is still God."

THE SAME God who healed Job of the very sores that He allowed Satan to put on his body is still God today.

THE SAME God who healed blind Bartimeus is still God today.

TELL SOMEBODY, "He is the same God."

THE SAME God who healed the centurion's servant is still God today.

THE SAME God who healed the woman from years of bleeding when she touched the hem of His garment is still God today.

THE SAME God who healed the Syro-Phoenician woman's daughter from demon possession is still God today.

IF YOU know what I am talking about, high-five three people and tell them, "He is still God."

THE SAME God who restored a woman who was deformed for eighteen years and a man crippled by the pool of Bethesda for thirty-eight years is still God today.

THE SAME God who healed a man from dropsy is still God today.

THE SAME God who raised up Jairus's daughter, THE SAME God who brought Lazarus back to life is still God today!

IF YOU understand where I am going, shout out, "God is still God!"

"IF you can have it, God can heal it!"

PROPHESY to someone and tell them, "Healing is coming. Deliverance is coming."

He may not come when you want Him.

But He will be there right on time!

IN fact, I FEEL like telling somebody that there is a miracle in the house.

The Word is in the house.

The miracle power of God is in the house tonight!

I AM A testimony of God's healing power.

And I may have shared the testimony that I am about to share with you some time ago.

BUT God said, "Share it again."

Because somebody in the service tonight needs to be reminded that no matter what, He is still God!

GOD is our healer, AND if you think God only heals sick bodies, let me remind you that THE SAME God who showed up in the fiery furnace with Shadrach, Meshach, and Abednego is still God.

THE SAME God who shut the lions' mouths in Daniel's den is still God.

THE SAME God who saved a wedding by turning water into wine is still God.

THE SAME God who took Joseph from the pit to the palace is still God.

IF you believe that God is still the same, find two people and tell them, "Don't you give up now. God is still God!"

I DON'T know what you came for tonight.

But your miracle is in this place!

YOU possibly felt like it would never happen, BUT it only felt that way because there is no victory without a fight.

And there is no testimony without a test.

IT only felt that way because there is no crown without a cross.

And there is no resurrection without a crucifixion.

IT only felt that way because there is no healing without a sickness.

And there is no deliverance without a fire.

THERE is a Jordan for every one of us.

YOUR Jordan may be different from mine.

But what is the same is the fact that it stands between my promise and me and between you and your promise.

AND the only way you or I can get through it is by faith.

You have to believe that God can and that God will.

YOU can't float over on feelings.

Feelings won't get you across.

THE only thing that can conquer Jordan is stepping out by faith on the promises of God.

I REMEMBER the children of Israel as they stood at the edge of a raging Jordan River, which was at flood stage.

JOSHUA gave the priest that carried the ark of the covenant a strange order.

HE said, "Start walking. Step into the water."

Start moving in the direction of your promise.

YOU see, you can't go by what you are seeing, by what you are hearing, by what you are feeling, or by what other people are saying.

YOU have to move because God says move.

YOU can't wait until you can see a break in the waves.

You can't wait until it makes sense or it feels good to your emotions.

YOU can't wait until you see the waters open up in front of you.

GOD says it is time to move from sight to faith.

It is time to move from "I hope so" to "I know so."

It is time to move from the milk to the meat.

IN other words, it is time to step out by faith.

YOU have got to have enough vision and enough faith in God to know that if you have it, God can heal it.

TELL your neighbor, "I am taking the step of faith."

IT may not make any sense to you.

The circumstances may be stocked up against you.

BUT it really doesn't matter as long as God is with you and you have a Word.

ALL you need is a Word.

You can bring down Goliath with a piece of leather and a rock with just a Word.

YOU can have your meal barrel full and your cruse of oil full in the middle of famine with just a Word.

THOUGH weeping may endure for the night, joy cometh in the morning.

LET me prophesy to somebody who has the faith to reach out and take what God has for you…

YOU are one step away from your miracle, one step away from your breakthrough, one step away from too much blessings.

YOU have put your time in toiling and trying and praying and confessing and waiting and watching.

BUT your time for miracles has come.

GOD is not a man that He should lie, neither the son of man that He should repent.

If He said it, He will do it. If He hath spoken it, He will make it come to pass.

THERE are some things that have been chasing you.

IN fact, they are things that have been threatening to drown you and take you under.

IT may be debt. IT may be sickness. IT may be fear.

IT may be a bad relationship.

I DON'T know what it is that has been chasing you, but there is a turnaround in the atmosphere.

And God is getting ready to flip the script.

And that which has been running after you, nipping at your heels, is going to be running from you.

POVERTY and lack are going to run from you.

Sickness and disease are going to run from you.

Hopelessness and discouragement are going to run from you.

Worry and anxiety are going to run from you.

Fear and confusion are going to run from you.

Deuteronomy 28:7 says, "The Lord shall cause thine enemies that rise up against thee, to be smitten before thy face: They shall come out against thee one way but they shall flee before thee seven ways."

TELL your neighbor, "Take a good look at me, because I am getting ready to do the impossible.

"I am getting ready to go where they said it was impossible for me to go.

"And I am getting ready to do what they said it was impossible for me to do."

YOU see, I am just crazy enough to believe God when He said, "With God all things are possible, and all things are possible to him that believeth."

High-five three people and tell them, "My faith is making a way for me." (Repeat.)

LISTEN. Whether you believe it or not, somebody is coming through on your praise tonight.

Somebody that wasn't going to make it is going to make it, because you praised God in the middle of your Jordan.

AND that is why it is so important that you lift Him up and praise Him and magnify Him.

Regardless of your situation, LIFT Him up like your life depended upon it.

YOU SEE, anybody can praise God after they have crossed over their Jordan experience.

Anybody can praise God after they made it out of the lions' den.

Anybody can praise God after they came out of the fiery furnace.

BUT there is something about a midway praise, a midnight praise, an in-the-middle praise that gets God's attention and pushes His hands in breaking things open.

YOU may be going through the worst trial of your life, but praise Him anyway.

YOU may be going through hell in your finances, but praise Him anyway.

YOU may be going through the valley of the shadow of death, but praise Him anyway.

YOU may be going through it with your family or your job, but praise God anyway.

PRAISE Him! For the Lord is your shepherd. You shall not want.

PRAISE Him! If you have it, whatever it is, God can heal it! PRAISE HIM!

CHAPTER 11

Forever I Do

In January 2015, the third year of my son's studies, he was finally able to move off campus, and we had secured rented accommodation for him in a home that made us feel safe that he was still being protected from the ills of the outside world.

Within two months of him living there, the homeowner's relative who was pursuing her PhD in pharmacy needed a place to temporarily stay to facilitate her doing her internship outside of her hometown. She took her in, and that was when Jordan met his soul mate.

They soon became friends and started dating, which resulted in him flooding my phone with photos of the girl that he could not stop talking about. My mom and I went up to spend our summer vacation with him as usual (it was now our routine to either spend summer with him, and then he comes to us for Christmas or sometimes we reverse the order). Plus, this time, our trip also allowed us the opportunity to meet her and her family. It was clear that they had bonded, and we loved the God in her and her sweet spirit.

By the summer of 2016, my mother and I had gone up again for our usual vacation time with Jordan, but this time, we also had another thing on our agenda. By this time, his soul mate had graduated, and Jordan had started thinking about marrying her in 2017. He wanted to commence the process by asking for her hand in marriage by way of a surprise engagement.

So within days of our arrival, we accompanied Jordan to help him in selecting the engagement ring. God planned ahead of us, because we will never forget the day we walked into a renowned jewelry store and asked to see wedding rings.

The manager of the store was on the floor that day, and she offered to assist us. We quickly learned that she was a Christian and was the daughter of the pastor of a church whose beliefs were similar to ours.

At the very moment after the rings (engagement and wedding band) were chosen, the glory of God came down into the store literally. The manager was packaging the rings to give to us, and then suddenly, I cannot fully explain what had happened except to say that the presence of the Lord was so heavy in the store that involuntarily, Mom burst out, speaking in tongues and rejoicing. And the lady, Jordan, and I were also rejoicing and giving God praise, unashamed. One thing was clear—God was confirming that He had sanctioned the move.

Jordan asked his soul mate, Dr. Robyn McCrae, to be his wife on her birthday in 2016, and she said yes! He graduated in December of that year and was immediately employed by his school based on his academic achievements. They got married in February 2017 to happily ever after.

What is most amazing about this story is that God allowed Mom to be a part of the choosing of the rings, the engagement, the graduation, and the wedding before He took her home to glory. She went home celebrating the victories of our faith walk, which is why we will always say, "Lord, forever, I do."

The Sermon

> Then said the LORD unto me, Go yet, love a woman beloved of her friend, yet an adulteress, according to the love of the LORD toward the children of Israel, who look to other gods, and love flagons of wine. (Hosea 3:1)

AND **the Living Bible Version** states it this way:

> Then the Lord said to me, "Go, and get your wife again and bring her back to you and love her, even though she loves adultery. For the Lord still loves Israel though she has turned to other gods and offered them choice gifts."

DEARLY BELOVED, we are gathered together here in the sight of God and in the face of this company to join together a man and a woman in holy matrimony.

THOSE are familiar words that often begin wedding vows, which usually end with the man and the woman saying, "I do" to each other.

AND SO I USE for a theme this morning the words **"forever I do."**

TELL your neighbor, "Get ready to experience the 'forever I do' love! It's all about marriage today."

WE are living in an age where most couples who walk down the aisle do so on the premise that they will stay together until trouble comes. Or until a partner messes up. Or until they find someone who is more beautiful, or someone who is more handsome or wealthier.

BUT HERE in the scriptures, we are directed to a story surrounding the life of a man named Hosea.

HOSEA was the first of the minor prophets, and often we do not recognize the derivation of these Bible names.

But this prophet's name would be Joseph in English, as his name is related to the name Joshua, which means "salvation."

HOSEA was a young preacher in the nation of Israel, and the nation was going through a difficult time when Hosea was preaching and prophesying.

PEOPLE were living it up," as we might say.

And they didn't make much time for God.

SO HOSEA had become extremely discouraged.

It seemed like the more that he spoke to the people about God, the more rebellious they had become.

AND so in the opening chapter of Hosea, in this little book of prophecy, we read a personal note about him.

HOSEA went to God with his concerns about the people.

And God had told him to do a strange thing.

GOD said, "I want you to get married."

NOW to the natural mind, that didn't make any sense.

Because here was Hosea, frustrated by the waywardness of God's people.

And in going to God to tell Him of his frustrations, God instructs him to get married.

TELL your neighbor, "God's ways are higher than our ways. So trust His ways."

SO God told Hosea to get married. And the truth is, Hosea, being a typical man, must have welcomed those instructions from the Lord.

LET'S be real for a moment.

Hosea was a frustrated bachelor.

And any man will tell you that a woman can be good medicine.

SO GOD, having listened to Hosea pouring out His frustrations on Him, said, "Hosea, I want you to get married. I have a girl picked out for you."

AND WHEN God mentioned her name, Hosea's heart must have fluttered.

Because the name of the girl that God had handpicked for Hosea was Gomer.

GOMER was one of the most beautiful girls in Israel.

And so Hosea was definitely interested.

YOU SEE, men are turned on by what they see.

BUT then God said, "HOSEA, I am going to be upfront with you. Because I want you to know the whole truth about this girl. YOU are going to marry her. But she is going to be unfaithful to you.

"IN FACT, she will become nothing but a common street prostitute. But I want you to marry her anyway."

NOW the instructions to get married was exciting.

But the truth about who he was to marry was a bitter pill to swallow.

UNDOUBTEDLY, Hosea must have been very puzzled by God's strange command.

Just as Abraham was puzzled by God's command to take his son up to the mountain and kill him.

YOU SEE, God does strange things at times.

Things that we don't always understand.

Things we can't categorize.

JUST like He has some very strange instructions to us.

For God, we must become empty to be filled.

Or we must become the least to be great.

Or we must die to live.

GOD does things that don't always make sense to the natural mind.

AND this is one of those strange things.

He told Hosea, "The girl that I picked out for you, SHE is going to be a harlot, a prostitute, but that is the one that I want you to marry."

TELL your neighbor, "Even when it makes no sense, if God said it, do it!" (**Repeat.**)

GOD'S instructions to Hosea must have really shaken up his personal dreams about the woman that he would have wanted to marry one day.

BECAUSE when most men pick someone to marry, they usually want someone who is upright.

Someone who they can boast to their friends and say, "I picked the best one."

Even after years of marriage, they want to still be able to say, "I picked the best."

BUT based on what God had said, Hosea's marriage would be broken before it started.

AND that wasn't all. God went on to tell Hosea that his wife would have three children—two boys and a girl.

But God would be the one to name them.

Because their names would serve as an object lesson to the people of Israel.

GOD was clearly up to something! AND perhaps that must have been the *only* glimmer of hope, the *only* light at the end of the tunnel that Hosea could see in the strange instructions that God had given him when He told him to marry a woman like Gomer.

YOU SEE, Hosea knew that it was customary in Israel to teach by symbols.

GOD often used this method of instructing His people, and he knew that names were very important, as God often used the meanings of names to teach Israel certain truths.

AND so when Hosea heard God say this about his children to come, it must have made him feel that all wasn't lost.

Because at least God saw it important enough to personally name his children.

AND SO in true woman-pursuing style, Hosea went after Gomer and started courting her.

And sure enough, Gomer was attracted to this shy young man.

And at last he summoned up the courage to ask her to marry him.

YOU SEE, Gomer was indeed a beautiful catch.

Plus she acted right, and she treated him right.

And so falling in love with her was easy.

AND SO when Gomer said yes to marrying Hosea, he was excited, possibly even forgetting about what God had told him of his future with Gomer.

And in no time, they were married.

AT first, their marriage must have been heaven on earth.

Hosea truly loved this girl, because there is no way that you can read the story without seeing that fact.

THEY must have been wonderfully happy together.

And then they started having children.

WHEN they had their first child, Hosea's heart must have been filled to bursting.

BECAUSE it is every man's joy to have a son, especially when his first child is a son.

AND so in keeping with what God had said, Hosea went to God for the name of his son.

And to his surprise, God named him Jezreel, which means "cast away."

And it was a name of shame in Israel.

IT didn't make sense to Hosea.

In fact, it must have broken his heart.

CAN you imagine what it feels like to have your first child labelled as a castaway?

IN FACT, many mothers and fathers here today, and some viewing by the worldwide web, have children who suffer with a low self-esteem because of alias names given to them or because of unkind things done to them.

SOME persons listening to me today, they themselves feel like a castaway.

So you can imagine how horrified Hosea must have felt.

YET in this story, we found that Hosea was determined within himself not to take it personally.

Because he knew that God naming his son Jezreel MUST have meant that it was God's way of warning the children of Israel that they would become castaways if they didn't turn from going after idols.

TELL your neighbor, "If you feel like a castaway, don't lose hope. Because God is up to something."

WHEN Hosea and Gomer had their second child, it was a girl this time. And Hosea must have thought surely his daughter must represent blessings.

And so yet again, he went to God for the name.

And God named her Lo-Ruhamah, meaning "not pitied."

IMAGINE naming your daughter "not pitied."

The child your prayed to have, the one you went through hours of labor to birth, the one that you thought would one day bring blessing into the family, God chose to name her "not pitied."

IN other words, even when she struggled, she would not be pitied.

SOME persons under my voice have been struggling for such a long time that you feel not pitied. In fact, you feel forsaken.

WHEN other's season of struggles end, you seem to just be experiencing season after season of frustrations and unhappiness, with no one extending a lending hand.

BUT somebody will find out today that God was there all the time.

IN FACT, tell your neighbor, "Even when it made no sense, Jesus was there all the time."

SQUEEZE somebody's hand and say, "Jesus was there all the time."

HOSEA, although distraught by name of his daughter, was determined once again to trust the ways of God.

Because he understood that for God to have name his daughter "not pitied," it must have been that God was giving the children of Israel another opportunity to change their ways by letting them know that they would not be pitied if they continued in their stubborn rebellious ways.

NO matter how wretched we become, God always gives us a chance to change.

TELL your neighbor, "Thank God for grace."

AND SO when this little girl was weaned, Gomer conceived again and bore their third child.

And Hosea must have thought that two names were about the children of Israel.

But surely God must make the name of his third child about him and his family.

But God named their third child and second son Lo-ammi, which means "not my people."

IT IS one thing to mess up. But when God warns you that He will disown you if you don't change, that's serious business.

GOD had become angry at the children of Israel's waywardness.

But all was not lost, because this was only a warning.

God always prefers to give mercy over judgment.

WE may not understand His ways of doing things, but we should be glad that He cares regardless.

SO if you feel like God has turned His back on you, it is because you have forgotten about the power of His mercy.

TELL your neighbor, "Mercy always says no."

FOR all the wrong that you have done, you don't deserve to be included in the family of God.

But mercy says no!

SAY, "Neighbor, thank God for mercy."

IN fact, let's take a praise break and open up your mouths and thank God for mercy!

YOUR husband may have walked out on you.

And by all accounts, you should have lost your mind.

But mercy said no!

YOUR children may have turned against you.

And by all accounts, you have suffered a nervous breakdown.

But mercy said no!

FOR all the struggles that you have been through, for all the sickness and pain that you had to contend with, YOU should have been dead and gone.

But mercy said no!

SAY, "Neighbor, if you knew my struggles, you would understand my praise. Mercy said no!"

Praise God for His mercies!

HOSEA must have been terrified about what would have been God's next move.

Because all the names that God had given to his children spoke of God's warning of judgment for His people.

BUT IF THAT wasn't bad enough, it wasn't long after Hosea and Gomer had their third and last child that Gomer began to fulfil the sad prediction that God had made when he had told Hosea to marry her.

WHAT a heartbreak it must have been to this young preacher and prophet as he heard the whispers that began to circulate about his wife and about what had happened when he was away on preaching trips.

PERHAPS even his own children may have unconsciously dropped some remarks about the men who visited the home when Hosea was away.

AND undoubtedly during those moments, the children were left uncared for whilst Gomer spent her time running around with other men.

AND THEN one day, reality struck!

HOSEA came home, and he found a note from Gomer.

SHE decided to find the happiness that she felt was lacking from her life, and she was leaving him and the children to go follow a man that she had met and had now thought that she really loved.

YOU know how those notes are usually written.

She must have written, "Dear Hosea, you are no longer exciting in bed. And I have not been truly happy because you have not been able to buy me the fancy things that I love. PLUS the children are stressing me out. Their names say it all. And I am bored with you and God. I want to go out on the town and live it up."

HOSEA must have been extremely broken, coming home to a note and children abandoned by their mother and his wife.

YOU can imagine how the gossip went across the back fences of the community.

YOU can imagine how the nosy neighbors and some church people must have laughed and said, "Serves him right. He is always busy telling people how to live. And he couldn't hold his own home together."

AND THEN there must have been others who, IN AN attempt to be there for Hosea, encouraged him by saying, "Hosea, don't worry. She has everything to lose by leaving you. So just forget about her."

BUT Hosea loved Gomer.

And he couldn't just simply forget her.

THERE IS something about love that will make you forgive the unforgiveable.

THERE is something about love that will make you want to walk away yet you cannot leave.

GOMER went from man to man until she fell into the hands of a man who was unable to pay for her food and her clothing.

HER first lover and husband, Hosea, had provided for her as best as he could.

Yet she had walked out on him, only to find herself with a man that could barely care for himself, much more for her.

MANY persons walk out on their marriage thinking it is for the best, only to find out that their lives took a downward path.

HOLD on to the hands of your neighbor and say, "I know that sometimes it's hard. But if it is worth fighting for, FIGHT!"

NEWS of Gomer's miserable state came to Hosea.

And he went in search of the man that she was living with.

IN FACT, he knew exactly where to find him.

He was down at the local bar.

And when he found the man, the conversation may have gone something like this:

"ARE you the man who is living with Gomer?"

And the man must have said, "If it's any of your business, yes, I am."

AND HOSEA, in response, must have said, "Well, I am Hosea, her husband."

UNDOUBTEDLY, a tense moment must have followed where the man must have clenched his fist and was prepared for a fight.

But Hosea said, "No, you don't understand. I am not interested in causing any trouble. But I know that you are having difficulty making ends meet. And I *love* my wife."

HOSEA pretty much said to the man, "Can you do me a favor? CAN you take some of my gold and some of my silver and buy for her the things that she needs? PLEASE buy her some clothing and plenty of food. And if you need any more money, I will give it to you."

LOVE made him do that!

BUT THE man must have probably thought, *There is no fool like an old fool. IF this man wants to help pay her expenses when I am the one getting the goods, that's all right with me.*

AND SO he took the money from Hosea and went and bought groceries and clothing for Gomer.

NOW you may still be saying, "That's a foolish thing for a man to have done."

But who can explain the madness of love?

Love exists apart from reason and has its own reasons.

LOVE does not act according to logic.

Love acts according to its own nature.

AND so Hosea acted on the basis of love.

THEN Hosea found himself watching Gomer from a distance.

HE wanted to catch a glimpse of the woman he loved.

And so as the man arrived home with the groceries, Hosea watched as Gomer rushed out the door to take the groceries from the man's arms and to thank him for what he was bringing to her.

HE didn't pay for them, but he got the praise for it.

AND this reminds me of the love of God.

Even when we don't deserve it, God still provides for us.

SOME OF you looking at me for the wrong that you did, you know that you don't deserve to be blessed.

But God blessed you anyway.

EVERY DAY Hosea kept watching Gomer from a distance.

And how long this went on for, we don't know for sure.

But finally, word came that the woman Hosea loved—his wife—had found herself in the hands of yet another man.

THIS time, it was a man who did not care for her at all.

As he had gotten tired of her, and so he decided to sell her into slavery.

BROKENHEARTED, Hosea didn't know what to do.

And so yet again, he went weeping to God.

AND God asked, "Hosea, do you love this woman in spite of all that she has done to you?"

And Hosea nodded yes.

THEN the Lord said to Hosea, "Go and get your wife again and bring her back to you. And love her, even though she loves adultery. For the Lord still loves Israel though she has turned to other gods and offered them choice gifts."

CERTAINLY this could not have been the instructions that Hosea was expecting from God.

HOSEA probably thought that God would say, "Don't worry, Hosea. You did well to have stuck out this long. I will find you another wife."

HOSEA probably thought that God would have said, "Don't worry, Hosea. I will perform a miracle for you. I WILL cause nobody to buy her and make her thereafter beg you to take her back."

BUT INSTEAD, God sent Hosea to go buy her back.

And so it must have been with much shame that Hosea showed up at the marketplace that day.

EVERYBODY had known how the preacher's wife, the prophet's wife, had backslidden and had chosen a life of prostitution and left him to care for himself and his children.

BUT HOSEA loved Gomer beyond his shame.

And so as he watched Gomer being brought up and placed on the dock to be auctioned.

HE held his head down in unbelief as they stripped her of all her clothing and made her stand naked before the crowd.

HOSEA must have thought then, *I must be crazy to love somebody this much. To allow myself to be so humiliated.*

YOU SEE, men see their women as their prized possessions.

They will sleep with many women, as wrong as that is, but they don't want their women sleeping with any other man but them.

AND added to that, they don't want any other man seeing their woman improperly clothed.

AND that is why men will run around WITH the scantily dressed women but never marry them because the ones that they marry must be for their eyes only.

AND THAT IS WHY I LOVE HOSEA!

YOU SEE, he wasn't totally fazed by the events of the day.

In fact, he strikes me as a dreamer.

Because only a dreamer can look at things as they are yet see them as how they want them to be.

HOSEA heard the auctioneer make his opening remarks.

And I believe that as he looked up, he must have thought, *Gomer, you may be a prostitute today. But I see you in the future. And you look better. I see you walking in favor and prosperity too.*

YOU SEE, you must be able to dream.

IF you don't have the ability to dream, then you don't have the ability to hope.

Because hope is dreaming.

ANYTIME you are a dreamer, you can be in one place yet see yourself in another place.

You can be in one situation yet see yourself elevated out of that situation.

DREAMERS aren't bothered by how rough things get right now because they know that where they are is not where they will remain.

HOSEA, whilst facing the events of the day, knew in the depths of his heart that this was not the end.

AS A dreamer, your spouse may have left you, but you know that your life isn't over because better days are coming.

AS A dreamer, you may be single right now, but you see a honeymoon.

AS A dreamer, you may be living in a small one-bedroom house right now, but you see yourself living in a big house with many rooms one day.

AS A dreamer, although they got you fired, you see yourself in a better paying job.

DREAMERS see stuff changing.

They have active imaginations.

AND that is why, as dreamers, you can't let the devil get a hold of your minds.

EVERYTIME that the devil speaks into your mind, rebuke him in the name of Jesus.

IF the devil, through his antics, takes your money, don't worry, because that is temporary.

You will get *more* money later.

BUT *never* let the devil have your mind.

KEEP your minds focused on God.

THAT IS what Hosea undoubtedly had to do in order to walk into that marketplace that day to buy back his wife.

HOSEA must have waited with great anticipation for the auction to get on the way.

He watched as the auctioneer pinched Gomer and prodded her to show how strong she was.

And then the bidding began.

THE auctioneer presented Gomer to men looking on, but she didn't look like much.

The beautiful woman that Hosea had married had lost her beauty to the men she ran around with.

She looked haggard and used.

AND SO none of the men were bidding on her until Hosea, without thinking, shouted out, "Gomer, I love you!"

AND at that point, somebody bid **three** pieces of silver, thinking if Hosea still loved her, perhaps she still had some value.

But Hosea raised it to **five** pieces of silver because he was determined to get her.

THEN SOMEBODY upped it to **eight** pieces of silver.

And then Hosea bid **ten**.

SOMEBODY went to **eleven** pieces of silver.

And Hosea went to **twelve**.

SOMEBODY else went to **fifteen**.

And Hosea offered **fifteen pieces of silver and a bushel of barley**. It was *all* that he had.

And the auctioneer's gavel fell.

Hosea had won the bid to get his wife back.

AND at that point, one of the men looking on said to Hosea, "Why would you do that? Why would you give your all for a woman who brought you so much disgrace?"

AND HOSEA said, "I did it because of who she is. And if you knew who she really is, had you been me, you would have done the same thing too."

AND the man asked, "Who is she?"

AND HOSEA said, "She is a chosen generation. She is a royal priesthood. She is a peculiar person. She is a holy nation."

THE MAN laughed and said, "Hosea, have you lost your mind? She is a prostitute."

But Hosea said, "No, she isn't. Prostitution is what she did. It isn't who she is. SHE is the apple of God's eyes. SHE is the head and not the tail. SHE is above and not beneath. SHE is a success and not a failure."

THE MAN said, "Hosea, you are not making sense."

BUT Hosea said, "I am making more sense than you will ever understand, because this is not about what she did. I bought her back because of who God says she is. SHE is God's righteousness. SHE is blessed and not cursed. SHE is rich and not poor. SHE is free and not bound!"

TELL your neighbor, "It's not because of what I have done. It's not because of who I am. But it's because of *whose* I am."

HOSEA bought back Gomer.

And the Lord said, "Tell My people that the kind of love that Hosea had for Gomer is similar to the kind of love that I have for My children."

JESUS IS our redeemer. And He paid the price to free us from a life of being slaves to fear.

He freed us from a life of being slaves to sickness.

He freed us from a life of being slaves to poverty.

He freed us from a life of being slaves to hopelessness.

JESUS freed us from a life of being slaves to SIN!

TODAY the Marriage Enrichment Ministry is recognizing and celebrating marriages.

But the greatest marriage is between Jesus and His church.

Because we are the Bride of Christ.

AND LIKE Gomer, we messed up.

Like Gomer, many have done some foolish things.

But whilst Hosea paid fifteen pieces of silver and barley for Gomer, Jesus paid a price far superior.

BECAUSE He paid for us through the shedding of His blood.

HOSEA went to Gomer, and he put her clothes on her.

And he led her away by the hand.

And he took her to his home.

AND in Hosea 3:3b, he says to her, "You must dwell as mine for many days; you shall not play the harlot, or belong to another man; so will I also be to you."

HOSEA pledged his love to her anew.

You see, for Hosea, his pledge to her in marriage was "Forever I do."

FOR better or for worse, forever I do.

IN sickness and in health, forever I do.

For richer or for poorer, forever I do.

And no wonder from there on, Gomer remained faithful to Hosea.

GOD's pledge to us is the same.

God says His love for us is "Forever I do."

Regardless of what you have do, God says, "Forever I do."

Regardless of where you have been, God says, "Forever I do."

GOD hates sin. But in spite of our sins, His love for us is "Forever I do."

"Forever I do" speaks of an unconditional love.

AND because He loves us unconditionally, the best is yet to come!

I FEEL like telling somebody that you will get past your past.

YOU are about to enter into the greatest season of your life.

God is about to move in your family.

He is about to move in your business.

God is about to move in your finances and in your personal life in a greater way than you have ever experienced in the past.

GOD sent me to tell you that you are closer to your breakthrough than you think!

YOU are closer to your breakthrough than you have ever been before!

YOU are closer to your miracle than you even realize.

THE truth is that you may not understand everything that is going on in your life at the present time.

But you are on the verge of a change.

IN spite of the fact that hell is hitting your marriage hard, in spite of the fact that you are going through the greatest trial of your life, the best is yet to come!

Because God's commitment to us is "Forever I do."

YOU SHOWED up for service today.

But God wants you to renew your marriage vows because He says, "Forever I do."

He Wants your "Forever I do" too.

"FOREVER I do" is a promise from God that you can take to the bank!

And God says, "The best is yet to come!"

YOUR dream is about to become a reality.

YOU may not have any evidence that a change is about to take place.

But God is an on-time God.

THE best is yet to come because you have a promise.

IF all you have is a promise, it is enough.

Because a promise is all you need!

YOU, too, have God's promise of "Forever I do."

And that is why no matter how things look, just know that the best is yet to come.

BECAUSE of your promise, your future will be better than your past.

BECAUSE of your promise, your situation is going to change.

THE world will not understand you.

YOUR family will not understand you.

EVEN some church people won't be able to figure you out!

AND the reason they will not understand you is because they see what you are going through.

But you still have peace and you still have a praise.

You are holding on to God's promise of "Forever I do."

TELL your neighbor, "I have a promise."

> He that dwelleth in the secret place of the most high shall abide under the shadows of the Almighty. (Ps. 91:1)

TELL someone else, "I have a promise."

> Yea though I walk through the valley of the shadow of death, I will fear no evil, because God is with me. (Ps. 23:4)

SHAKE somebody and say, "I have a promise."

> A thousand shall fall at thy side and ten
> thousand at thy right hand, but it shall not come
> nigh thee. (Ps. 91:7)

YOU have a promise. The promise is that God is about to bring you out of what you are in.

YOU are on the verge of a change, and your promise is about to be fulfilled.

YOU may be having a hard time trying to figure out what is going on in your life at the present time.

YOU are probably in a time when your mind is telling you one thing and your spirit is telling you another thing.

YOUR body is still in your present situation, but your spirit has somehow stepped into your future, and your mind is a little confused because it is trying to figure out what is going on.

YOUR spirit knows things about your future THAT your mind does not yet know.

> BUT as it is written, Eye hath not seen, nor
> ear heard, neither have entered into the heart of
> man, the things which God hath prepared for
> them that love him. (1 Cor. 2:9)

WHILE your body is still in your present, in your today, your spirit has stepped into your future, into your tomorrow.

YOUR spirit has stepped into a place of revival.

IT has stepped into a place of restoration.

IT has stepped into a place of renewal, a place of provision and prosperity.

AND your mind is a little confused because it does not yet understand what is going on.

BUT YOUR body is about to catch up with your spirit.

TELL your neighbor, "My body is catching up with my spirit."

AND in return, you are going to walk into a place of victory.

You are going to walk into a place of blessings and prosperity.
Greater than anything you have ever experienced.
Because God says, "Forever I do!"
YOU don't have time for man's foolishness.
You don't have time for the drama.
You don't have time for the strife and the negative talk.
AT THIS season of your life, you cannot afford to have people in your life that always talk negative.
YOU do not need people telling you that you cannot have what God says you can have OR that you cannot do what God said you can do OR that you cannot go where God said you can go.
YOU must have people in your life that believe in you.
Like Hosea believed in Gomer.
YOU need people in your life who believe in your future.
People who will celebrate you and not people who will simply tolerate you!
THE love of God is greater far than tongue or pen can ever tell.
It goes beyond the highest star and reaches to the lowest hell.
WHY do you think hell is hitting you so hard?
WHY do you think you are going through what you are going through?
WHY do you think you are experiencing strange trials in your life?
THE scriptures says, "Beloved, think it not strange concerning the fiery trial which is to try you, as though some strange thing happened unto you."
WHAT you are going through is because the enemy is upset about what is to come.
WHY do you think there is an increase of demonic activity against you, against your family, against your ministry, against your business?
IT IS because like Gomer, you have decided to be faithful to the One who redeemed you.
You have decided that come hell or high water, you are not giving up.
You are not throwing in the towel.

You are not turning your back to Jesus.

Because He paid the price you could not pay, you are redeemed by a love that says, "Forever I do!"

AND so from hereon, you are sealing your ministry with a commitment of "Forever I do!"

NO BACKSLIDING.

NO PLAYING CHURCH.

NO COMPLACENCY.

NO BACKBITING.

NO MALICE-KEEPING.

"FOREVER I DO" means that you are committing to show up.

You are committed to stand up and to speak up!

"FOREVER I DO" means that YOU are committed to loving your enemies.

YOU are committed to blessing those who curse you.

YOU are committed to bless those who spitefully use you.

AND when somebody asks you, "How much do you love me?" Tell them, "Forever I do."

Forever I do love you regardless of your imperfections.

Forever I do love you regardless of your status in life.

FOREVER I DO!

CHAPTER 12

Provoke Your Rainfall

Despite the financial struggles and difficulties that I have encountered in life, I am blessed because of the many persons that God had used and continues to use to be a blessing to me.

One thing that I have learned throughout the years is that God takes us through different seasons (good and bad). And for each season that He takes us through, He provides a person or persons to help us or to celebrate us through our seasons. And if you feel alone whilst going through a season, it is because He has not yet provided the person or persons.

God is a provider. However, the ways that He provides are not always predictable. It is true that "without faith, it is impossible to please God." And as such, we must be prepared to stand in faith, believing God to supply all our needs, regardless. It is designed to stretch us and to pull us closer to Him so that in the end, we provided for and He is glorified.

Prayer is a powerful weapon, and I have found that for every financial struggle, for every difficulty, for every hardship, a prayer that I either prayed in the past or had prayed in the crisis preceded the provisions.

I remember waking up one morning to having only a one hundred Jamaican dollar bill in my purse with bills to pay that had become due and some past due. I prayed that morning with tears streaming down my face. I said, "Lord, I need your help." I was broken because it seemed like I was moving from "hand to mouth" to having nothing in my hand to take to my mouth.

Just after I got through praying, my cell phone rang. I initially did not want to answer the call because I did not want the person to know that I was crying, but the more the phone rang, the more I felt the urge to respond. And so I did. When I answered, the person said, "Minister, I was just praying, and I saw you praying and telling God that you needed His help, and God told me to take some money and give to you." The person arrived at my home that morning within twenty minutes, and the money that she gave me was able to pay the bills that were due with money to spare. This was just one of many instances that God used this individual as well as others to bless me during a crisis.

It was not easy, but I know how it is to pray until something happens. I had to pray until God opened the door and provided for the payment of my mother's mounting medical bills. On one occasion, God had the hospital write it off. I had to pray until God opened the door by speaking to the heart of a friend who, during one of the lowest seasons in my life, wrote me a check, which I was able to use to pay outstanding loan payments.

There was a time that I needed over one hundred thousand Jamaican dollars to pay my annual car insurance premium, and when I prayed, God caused the exact money that I needed to miraculously show up in my savings account. When I had called the bank to point out what I had thought to have been an error on their part by placing the sum in my savings account, the bank made checks and told me that no error had been made, as they saw that the sum was legitimately deposited to my account, only that they did not know who had deposited the money.

On another occasion, I needed five thousand Jamaican dollars to allow my mother to do some blood tests, and all that I had was two thousand Jamaican dollars. I went to the ATM to withdraw the two thousand Jamaican dollars, thinking that I would pay for her to do some of the tests. And when I got the remainder of the money, I would pay for her to do the remainder.

Upon arrival at the ATM, the machine was already in use as the door was locked, and so I waited with a line starting to form behind me. Within a few minutes, a lady came out and I went in. As soon as I went in and was about to use the machine, I saw money pushing out of the machine. Without touching the money, I immediately reopened the door to call back the lady to let her know that she had left money behind. When I looked, the lady was nowhere in sight. I even asked the persons standing in line waiting to use the machine if they had seen the lady who came out before I went in, and they told me that they had not seen a lady, and so I went back in and took up the cash and counted it, only to find that it was exactly five thousand Jamaican dollars.

I did not allow this to stop me from withdrawing the money that I had gone to the ATM for. However, as soon as I withdrew it, I headed straight to the ATM's bank to report that a lady had mistakenly left the money behind. When I told the lady at the bank's customer service desk, she looked at me as if I was crazy. And so I asked to speak with a supervisor or manager. Hesitantly, she called the manager, to whom I explained again what had happened. She, too, looked at me as if I was crazy and then suggested that I could leave the money and they would place it in a suspense account just in case someone came to claim it. Instead, I gave her my contact details and told her that I would keep the money. And if anyone ever came to claim it, she should call me. No one ever called me, and yes, I paid in full for my mother to do all her blood tests because it had by then become clear to me that it was God who had provided.

Then how can I forget the tender care of God during a season of pain? We had received a dog as a pup, and he grew to become a member of our family. He was our joy. One day, he went over the fence between our neighbor's yard and ours, and they had left their front gate open. He went through their gate and was hit by a car, which broke his two back hips. We were devastated by it. Plus, it also happened at a time when we had very little money.

I remember us rushing him to the doctor early the following morning after he had suffered all night in pain, as all the vets were closed when he got hit that night. The doctors treated him, and the cost for his treatment took all the little money that I had.

When we got home, I went into my room, and I cried whilst praying and complaining to the Lord. We needed grocery and money, and I just had to pay a bill for our dog who, through my frustrations, I felt was responsible for his injuries by having gone on the road. And so now not only did we not have any money, but we also had the task of nursing him back to health, as he would be unable to walk for the next six-week period. I was hurting.

As soon as I got through praying, I heard my mom shout out excitedly, "Denise, I found money!"

I said, "What? Where did you find money?"

She responded, "Come here." And I rushed to her to find her holding money in her hand.

Mom explained to me that she, too, had become heartbroken, especially when she heard me praying and complaining to the Lord how our dog's doctor bill had taken away all the little money that we had to keep until I had gotten paid. She said when she finished praying, she opened her eyes, and when she did, the focus of her eyes were on her drawer, and she heard the Lord say, "Look under the vase." She said that she immediately got up and looked under the vase on the drawer, and she found money. Mom couldn't recall if she had put the money there, but even if she did and had forgotten, it was the Lord who had led her to it at a time of great need. God had provided once again.

One day during one of our church services, I was challenged to sow a seed of five thousand Jamaican dollars after the guest speaker was through ministering. The five thousand dollars was all that I had, and so I was hesitant to obey when the Lord kept nudging me. I walked out in faith, and I sowed the seed. And for the rest of the service, I kept wondering if I had heard the Lord correctly. I was troubled because I needed the money—it was a big sacrifice for me at the time. The following Sunday after the service, I was chairing a meeting when a lady walked up to me and asked if she could speak with me briefly. I wondered to myself if she had not seen that I was chairing a meeting. However, she looked desperate, so I asked someone to continue the meeting for me while I stepped away and quickly spoke with her.

The lady said, "Minister, I was looking for you after the service last Sunday and did not see where you had turned. The Lord had instructed me to give you some money after the service last week, and when I did not find you, as much as I wanted to spend the money during the week, I could not. It was as if something would have happened to me if I did, and so I brought it for you, and I just could not leave this week until I give it to you." So she held my hand and secretly placed the money in the palm of my hand. When I opened my hand and looked at it, I realized that she had placed a five thousand Jamaican dollar note in the palm of my hands. And immediately, I remembered my seed of obedience from the previous week, and I realized there and then that the act of God having nudged me to give the week before was a test that thankfully, although initially hesitant, I had somehow passed.

By the time the meeting had ended and I was leaving the church sanctuary, another lady walked up to me and placed two thousand Jamaican dollars in my hand and said, "The Lord told me to give it to you."

Tears filled my eyes, and immediately I heard the Lord say, "You lose nothing by giving to me."

If that was not enough, I had preached at church one Sunday morning, and toward the end of the sermon, the Lord led me to give away a one-thousand-dollar bill as a way of showing the people how God would surprise them with blessings. The truth was that I also needed surprise blessings from the Lord, as I was going through a rough season. But in obedience to the Lord, I gave away the one-thousand-dollar bill, knowing very well that I, too, had a desperate need for it.

By the time the service had ended and I went to my car, a lady quickly stopped me before I could enter my vehicle. She was trembling with tears streaming down her face. It was clear that the anointing of the Lord was heavily upon her. She said, "Minister Samuels, this is the first time that I am coming to this church, and it is the first time that I am hearing you minister, but as soon as you got through ministering, the Lord said that I should find you and give you this money. Please take it." I took it from her shivering hand, and when I counted the money, it was three one thousand Jamaican dollar bills. God had instantly tripled the seed that I had sowed in the service!

What is clear from experiences such as these is the importance of "provoking our rainfall." Our rainfall meaning our blessing, our healing, our deliverance, our provisions. God has already provided. He has already made a way. All that is left is for us to do is to provoke (trigger, activate) our rainfall with our prayers and with our seeds of obedience.

The Sermon

And Elijah said unto Ahab, Get thee up, eat and drink; for there is a sound of abundance of rain.

So Ahab went up to eat and to drink. And Elijah went up to the top of Carmel; and he cast himself down upon the earth, and put his face between his knees,

And said to his servant, Go up now, look toward the sea. And he went up, and looked, and said, There is nothing. And he said, Go again seven times.

And it came to pass at the seventh time, that he said, Behold, there ariseth a little cloud out of the sea, like a man's hand. And he said, Go up, say unto Ahab, Prepare thy chariot, and get thee down that the rain stop thee not.

And it came to pass in the meanwhile, that the heaven was black with clouds and wind, and there was a great rain. And Ahab rode, and went to Jezreel. (1 Kings 18:41–45)

I USE for a theme tonight the words **"provoke your rainfall."**

SOME of you have been praying and fasting from the beginning of the year.

But your season is still dry.

SOME of you here tonight are at your lowest hour.

YOU are totally down and you really need help.

YOU didn't come here tonight because you don't mind losing a night's sleep.

YOU came because you are desperate for a change in your circumstance.

YOU came because you need something tangible from God.

YOU came because you are not satisfied and you need a greater anointing.

YOU need a supernatural touch from the Lord.

YOU need to experience a change in your financial situation.

Your income has dried up, and you don't know what next to do.

YOU have done everything you know how to do, but there still seems to be no solution to your problem.

BUT God sent me to tell you to provoke your rainfall.

DROUGHT was on the land. It had not rained in three and a half years.

And Elijah needed the rain to fall as a sign of the miraculous power of God.

IF the rain didn't fall, it would have been a disaster in the land.

And So Elijah had to provoke it.

IF the rain refuses to fall in your circumstance, you have to take some actions to provoke it.

TO provoke means to deliberately annoy.

IT means to incite something to do something.

IT means to incite by arousing anger.

IT means to stimulate into action.

ELIJAH said, "I hear the sound of the abundance of rain."

He heard it in his spirit, and he spoke a language of faith.

AS far as Elijah was concerned, the rain was on the way.

But there was work to be done.

So Elijah went to pray.

ONE sure way to provoke your rainfall is to pray.

GOD does nothing except in answer to prayer.

So if things seem to be stagnant around you, nothing seems to be moving, you need to check your prayer temperature.

FOR every miracle, FOR every breakthrough, FOR every prodigal who comes home, somebody had to pray.

ELIJAH got himself in the birth position.

He placed his head between his knees, and he began to labor in prayer for what he heard in the Spirit.

ELIJAH'S birth position signaled his expectancy of a breakthrough.

A WOMAN only assumes a birth position when she knows that her baby is fast approaching and that she is about to give birth.

AND SO after Elijah prayed the first time, he sent his servant out to look toward the sea for an answer.

BUT Elijah's servant returned and told him that he looked, but he didn't see any evidence of an answer to his prayer.

MOST people would have given up right there.

But Elijah understood the importance of provoking the rainfall.

He understood the importance of determination.

SO Elijah kept on praying.

And then he sent his servant back to the sea.

And while the servant was running to go see if the answer had appeared, Elijah kept on praying.

YOU have to keep on praying.

Elijah received the Word from God in his spirit.

And although there were no physical signs of rain, he held on to God's Word.

And he kept provoking the rainfall by praying.

WHEN you have a Word from God in your spirit, you just have to keep on praying.

DANIEL prayed for twenty days with no evidence whatsoever that God had heard him.

But on the twenty-first day, the breakthrough came.

KEEP on praying. KEEP on praising. KEEP on confessing.

KEEP on tithing and sowing. KEEP on singing and dancing.

NEVER accept your present position as final.

DON'T let the devil see you sweat. Delay is not denial.

ABRAHAM was delayed twenty-five years for the birth of his promised son, but he was not denied.

JOSEPH was delayed fifteen years before being seated on the throne, but he was not denied.

LAZARUS was delayed by death for four days, but he was not denied his miracle.

Habakkuk 2:3 says, "For the vision is yet for an appointed time, but at the end it shall speak, and not lie: (though it tarry) wait for it because it will surely come, it will not tarry."

Numbers 23:19 says, "God is not a man that he should lie, nor the son of man that he should repent: if he said it he will do it and if he hath spoken it, he will bring it to pass."

EVERY time you pray, you put pressure on the spiritual realm, and you fill the clouds that are bringing you blessings with expectancy.

WE ought not to pray just because we feel like it.

WE ought not to pray just because it's the Christian thing to do.

Or because it sounds like a good idea.

WE should pray because we have an objective that can only be reached and can only be won and conquered through prayer.

ELIJAH was still praying with his head between his knees.

Prayer is serious business and hard work.

SOMEBODY once said, "Many Christians pray with such lukewarmness and indifference and uncertainty that they wouldn't even recognize the answer to their prayer when it arrived."

ELIJAH'S servant brought back another negative report.

But Elijah kept on praying.

TELL your neighbor, "Keep on praying."

BUT Elijah told his servant to go back to the sea to look again.

Six times Elijah sent his servant to look for the answer.

And each time, he brought back a negative report.

But Elijah kept on praying.

AND then on the seventh time, the servant came back with the report.

He said, "Behold there ariseth a little cloud out of the sea like a man's hand."

SEVEN is God's number of completion.

TELL your neighbor, "When you provoke your rainfall, it forces God's hand into completion."

ELIJAH'S servant brought back the answer to the prayers prayed.

ELIJAH had successfully provoked the rainfall.

WHAT the servant saw at the time didn't look like much.

He said it looked like a "man's hand."

BUT Elijah's faith grabbed ahold of it, and that was all he needed to hear to confirm that the rain would be falling very soon.

THERE is something about faith that lets you see the greatness in little things.

LIKE SAMSON, FAITH can see a weapon of mass destruction in the jawbone of an ass.

BECAUSE OF faith, Jesus saw a meal for a multitude in a sack lunch.

LIKE Elisha, FAITH can see an oil business in a roomful of empty jars.

LIKE Samuel, FAITH can see a king in a simple smelly shepherd boy.

THE servant saw a little cloud, but Elijah saw a river filling.

He saw the ground soaking.

He saw a drought-busting rainstorm.

=I DON'T CARE how big the problem may seem to you or how long it is has existed.

THE promises of God come in concentrated form.

All you need to do is to provoke your rainfall by standing on those promises.

And keep praying until something happens.

JESUS said, "All it takes is faith like the size of a mustard seed. And you can command mountains to jump into the sea. And they will have to go."

TELL your neighbor, "Provoke your rainfall!"

SAY like Jacob, "I will not let you go until you bless me."

I am desperate for my breakthrough.
I am desperate for my healing.
I am desperate for my miracle.
I am desperate for an outpouring of God's anointing upon my life.

TELL somebody else, "Provoke your rainfall!"
Say like Esther, "If I perish, I perish. But I must see the king."
YOU MUST see the answer to your prayers.
YOU MUST see a turnaround in your circumstance.
YOU MUST see the chains of financial lack being destroyed.
YOU MUST see the salvation of your loved ones.
HOLD on to somebody's hand and say, "Provoke your rainfall!"
SAY like David, "Hear my cry O, Lord. Attend unto my prayer. From the ends of the earth will I cry unto thee. For when my heart is overwhelmed, lead me to the Rock that is Higher than I" (Ps. 61:1–2).

PROVOKE your rainfall and say like James, "Blessed is the man who perseveres under trial, because when he has stood the test, he will receive the crown of life that God has promised to those who love him" (James 1:12).

PEOPLE of God, provoke your rainfall.

When 120 men and women had gathered in the upper room, waiting for the promised power, the Bible says, "Suddenly there came a sound from heaven like a mighty rushing wind. And it filled all the house where they were sitting" (Acts 2:2).

THERE was a sound.

The sound was an indication that something was coming.

AND suddenly, cloven tongues as fire appeared on each of them.

And they were all filled with the Holy Ghost.

And they began to speak with other tongues.

As the Spirit gave them utterance. (Acts 2:3–4)

I HEAR the sound of an abundance of rain.

Elijah spoke those words in a place and at a time where there had not been one drop of water from the sky nor dew on the ground in three and a half years.

GOD sent me to prophesy to you and to tell you that it is getting ready to rain.

The rain is on its way.

NOW THAT may not mean anything to some of you, but for somebody listening to my voice, it means everything.

IT means there will be joy where there has been sorrow.

IT means there will be laughter where there has been weeping.

IT means there will be victory where there has been struggles.

THE rain is on its way. Can you hear it in your spirit?

HELP is on the way.

THE answer to your prayers is on the way.

YOUR breakthrough is on the way.

THERE is just something powerful about knowing that the answer is on the way.

IT puts a fire back in your belly and a fight back in your spirit.

IT gives you the strength to hold on and to persevere in provoking your rainfall."

I DON'T know who I am talking to, but you have prayed.

And you have fasted.

And you have cried.

And you have confessed the Word.

And from every natural evidence, nothing has changed.

AND if the truth is known, for many of you, it has gotten worse.

BUT I came to tell you that change is in the atmosphere.

The rain is coming.

Restoration is coming.

Healing is coming.

Peace is coming. Joy is coming. Money is coming.

"Provoke your rainfall!"

You may not see any evidence right now.

You may not see any physical sign just yet.

But don't give up! Don't quit on God.

Keep praying until something happens.

THE Word that I am giving to you tonight is a sign.

TELL your neighbor the words *provoke your rainfall* is a sign."

IF you are hearing this Word, just remember that "Faith cometh by hearing and hearing by the word of God."

SOMEBODY'S faith is going to another level tonight.

Somebody who has been struggling through the wilderness of just enough and barely getting by is getting ready to go into overflow.

SOMEBODY is going to change address in the Spirit tonight.

SOME of the stuff that used to hinder you and used to pull you down won't bother you after this service.

ELIJAH said, "I hear the sound of the abundance of rain."

What is the rain to you?

THE rain is God's power visiting your life in the area or areas that are in drought or in lack or broken or empty.

THE rain is God taking every plan, every plot, every scheme, and every weapon that the devil has launched at you and turn it around for your good.

THE simplest definition of "provoke your rainfall" is your answered prayer.

THE drought is about to break. Provoke your rainfall!

YOUR spirit has been dry for so long, and you have felt so distant from the presence of God.

But that drought is going to break.

The wind is blowing.

And the rain of God's supernatural presence is flooding your soul right now.

Just open up and let it fall on you.

THE drought is about to break. Provoke your rainfall.

YOU have been fighting a long battle with your health, but it is going to rain—.

And there is healing in the rain.

YOU have been fighting with peer pressure.

YOU have been fighting with some private struggles.

But it is going to rain.

And there is deliverance in the rain.

Receive your miracle.
Receive your breakthrough.
Provoke your rainfall. It is the time of rain.
THE anointing is here. Yokes will be destroyed.
Burdens will be lifted.
ELIJAH got off his knees and told Ahab, "The rain is here! If you don't get that chariot rolling, you won't get off this mountain."
AND while Elijah was prophesying, the wind blew.
And the clouds turned black and the rain came.
Elijah heard it with his spirit.
He prophesied it with his mouth.
And then he saw it with his eyes.
I PROPHESY right now that somebody is getting ready to see a manifestation of what you have heard God say in your spirit.
YOU have been confessing it and believing it.
And a lot of people thought you were crazy.
But you are getting ready to see it because as you provoke your rainfall, you will see that the drought is over—the rain is here.
NOW stand on your feet, open your mouths, and begin to provoke your rainfall!
BEGIN to pray. Talk to God about the drought—the dry situations in your life.
BEGIN to pray. Talk to God about the things that have been hindering your breakthrough.
BEGIN to pray.
Talk to God about your difficulties, about your struggles.
PROVOKE the rainfall!
Trouble the skies. Trouble the heavenlies.

For the weapons of your warfare are not carnal but mighty through God to the pulling down of strong holds. (2 Cor. 10:4)

PROVOKE the rainfall and pull down every stronghold.
PROVOKE the rainfall. Defeat the plans of the enemy.
PROVOKE the rainfall. War against principalities and powers.

FOR God is our refuge and strength—a very present help in times of trouble.

IT is going to rain again. The rain is coming.

Open your mouths and pray the following with me.

Prayer Points

1. I provoke my heavens to open, in the name of Jesus. (Pray this seven times and shout seven Hallelujahs.)
2. Every power that has locked me up, die, in the name of Jesus.
3. My rain of marital, business, and career breakthroughs (whatever it is, be specific).

I provoke you by the blood of Jesus Christ of Nazareth.

Fall in the name of Jesus!

IT IS raining! IT IS raining! IT IS raining!

If you believe it, praise God for the rain!

CHAPTER 13

Lord, Give Me a Double Portion

As a little girl growing up, I rarely played dolly house, but instead I found that I loved teaching. I would go home from school, and my playtime would be me teaching my mother's plants in the yard and at times beating them if they did not answer my questions correctly. I also found that I would go home from church on Sunday mornings, and I would open my Bible and preach full sermons to the plants and then lead them into repentance. Another favorite playtime activity would be going into my room and pretending to be a grown-up. I would talk to myself in the mirror about the issues of life, all the while speaking positive words to the person in the mirror. As a child, this came naturally to me. Looking back, it is clear that I was acting out my purpose.

I had known from an early age that the call of God was upon my life. I grew up in the church, and I was always actively involved in ministry. In fact, it is the only life that I have known.

Singing is one of my passions, and so the first ministry that I got involved in at church was the choir ministry. I was about eight or nine years of age at the time, and to this day, I credit our then minister of music with helping to shape our spiritual development, as from those early years, we were mandated to attend regular half-day fasting services and all-night prayer meetings hosted by the music ministry. In fact, it was after having attended one of those all-night prayer meetings that I went home still under the influence of the anointing, and right there in my home, I started speaking in tongues. I was filled with the Holy Ghost. I was twelve years of age at the time, and I remained a part of the choir ministry for many years thereafter into adulthood.

I love the youth ministry, and so I had hardly ever missed attending our church's weekly youth meetings, coupled with the fact that as a youngster, from as early as the age of twelve or thirteen years, I was attending three-day fasting services with my mom, which I did for many years thereafter. I was always known as the youngest person in attendance at those fasting services, and it was because I always had a hunger for more of God and for seeing other young persons like myself grow in God. It therefore did not take me long to realize that another passion of mine is helping to nurture and develop young people. And so it was no surprise when through the divine leadership of Bishop Herro Blair, I was appointed a member of our church's youth board, a position that I held for over three years before I was appointed the youth director, a position that I held for over ten years.

In going back a bit, I recall that at the age of twenty-seven years (within two months of being separated from my then husband), I started seeing myself in my dreams and visions, preaching to large crowds of people. I would often awake feeling puzzled, as prior to that, with the exception of me preaching a sermonette ("Meeting Christ Empty-Handed") as a teenager and being active in the youth ministry, I had had no inclinations to be a preacher or a teacher of the Word.

I kept having the dreams and visions to the point when I woke up, I would be able to write the title of the sermons that I preached in my dreams and visions, and I would share them with my mom. And as I did so, we would feel the distinct presence of the Lord. This happened for a couple years before I preached my next sermonette in 1999, entitled "Obedience," at a small women's group meeting called the Women of Vision—a women's group started by the co-pastor of our church, Dr. Alma Blair. The first full sermon that I preached was in church later that same year in our Sunday evening service. It was entitled "Does God Have Your Soul?" The impact was so divine that it was what had launched the beginning of my preaching ministry, which has since seen me not only preaching in our church on a regular basis but has also seen me preaching in almost all the parishes in our island Jamaica and in the United States of America, Canada, and Grand Cayman.

God also opened the door for me to do television ministry when He inspired our co-pastor to recommend me to Bishop Delford Davis, senior pastor of the Power of Faith Ministries International, to serve as a guest on his program dubbed *Strength for Today*. That one encounter led to me being asked by Bishop Davis to serve as cohost of the program and to at times serve as host of the program. It further paved the way for me to go on to serve on other television programs on his PFM Television ministry to include *The Bible Speaks*, *The Hour of Prayer*, and *Community Connection*. God is purposeful. When He opened the door to me serving as a presenter on the TBC radio program *Reflections* a couple years before that, I had not known that it was His way of launching me into media ministry.

Soul-winning became my focus and added passion, which again through the divine leadership of my bishop resulted in me being asked to serve as the director for the young converts/new members class. It was a position that I held for over ten years as I taught and provided critical leadership to the hundreds of souls won for Christ throughout the years.

God was not through with me, as what had shifted me from the direct leadership of the young converts/new members portfolio was when I was asked to serve as associate pastor with responsibility for assisting with the birthing of new ministries and the development of other ministries. In the end, I was given direct responsibility for the thirty-six ministries in our church.

It was not until I had assumed this portfolio responsibility that our ministry leader for media found and sent to me videotapes of a prophecy that had been spoken over my life openly before the church one Sunday morning about seven years prior. The prophecy spoke on how God would have elevated me in the ministry. Up until that time, I had totally forgotten about the prophecy and the other prophecies that I received throughout the years where God shared openly about His call upon my life and how He would be using me to do His work.

As God used me and continues to use me to preach and to teach His Word to hundreds of people, my prior dreams and visions of yesteryears began to make sense. I was no longer puzzled by why I had them. I now understood that God, at times, shows us the end result before the beginning so that when we get there, we will know without a shadow of doubt that it was all God's doing.

The numerous testimonies of persons being healed, delivered, and receiving financial breakthroughs, the many marriages and relationships that were restored all because of how God used me in ministry oftentimes leave me in awe. All glory and honor is due to God and Him alone. He did it through me.

I could not have made it this far without some key persons in my life. They include the undying love and support of my senior pastors and other supporters of my ministry, headed by my mom, who had often traveled around the island of Jamaica with me as I went to preach the Word. My church family is my rock, and the many who stand in the gap for me, always praying for me and giving me words of encouragement. I wake up and show up for you all. I believe that God blessed our church with some of the sweetest people on earth.

When we commit our lives to the Lord, we experience divine providence, and we allow ourselves to be taken on a journey that is totally charted and directed by God. For all that God has been doing in my life, for all that He has been using me to do and continues to use me to do, I am humbled and know that there is no way that I can continue each day without a daily outpouring of a double portion of His anointing upon my life.

The journey has not been easy, but it was worth it. I don't know what else the Lord has in store for me, but as the journey continues, my daily prayers have been and will continue to be "Lord, give me a double portion." You know why? Because I am not satisfied. I will never be satisfied with living in yesterday's anointing.

The Sermon

Scripture: 2 Kings 2:9–10
Whether you know it or not, we are on a journey, and many tests will come.

TESTS that are geared at determining our faithfulness or our lack thereof.

I HEAR the physical prosperity doctrine preached every so often.

And whilst that is good, I believe that God wants us to have much more.

YOU see, it is time for us to grow into the eternal!

I RECENTLY read about a dream that a man had.

And in the dream, Jesus was crying.

JESUS had just finished hearing one of His elite deliver a sermon on "Claim Your Jet!"

The congregation had gone wild and was jumping in praise!

AND THE man stated that in the dream, he asked Jesus why He was so sad.

AND that Jesus replied by saying, "The number one request from people is for SUVs, houses, and money." And that thereafter, they would go to sleep.

THE man stated that in the dream, Jesus's eyes looked so broken that he found himself awoken out of his sleep, crying.

"God, may my heart be broken for what breaks your heart. May my tears be for lost souls!"

THESE days, I find that people are not concerned about the lost and dying.

YOU know, some people may find it hard to believe, but there was actually a time when the main purpose of the church was for the salvation of mankind.

I KNOW that some of you who are more concerned with prosperity may find it hard to believe.

BUT THE driving force behind Jesus's coming into this world was to save souls.

FOR far too long, the church tried to operate in the machinery of human wisdom and power.

AND AS a result, we have lost the power of God that made us remarkable!

SOMEONE once commented that without the ministry of the Holy Spirit in the early church, 95 percent of what the *early* church did would have ceased.

THIS person then went on to say that if the Holy Spirit were removed from our churches today, 95 percent of what we do in the *modern* church would continue unchanged!

AND THIS is an indictment on us all as people of God.

IN TODAY'S CHURCH, after very real moves of God, some people remain stuck in the fast-food lane.

THEY are stuck on wanting fast prayers, fast preaching, and fast leaving. Fast leaving the church, that is!

AND so after an extremely dynamic move of God in church, as they say, "The anointing wears off."

MANY are content to leave and to act as though its business as usual.

BUT where are the ministries?

Where are the testimonies?

TURN your Bibles with me to 2 Kings 2:9–10:

> And it came to pass, when they were gone over, that Elijah said unto Elisha, Ask what I shall do for thee, before I be taken away from thee. And Elisha said, I pray thee, let a double portion of thy spirit be upon me.
>
> And he said, Thou hast asked a hard thing: nevertheless, if thou see me when I am taken from thee, it shall be so unto thee; but if not, it shall not be so.

I USE this for a theme this morning: **"Lord, give me a double portion."**

HAVE you ever eaten food and not felt satisfied?

HAVE you ever drank water and still felt thirsty?

WELL, that's nothing to be compared with what our spiritual hunger and thirst should be like.

BUT if you have ever felt a desperate need for more, then just raise your hands toward heaven and make the plea, **"Lord, give me a double portion. I am not satisfied!"** (Repeat.)

I WANT US to examine a biblical experience this morning.

AND IF you really tap into what the Lord is saying, your life will be radically changed forever!

ARE you ready?

THE books of 1 and 2 Kings record the history of the nation of Israel.

And the nation of Israel WAS divided into the Southern Kingdom and the Northern Kingdom.

IN THE Northern Kingdom of Israel, the kings were evil, and there were no true revivals.

IN fact, these kings did evil in God's sight.

AND SO in the midst of this degenerate and idolatrous kingdom ruled by vicious, cruel, and corrupt kings, THE Lord called two men, one the successor of the other.

AND these two men—Elijah and Elisha—stood as the heralds of God and His Word.

THE verses that we have just read points to the homegoing of one of these men, who happened to have been one of the greatest men in the Word of God.

ELIJAH was greatly used of the Lord in his generation.

But his time on the earth had come to an end.

AND the day came when it was time to pass the baton to a new generation.

TELL somebody, "We are the new generation!"

IF YOU still have a purpose to fulfill, you are a part of the new generation!

SO THIS was how Elisha had come into the picture.

Elisha had a purpose to be fulfilled.

AND our text tells us that Elisha was a man hungry for all God could give him.

HE wanted the Lord and His power in his life, and he was willing to pay the price to get it!

SO the Question is, Are you willing to pay the price for more of God?

IF you have a purpose to be fulfilled, you should be!

AND SO IN examining verse 9 of our text, I wish for us to take note of the fact that Elisha's request was a spiritual request!

THE request was not for double the fame or for double the wealth.

But rather, the request was for double the spirit, double the anointing, a double dose of God.

AND I know that people like to get excited when they hear that they can get double of anything just by doing one thing.

BECAUSE two for the price of one is a good thing!

This kind of sales pitch really sells products fast.

I DON'T know about you, but I am all for getting two pairs of shoes for the price of one.

How about you?

I AM all for getting two of my favorite things for the price of one.

SO two for the price of one is a good thing.

But it only applies to the physical.

YOU see, THERE is no such thing as a sales pitch in God's kingdom.

GOD isn't into the selling business.

HE IS not a salesman working on commission.

WOULDN'T it be nice to know that all you need to do is to attend one church service per month and still get the blessings of the next two services?

FOR some people, that would be just dandy!

AND WOULDN'T it be just great to be able to never fast, to never have to sacrifice food and to still get the blessings of those that do?

HOW wonderful that would be for some people!

AND how about you praying once per week or every other week whilst having somebody pray for you constantly throughout each week, and you still reap the rewards?

THAT sounds good, doesn't it?

BUT God is really not into the two-for-the-price-of-one thing.

YES, He paid the ultimate price for all our sins.

And that is a good thing!

BUT IF WE want to grow and to develop spiritually, if we want a double outpouring of the spiritual, WE must be willing to do more than the average.

THE average Christian may only pray once or twice per day.

BUT if you want more, IF you want double the Spirit, you have to be prepared to pray throughout the day.

In your spirit, YOU are on the job.

But each chance that you get, you pray in the Spirit.

You are cooking dinner, but you are praying.

You are washing the car, but you are praying.

You are cutting the yard, but you are praying.

IF YOU want more than the average, you have to be prepared to do more than the average!

GOD'S blessings don't come cheap!

There are no discount offerings, no coupons for you to trade in.

TELL your neighbor, "God's blessing doesn't come cheap!"

THE scriptural experience that we are examining today IS really about the mantle of ministry.

And the mantle of ministry rests upon you and me.

IF we are going to be as effective as we should be for the glory of the Lord, THEN we, too, need the power of God's Spirit in double, triple, or even in quadruple amounts.

ELISHA spent time with Elijah.

And he understood the principle of doing more to get more and not doing less to get more.

ELISHA, being a young man, was fascinated by what Elijah was able to do by the power of God.

AND Elisha decided that he wanted to do more.

Because if Elijah could have done so much even in his golden years, at a time when Elijah was completing his ministry, completing his purpose, THEN as far as Elisha was concerned, he could do even greater!

AND this concept is not foreign because when Jesus Himself was leaving this earth, He did say that we would be able to do even greater works than He did.

SO Jesus left a system in place that would allow us to do even more than He Himself did!

Elisha wanted to do more.

He was not satisfied. He Wanted More!

AND Elisha knew that a double portion of God was the most valuable tool and goal that could ever be sought by God's people.

YOU SEE, back then, the law of the land dictated that the double portion was reserved for the firstborn.

SO what Elisha was asking for was what he was really entitled to!

LET me show you. ELISHA referred to Elijah as "father."

AND he did so because of his close association with Elijah.

And because of the fact that God had made him a firstborn, as God had appointed him to succeed Elijah.

AS Christians, God is our Father.

And regardless of when we were born into the kingdom of God, we are considered God the Son's firstborn.

CONTRARY to what some people think, Jesus had no second-born children.

He has no grandchildren.

He has no stepchildren.

He has no bastard children.

WE are all His firstborn children.

AND BY nature of that fact, we are entitled to at least a double portion of God's Spirit.

THE problem is, many have been settling for less than they are entitled to!

NOTICE SOMETHING WITH ME.

ELISHA wasn't interested in inheriting Elijah's trinkets and treasures.

Some people fight over what their loved ones leave behind.

ELISHA was more interested in the things of the Spirit, and he must have known that a double portion would have cost Him more.

HE must have known this because he knew what was expected of Elijah, who had been operating on less than the double portion.

BUT Elisha was still willing to exert all his efforts to attain the perfect will of God for his life.

THE question is, are you willing to exert more?

ELIJAH told Elisha, "You must STAY WITH ME."

Like it or not, understand it or not, YOU have got to stay with me if you are going to ever get the double portion.

YOU have to be at that place so that when the anointing is flowing, you are ready to receive it!

ELIJAH said, "The only way you can be guaranteed the double portion is if you are there when I am taken up by a whirlwind. Is if you are there when God is ready to do the supernatural."

YOU see, God had a plan. He always has a plan!

GOD'S plan for your life is in keeping with what He destined for you!

A greater anointing belongs to you.

It is rightfully yours, but you have to be ready to receive it!

YOU SEE, from the time that it became apparent that Elijah was leaving until the moment that he left and Elisha received the blessing, SEVERAL trials crossed Elisha's way that attempted to hinder his request for more.

ELISHA, however, remained focused on obtaining the double portion.

He remained focused on obtaining his inheritance.

TELL somebody, "If you want it that badly, you must remain focused!"

GOD revealed to Elijah that he was to set out on the final chapter of his life—his last day on earth.

SO early in the morning, maybe a day like today, Elijah found himself having to face his last day on earth.

And God had given him an assignment.

ELIJAH'S assignment from God was to have taken Elisha to some places of significance.

AND Elisha was to be taken to *all* these places in one day.

EVERY time that Elijah and Elisha passed through the places, Elijah would attempt to get Elisha to stay.

AND it wasn't an effort on Elijah's part to hinder Elisha's progress.

BUT it was in an effort to test Elisha's determination/resolve.

YOU see, GOD always tests us before a promotion!

BEFORE an increase, God wants to see what you will do with what you already have!

IN ORDER to get a double portion of the anointing, in order to get more of God, THERE is a trail of the anointing that we must follow.

THERE is a road that we must journey on to get there.

THE journey does not have to be long.

THE journey just has to take you on the right pathway.

BECAUSE THERE are no shortcuts, there is no hiding behind the scenes.

GOD was about to test Elisha TO see if what he had asked for, he was really ready for.

SO the first place that God had Elijah take Elisha was to **GILGAL, the place of beginnings.**

ELISHA'S first trail of anointing led him through Gilgal.

GILGAL is where the Israelites first celebrated the Passover in the Promised Land.

IT was at Gilgal where the males who were born during the wilderness wanderings became circumcised and the covenant renewed.

SO IT IS easy to think that being at Gilgal is a good place to stay.

BUT GILGAL also represents restlessness, rolling stone, surface, no root system.

And we all know that a rolling stone never grows moss.

GOD wanted to see if Elisha was willing to go beyond the mentality of pleasure-seeking and emotional highs.

LORD, have mercy.

A lot of people today have a feel-good mentality.

IF THEY can come to church and feel good, then all is well.

IT has nothing to do with depth.

It is just about feeling good.

BUT TELL your neighbor, "Feeling good is not enough!"

GOD wanted to see if Elisha would be satisfied with just being in a place of beginning, a place of surface worship.

SO Elijah took Elisha to Gilgal.

And when Elijah was ready to leave Gilgal, as a test, he said to Elisha, "Stay here. I release you from your call. You don't have to go any further with me!"

BUT Elisha was determined for more.

He wasn't satisfied with the thought of just staying at Gilgal.

SO he told Elijah, "I am not staying here."

ELISHA said, "As surely as the LORD lives and as you live, I will not leave you."

I AM not Leaving without first receiving that which I am entitled to!

GOD says there are persons here today who are still at places of beginnings.

PERSONS are restless. You are still searching.

PERSONS are operating on the surface level.

You are not firmly rooted in God.

Yet you are satisfied to stay where you are.

You are satisfied to stay at Gilgal.

YOU are satisfied with just going through the motions.

YOU are satisfied with a little shake in your bodies.

Two spins and a roll.

YOU are satisfied with just showing up for ministry!

YES, choir! You are always in your place for ministry.

But don't you want more than just being in your places?

ELISHA was always in his place right beside Elijah.

But he still wanted more!

DON'T you want more than Gilgal?

USHERS, you are always ushering people to their seats.

But don't you also want to be the one to usher in God's presence?

GOD says TOO many people have settled at Gilgal.

FAR too many believers spend their entire Christian lives at Gilgal. They never grow.

And they never leave the place of beginnings.

TOO many are satisfied with just showing up for services on a Sunday morning and doing nothing else.

YOU NEED to leave Gilgal!

TELL your neighbor, "You need to leave Gilgal!"

You've stayed there long enough!

ELIJAH told Elisha, "THE Lord is now leading me to **BETHEL**."

AND Elisha said, "I'm not staying at Gilgal. I am going with you to Bethel!"

IN OTHER WORDS, Elisha was saying, "Wherever the Spirit of the Lord leads, I am going to follow."

GOD! WHEREVER you are, that's where I want to be!

LORD, IF YOU say it is time for me to leave GILGAL, IF you say it is time for me to achieve more, THEN I am willing to follow your lead!

THE trail of the anointing led Elijah and Elisha to BETHEL!

Bethel is the **House of God**—the altar of the Most High.

BETHEL is where you bury yourself in the Word of God.

IT IS where you learn the things of GOD.

IT is where you develop the fruits of the Spirit.

MANY people think that they can bypass faithfulness.

YOU can barely find faithful and committed people these days.

YES! They will show up for the fanfare.

BUT they are never around for the deeper things, for the more spiritual things.

MANY of you are here this morning because of tradition.

It is tradition for you to be in church on a Sunday morning.

SO once you have fulfilled your need to maintain your tradition, nobody sees you again until the next Sunday.

ASK your neighbor, "IS she talking about you?"

BETHEL, the house of God, is also a place of dreams.

IT was at Bethel that Jacob met God and dreamed of angels descending and ascending out of heaven.

LET ME see the hands of the dreamers in the house today.

Well, maybe you would be satisfied with staying at Bethel.

BECAUSE ALL dreamers want to do is dream of all the wonderful things that God can do.

All they want to do is dream of all the great work that can be accomplished.

MANY OF YOU are at Bethel.

You catch the vision of God's great work which must be done.

YOU see the needs, you feel the tug, but you never get past the place of dreaming about what you might do.

YOU never take the next step of making those dreams and visions a reality!

BECAUSE all you want to do is dream.

THE song says, "Dream, dream, dream, dreeeam."

(That's how the song goes?)

IT IS almost like a child not wanting to leave the comfort of home.

YES, you dream of owning your own home.

You may even buy a home of your own.

But you never want to leave the comfort of your parents' home.

BECAUSE it is your place of comfort.

You don't want to know what it feels like to be out there on your own.

YOU don't want to know what it feels like to have to depend on God for yourself.

BECAUSE exercising trust requires complete dependency.

And you don't want to learn how to do it.

BUT GOD SAYS TODAY you are being called to a higher place of service.

WHILST Bethel is a good place, that's not where God wants you to stay.

IT IS time to realize your dreams!

It is time to put action to your dreams!

GOD is calling you to affect lives.

HE is calling you to tear down idols.

HE is calling you to destroy demonic territories.

HE is calling you to trample on principalities and powers.

THE days of dreaming are over. It is time for action!

TELL somebody, "Wake up and stop dreaming!"

IT is time to realize your dreams.

There is work to be done!

YOU should be asking God to open your spiritual eyes.

DEMONS are on assignment to wreak havoc in this nation and in the nations of the world.

ASK GOD to open your spiritual eyes.

There are demons assigned to destroy families, and that is why so many are falling apart.

ASK God to open your spiritual eyes.

There are demons assigned to instigate criminal activities.

And while you are playing the blame game, innocent lives are being snuffed off out of this world.

WHOSE life will be the next devil's sacrifice?

Open your spiritual eyes.

There are demons of lust that have been assigned to inflict the people of God.

(COVER me, Jesus!)

THAT woman who has swayed you away from the things of God was assigned by the devil.

DON'T you see that every time that you are with her or you hear her voice, you start doing fooling things?

AND you start doing the sinful things of the flesh?

THAT man who keeps calling you all hours of the night for sex, telling you how good you look, THAT man who keeps asking you out and promising you the world, THAT man that you have been dating against your Christian belief was assigned by the devil to destroy you!

He was assigned by the devil to destroy your ministry.

He was assigned by the devil to keep you from fulfilling your purpose.

TURN off the telephone.

Shut the door in his face.

Stop the devil in his tracks.

TELL the man, "No God, no marriage, no sex!"

GOD wants to take you to the next level.

THERE IS work to be done!

DEMONS of frustration and depression are unleashed.

THEIR aim is to rob you of your finances and to destroy your faith.

THEIR aim is to rob you of your integrity and to destroy future.

IT IS time to leave Bethel.

BETHEL is a good place, but duty calls!

TELL two people it is time to leave Bethel.

It is time to leave your comfort zone.

It is time to tear down Satan's kingdom!

ELISHA had to face another test.

Either to stay in Bethel or to move on in keeping with God's leading.

BECAUSE now God was leading ELIJAH to move on to JERICHO.

AND SO Elisha decided, "IF I didn't stay at Gilgal, the place of beginnings, I am sure not staying in Bethel. Not when there is a greater anointing awaiting me."

ELISHA decided that he was going with Elijah to Jericho!

TELL somebody, "I am going to Jericho!"

I DON'T just want to be filled with God's Word.

I also want to conquer territories!

I want to tear down some walls! I am going to Jericho!

JERICHO was the third city on the anointing trail.

JERICHO represents what can be accomplished when God's people unite, when God's people come together.

OH! If the church would be on one accord…

ON THE day of Pentecost, they were all on one accord.

AND so the Holy Spirit filled the place.

THE Holy Spirit baptized everyone present!

HOLD somebody's hand and say, "We need to unite in the Holy Spirit today."

WE need to live overcoming lives.

WE need to conquer our fears.

WE need to live out our purpose.

SAY, "Neighbor, unite with me against the forces of evil. Unite with me against spiritual wickedness in high places. Unite with me against the weaknesses of the flesh."

IF THE church is on one accord, then we will hear a sound from heaven like a mighty rushing wind.

PEOPLE will be filled with new tongues.

People will receive new gifts of the spirit.

PEOPLE'S strength will be renewed!

WHEN the children of Israel were faced with the walls of Jericho, GOD made it clear that the only way the walls would be destroyed would be through the unity of the people.

THE people had to work together.

There is too much of a competitive spirit in the church!

WHY are you working against your brother when you both should be working together?

TOO many bad-minded people are still in the church.

Why should you be the only ones that progress?

TOO many news carriers and hypocrites are still in the church.

WE should seek to correct our brothers and sisters in love.

WE should seek to build them up and encourage them instead of tearing them down.

IT IS time to unite to destroy the walls of Jericho!

AND IF YOU see a wall before you, it means you should have a praise!

BECAUSE God would not have led you to Jericho if He knew you could not gain the victory over your situation.

I WONDER IF there is anyone here today who is willing to take a spiritual look at the walls of Jericho and command it in the name of Jesus to come down!

ANYBODY willing to look into the spiritual realm and say, "**Walls of Jericho!** I see that you are built up against the people of God. BUT it is time for you to go. YOU are coming down in Jesus's name!"

Shout out!

Jericho walls, you must come down in Jesus's name!

FOR no weapon formed against the people of God shall prosper!

Walls of opposition!

I see you keeping back the people of God, BUT it is time for you to go.

YOU are going to be destroyed in Jesus's name!

SHOUT out! Walls of opposition!

You must be destroyed in Jesus's name!
FOR the people of God are moving forward.

FOR the earth is the Lord's and the fullness
thereof, the world and they that dwell therein.
(Ps. 24:1)

Walls of confusion!
I see that you are on a mission to confuse the minds of God's
people and to overthrow the willpower of the people of God.
BUT it is time for you to go.
YOU are being torn down today in Jesus's name!
SHOUT out! Walls of confusion!
You are being torn down in Jesus's name!
OUR minds are covered under the blood of Jesus.
Tell somebody, "My mind is covered under the blood of Jesus!
My will is wrapped up in the will of God!"
For the fear of the Lord is the beginning of wisdom.
AND I fear God.
COMMAND your wisdom to increase in the name of Jesus!
COMMAND your minds to be renewed in the name of Jesus!
COMMAND your willpower to be revived in the name of Jesus!
Say, "Devil, you can't have me!" (Repeat.)
Walls of doubt and fear!
I see that your aim is to keep the people of God in bondage.
But it is time for you to go.
SET God's people free in Jesus's name.
SHOUT out!
Doubt, set me free in Jesus's name!
Fear, set me free in Jesus's name!
WE are free through the blood of Jesus!
SHAKE yourselves and say, "LOOSE me and let me go!"
I want to be free to fulfill my purpose.
I want to be free to do God's will.
THE Lord shall preserve us from all evil.
He shall preserve our souls.

THE Lord shall preserve our going out and our coming in.
IF we are out there, God will be with us.
IF we are in here, God will be with us.
BECAUSE FROM this day forth, WE ARE going to unite in praise and worship.
SOUND the trumpet! Sound the alarm!
THE walls must come down.
THE enemy must be defeated!
SOUND the trumpet! Sound the alarm!
FROM this time forth, WE are conquering territories.
FROM this time forth, we are taking back what the devil stole from us.
FROM this time forth, we are going to get what we have been praying and fasting for.
SOUND the trumpet! Sound the alarm!
For the steps of a good man are ordered by the Lord.
SOUND the trumpet! Sound the alarm!

➢ Praise God in His sanctuary.
➢ Praise Him in the firmament of His power.
➢ Praise Him for His mighty acts.
➢ Praise Him according to His excellent greatness.
➢ Praise Him with the sound of the trumpet.
➢ Praise Him with the psaltery and harp.
➢ Praise Him with the timbrel and dance.
➢ Praise Him with stringed instruments and organs.
➢ Praise Him upon the loud cymbals.
➢ Praise Him upon the high-sounding cymbals.

LET everything that hath breath (repeat).
Praise the Lord. Praise ye the Lord!
PRAISE God in one accord. Praise Him in unity.
FOR NO walls (repeat) shall prevent us from moving forward!
WE are children of the King!
LISTEN.
JERICHO also represents a place of past victories.

IT was here that Israel had its first military victory in the Promised Land.

BUT GOD did not want Elijah to settle in Jericho.

YOU see, IT IS okay to tear down walls and to conquer territories.

BUT then you must move on!

ELISHA was not about to be satisfied with staying in Jericho BECAUSE he realized that God was now leading Elijah to another area.

YOU see, JERICHO is also a border town.

To pass beyond this location was to enter wild new territory.

AND God knew what it would take to function in a wild/ uncertain new territory.

SO God told Elijah to move on to JORDAN.

And of course, Elisha followed.

JORDAN represents complete surrender—a place of death, death to the flesh.

IT is the barrier between the self-life and the spirit life.

FEW people ever take that final step of faith and sell out to go with God all the way.

THE prodigal son had said, "Dad, give me my inheritance" as he left.

BUT HIS trail, his Jordan, taught him a new attitude.

WHEN he came back, HE said, "DAD, MAKE ME one of your hired servants."

JORDAN is where you fully decide that you are going to quit chasing after trophies and men's applause.

IT IS that time when you are prepared to go through humiliation just for the cause of Christ.

IT IS that time when you become so humble before God THAT God has no other choice than to lift you up!

JORDAN teaches FAITH, OBEDIENCE, AND COURAGE.

AND THIS more than anything else was what Elisha was after.

ELISHA wanted a double portion of **the spirit of faith!**

YOU see, Elisha had seen Elijah walk by faith.

And he had seen him operate in complete trust in the presence and power of God.

ELISHA knew how Elijah had caused rain to cease for three and a half years.

ELISHA knew how Elijah had called the widow's son back to life.

ELISHA knew how Elijah called fire from heaven on the altar.

AND SO Elisha wanted the ability to cause even greater miracles to happen.

HE wanted a double portion of Elijah's faith.

HE wanted a double portion of the spirit of faith.

I WONDER how many are here today who are willing to say, "LORD, give me a double portion. I am not satisfied! AND LORD, IF it be possible, give me more than a double portion."

ELIJAH was able to perform at least seven miracles.

Elisha was able to perform at least fourteen miracles.

BUT, Lord, the times that we are living in require more than me performing just fourteen miracles.

The times that we are living in require an unlimited supply of miracles.

SO, Lord, GIVE me more of the anointing to stand in faith!

To speak your Word in faith and to see situations change.

LORD, give me more of the anointing to believe that the dumb will talk at the command of Thy Word.

LORD, give me a double portion, for I am not satisfied!

ELISHA also wanted a double portion of **the spirit of obedience.**

ELISHA recognized that one of the things that had caused God to respond to Elijah's prayers was not only Elijah's faith but also Elijah's obedience to God.

ELIJAH always instantly and without question obeyed God, even when the commands of God made no sense to him at all!

YOU SEE, being fed by ravens made no sense to Elijah.

But in obedience, he ate the food that the ravens brought him because he left himself open to the unusual ways of God.

THE spirit of obedience needs to be more evident in the churches.

IT doesn't have to make sense for you to obey God.

If God says to do it, just do it!

MANY people are not able to reach their full potential in God because they are too disobedient!

IT was disobedience that cost Saul his throne.

It was disobedience that prevented Moses from going into the Promised Land.

Disobedience played a key role in keeping the children of Israel wandering in the wilderness for forty years.

GOD says fast and you eat.

God says get up and pray, yet you sleep.

God says apologize for your wrong, yet you refuse to submit.

IF YOU desire more from the Lord, you must be willing to obey His commands!

ARE YOU ready for an outpouring of the spirit of obedience?

THEN say, "Lord, give me a double portion. I am not satisfied!"

THE third and final double portion that Elisha wanted was a double portion of **the spirit of courage**.

ELIJAH's faith in God and His obedience to God had combined to give him the courage to stand for God, even when others ran away.

AND Elisha wanted a double portion of that courage.

LET ME see the hands of those who require at least a double portion of the spirit of courage.

WE ARE living in serious times, and it will take lots of courage to persevere.

ELISHA wanted to take over where Elijah had left off.

He wanted to be the next prophet of Israel!

WHO wants to be the next renowned prophet of Cayman?

WHEN Elisha asked Elijah for a double portion of his anointing, Elijah immediately remarked that what Elisha had asked for was a hard thing.

IN OTHER words, IT was beyond the power of Elijah to grant such a request.

Only God could raise up prophets and give positions of power and influence.

ON THE surface, Elisha's request may have seemed a little selfish!

It may have seemed as though he was asking for twice the power and twice the glory.

BUT in truth, his request was most humble in nature.

ELISHA knew that Israel needed a man of God to deliver the Word of God and to do the work of God.

JUST like Cayman needs men and women that God can depend on, ELISHA also knew that if he was to be that man, then he needed power that he didn't possess!

HE needed the power of God working in him and through him if he was to accomplish his ministry.

WHEN Elijah and Elisha initially arrived at the banks of the Jordan, Elijah decided to flex his faith one more time because he was now pretty much at the end of his life's journey.

HE knew that the time had now come for Elisha to receive a double portion of his anointing.

HE knew that there was no turning back because Elisha remained faithful.

Elisha remained determined to receive a greater anointing.

AND SO Elijah flexed his faith one more time.

AND he took his mantle and he wrapped it together, and he smote the waters and they were divided SO that both he and Elisha could go over on dry ground.

THE MANTLE was a coat worn by biblical prophets.

AND After Elijah was taken up into heaven in a whirlwind, his mantle fell from him.

AND ELISHA took up his mantle, and he went back to the Jordan River where Elijah had performed his last miracle.

AND Elisha did what Elijah had done.

HE used Elijah's mantle to part the Jordan River.

WHEN the Lord led me to deliver this message to you, He told me to take off my coat, my jacket.

IT is soaked with God's anointing as I preached this Word.

MY coat, my jacket is soaked with God's anointing.

AND the color of the coat/jacket represents the blood of Jesus Christ.

GOD told me to place it over the head of some people.

AND that as I do it, IF THEY are truly at their Jordan, ready to cross over, they will receive a greater anointing.

IF THEY are truly at that place of readiness, IF they are desperate enough like Elisha was, IF THEY truly hunger and thirst for God's righteousness, THEN they will receive at least a double portion of God's anointing.

I DON'T know how many people can get down here first because I probably can't get to everybody.

BUT I believe that today, sick bodies will be healed.

I believe that today, broken hearts will be mended.

I believe that today, revival will take place in people's hearts and lives.

JUST because you choose today to exercise the faith coupled with obedience and courage!

LORD, give me a double portion. I am not satisfied!

CHAPTER 14

Live Full, Die Empty

My mother, my best friend Beverley Elaine Walcott, was born Beverley Elaine Valentine on October 19, 1943, to Emelia Edwards and Ephraim Valentine.

She was the first of two children from this union. Her sister predeceased her. Mom also had four half-sisters—three deceased and two half-brothers. Mom never knew her mother, as she died when she was only three years of age, and I think that her experiences thereafter propelled her into ensuring that when she had children, she would be the best.

Mom was brought up with traditional values and learned the skills that a woman of her era had to learn, such as cooking, sewing, and embroidery. Mom also had an absolute love for gardening. Her flowers meant everything to her, and it became the norm for Mom to attend the annual horticultural shows just to see the latest blooms and to make purchases to expand her garden. Her love for gardening extended to the love of planting crops in our backyard. Whether it was yam, banana, gungo peas, pumpkin, melon, you name it, and Mom would plant it and then proudly share it with the neighbors, friends, coworkers, and of course her family members.

She loved reading the daily newspaper. I had to take it home to her every day, and when she wasn't watching Gospel TV or a documentary highlighting persons in need and how viewers can help, Mom would be watching *Judge Judy*. She loved the varied interpretations of the law, and she would often recall its application when situations arise.

Mom spent many years working outside of the home, with her last place of local employment being with the Seprod Group of Companies. To the day she died, she still shared lasting friendships with a number of her former coworkers. Mom thereafter lived overseas for over three years where she formed other lifelong friendships before returning home.

Mom had three children. The first, my brother Dean, was born as a result of a union that Mom often referred to as her first real relationship. However, when that relationship fell apart, Mom met and married my father, Walzie Walcott. The union produced two children, with me being the older of the two. I was five years older than my brother Brian, who died at five months old.

My mother had an active fear of God which she attributed to her father's insistence that both her and her sister attend church throughout their childhood and early adult years, although he never did.

This level of persuasion was passed on to my brother and me. And so even before my mother got saved, we had to attend Sunday school every week—no questions asked.

My mother was a warm, compassionate, and vibrant woman who always went out of her way to help others no matter what. It was not unusual for my mother to take in others in our home and made it their home.

Throughout our childhood, teenage, and young adult years, my brother and I had to share our home and often our beds with others. In preparing this remembrance, I attempted to count the number of persons that my mother helped to raise or provided short-term shelter for, and I almost lost count. Suffice to say, it included her nieces, nephew, sisters-in-law, brother-in-law, our housekeepers' children, my high school friends, her friends, and of course, a couple members of this church. My mother helped so many persons that one day, my father said, "Bev [which is what he called her], why don't you just put up a sign at the gate stating, 'If you need somewhere to stay, apply within!'"

However, one thing that those experiences taught my brother and me is the importance of sharing and giving until it hurts. Because often my mother would do without just to help somebody.

My mother's love for God consumed her. She loved to fast and pray, and growing up, I participated in many three-day fasting services with her. My mother taught us how to pray. She was my prayer partner. She taught us about Jesus not just in words but more so through the life that she lived. She was faithful in her service to God when she served as a member of the missions department and thereafter as a member of the choir.

There was never a bone of pretense in my mother. She had a genuine heart of love. She was a strict no-nonsense person who believed in upholding the principles and teachings of God. She had no problem telling you like it is, and she had no hesitations in loving you like she should. If she offended you in anyway, she would apologize, and if you offended her in anyway, she would also apologize. She was a true servant of God who loved to smile and make people happy. I often tell people that if Mom had any fear in life, it was the fear of going to hell. And as such, she lived a life that guaranteed her going to heaven.

As an adult, Mom transitioned from just being my mother to becoming my best friend, my advisor, and my confidante. We shared everything and anything—good or bad, huge or small. If you hurt me, you hurt her, and vice versa. She was my greatest cheerleader and avid supporter, especially when I had to do outside ministry.

Family was everything to my mother, and we always spent quality time together as a family, including vacations overseas. My brother would tell you that a part of Mom's quality time with him was always preceded with a counsel about his soul. She prayed for him tirelessly, and I think if she died with any regrets, it would be not seeing my brother give his life to the Lord. But God is intentional, as her passing greatly nudged him and brought within him a greater level of urgency so to do.

Mom's love for her only grandchild was unsurpassable. When my marriage fell apart, my mom stood in the gap and made transitioning back to single life almost effortless. She became more than a grandmother to my son. Our little family was close-knit, and nothing or no one could penetrate us. We lived so that each other could live.

As the years went by, our family was further reduced to just my mom and me living together, as my brother migrated and my son went overseas to pursue tertiary studies. I didn't know that it was possible for Mom and me to get any closer, but we did.

My mother experienced many miracles and healings in her lifetime—spiritually, emotionally, financially, and physically. And then she experienced the ultimate healing. I have so many testimonies of how she overcame. She was strong. She was a fighter. She never gave up easily, and when she became ill the last time, I was praying for a similar outcome to the other times God turned things around, but God chose to move things forward instead.

The truth is, in hindsight, God was preparing me for that moment. Mom was miraculously healed from a bowel obstruction in February of 2017. However, by the following month, I observed that although Mom had overcome that ailment, she was just not her usual self in terms of strength and feelings.

I remember driving home one evening in April of this year and talking to God aloud in my car. I prayed fervently for my mother with tears streaming down my face. I pleaded with God for another miracle, and God's only response was "You will be all right."

To be honest, I got a little upset with the Lord and I said, "God, what do you mean I will be all right? This prayer is not about me. It is about my mother. I want you to tell me that my mother will be all right." And He answered not a word. Yet shortly after, I felt a peace come over me which left me speechless for the remainder of the journey home.

Two Sundays before my mother passed, I had a vision. And in the vision, I received word that my mother had died. I didn't see her dead. I only heard that she had died, and the most intense feelings of sorrow came over me. But just before I awoke from the vision, I saw my mother, and she was looking radiant. She was happy, she was alive, and I remember saying to her in the vision, "Mommy, you have come back to life. You have come back to life!" Then

I awoke from the vision, and the interpretation that I applied to the vision was that it didn't matter how sick Mom would become. God would, at the very last moment, turn things around. You see, I didn't want any other outcome. In hindsight, I now realize that God was telling me that she was going to die but wake up on the other side.

On Saturday, May 6, 2020, my parting words to Mom before I left her bedside at the hospital were "Mom, tomorrow is May 7, the day of completion when your healing will be complete. And Monday is May 8, and as you know, the number eight signifies new beginnings, and you will get out of this hospital completely healed and go home as a mark of new beginnings."

I along with others from this church were with Mom up to 9:00 p.m. on Monday, May 8. And Mom kept saying to us, "I am ready to go home. I want to go home." She even said, "Give me my slippers. I am ready to go home."

I somehow thought that Mom was referring to our physical home, and so I comforted her by saying, "Mom, you will soon get to go home." In hindsight, I now realize that she was telling us that she was ready to go to her heavenly home. In hindsight, it made what I had said to her on Saturday, May 7, prophetic without me realizing it at the time.

Mom passed at about 11:00 p.m. on Monday, May 8. Indeed, it was her day of new beginnings, as on Thursday, May 11, when I went to identify Mom's body for the funeral home, the Lord gave me such peace as He said to me most audibly, "Your mother is not here. She is elsewhere resting. This is just the casing that carried her whilst she was here, but she is not here. She is elsewhere resting."

I find comfort in knowing that my mom completed her God-given assignment on earth and is now with her Savior.

This is not goodbye, Mom. This is "we will see you again, my mom." You are irreplaceable. You loved, and you served. You lived full and you died empty. Your legacy will live on forever. We will forever cherish the memories that were uniquely created because of you.

The Sermon

Scripture: 2 Kings 13:20–21

I ABSOLUTELY love the theme "Live Full, Die Empty."

Because what the theme is actually saying is "Live a full life. Live out your full potential. Live your purpose."

Do everything that God has created you to do.

Do everything that God has gifted you to do.

So that when death comes, you would have completed your God-given assignment.

And nothing would have been left undone.

And you would be able to say like Paul, "I have fought a good fight. I have finished my course. I have kept the faith."

THE theme is reminding us not to go to our graves with unfinished work still stuck inside of us.

But rather, we should live and leave behind a legacy for others.

NOW there is a difference between reputation and legacy.

YOUR reputation is who you are supposed to be, but your legacy is who you are.

YOUR reputation is what you have when you come to a new community, but your legacy is what you leave behind when you go.

A Reputation is made in a moment. But a legacy is built in a lifetime.

A single newspaper report or careless gossip can give you your reputation.

But a life of toil gives you your legacy.

AND OF course, reputation is what men say about you on your tombstone.

But legacy is what your children will live with for the rest of their lives.

SO RIGHT now, we should all be working on our legacy because reputation is short-lived.

But legacy lasts forever.

AND SO as I thought about the theme, which I will also use as the theme for my discourse, **"Live full, die empty,"** THE Lord led me to a passage of scripture recorded in **2 Kings 13:20–21**.

Please turn there, and it reads thus:

> And Elisha died, and they buried him. And the bands of the Moabites invaded the land at the coming in of the year.
> And it came to pass, as they were burying a man, that, behold, they spied a band of men; and they cast the man into the sepulchre of Elisha: and when the man was let down, and touched the bones of Elisha, he revived, and stood up on his feet.

WHEN I read this, it hit me for the first time that as great a prophet that Elisha was, he didn't die empty.

He died with unspent power still stored within him.

WE KNOW the story of how it all began.

Elisha followed Elijah everywhere he went, as Elisha's greatest ambition was to be a prophet like Elijah.

IN FACT, Elisha wanted a double portion of Elijah's anointing.

And after he received it, because Elijah left empty, Elisha performed twice as many miracles than Elijah.

HOWEVER, IT WASN'T until after Elisha had died and his bones caused a dead man to be resurrected that Elisha had fully completed his God-given assignment.

WHICH meant Elisha died before completing the work of the anointing upon his life.

AND this got me thinking of the many persons alive today who are not fulfilling their God-given assignments.

IT GOT me thinking of the many persons today who are not living out their full potentials.

AND as a result, many persons are being denied a miracle, being denied a breakthrough, a healing, a deliverance because gifted people are failing to live their purpose.

St. JOHN 12:24 speaks about the potential of a grain of wheat: "FOR a grain of wheat to produce and multiply. It must be planted in the earth."

YOU never realize the full potential of a seed until it is planted.

AN orange seed is potentially an orange tree, capable of having many orange fruits.

But it will never manifest its full potential of becoming an orange tree and having many fruits until it is planted in the soil and cultivated.

SUCH IS the life of an individual.

Many people are born with lots of talents, gifts, and potentials.

But potentials that are not released cannot produce fruits.

GOD did not create you just so you could live and die for yourself.

GOD did not endow you with gifts and resources just for you to hoard them and die with them.

YOUR life is a seed waiting to be planted.

And your God-given talents, gifts, and resources are also seeds waiting to be planted.

UNTIL you are willing to die for yourself and live for a cause bigger than self, you will never release or realize your full potential for increase.

SOMEONE can be gifted yet end up with nothing.

I have seen some gifted people with no desirable or corresponding results to show for their gifts.

A GIFT that is not committed to useful and productive engagements will eventually become a liability.

WE see the video clip of the St. Catherine High School students whose gifts were not committed to useful and productive engagements. AND as such, they have become a liability to their school and selves.

PEOPLE can be gifted but bound.

Gifted but bound by sexual perversion.

Gifted but bound by man's opinions.

Gifted but bound by low self-esteem.

Gifted but bound by a lack of determination.

YOU HAVE been gifted for a purpose.

But until you realize that God gifted you to meet a need, until you realize that you are not gifted for yourself but your gift is for somebody else to enjoy, you will never truly begin the process of living a full life.

WE are unique and specially created for a purpose.

God spoke everything into existence.

But when it came to man, God said, "Let us *make* man into our own image."

HE didn't speak man into being.

He formed man into being so that we would become a reflection of Him.

GOD formed us for HIS purpose.

It is not about what *we* want to do.

It is about what *He* wants us to do.

SO we don't live for ourselves.

We live so God's will and purpose can be accomplished through us.

AND sometimes there is a conflict.

BECAUSE we want to do one thing, but God wants us to do something else.

And the process of God getting us to do what He wants is not always easy.

YOU see, God has to get *your* purpose out of you so that He can get *His* purpose working through you.

YOU may want to sing secular songs because you say that pays more money.

But God wants you to sing gospel songs because there are souls waiting on your singing to be saved.

YOU may not believe it, but somebody's future is dependent on you.

ALL the mess that you went through, all your failures, all your struggles helped to prepare you for your purpose.

It helped to prepare you to help somebody.

YOU see, you think that God only began dealing with your life when you started coming to church.

BUT God was working in your past to make your purpose more powerful.

SOME PERSONS are afraid to admit where they are coming from.

But it is where you are coming from that prepares you for your God-given assignment!

YOU see, before you were born, God predetermined your purpose.

He predetermined your gifts.

He established it in eternity.

But then it must be revealed in time.

GOD says in Jeremiah 1:5, "Before I formed you in the womb, I knew you."

IF YOU could see your potential and where God is taking you, you would understand the reason the devil doesn't want you to live fully.

You are pregnant with destiny, and Satan knows it.

EVERYTHING that God purposes is challenged by the enemy.

Because the enemy wants to stop the work of God through your life so that you will die full and not impact lives.

IF THERE is anything Satan desires to do today, it is to keep you from living your full potential.

SATAN does not care if you live in your past.

It is not even your present that is Satan's greatest fear.

Satan's greatest fear is you living your purpose and becoming who God destined you to be.

SATAN does not want you to have what God said you would have.

He doesn't want you to do what God said you would do.

He doesn't want you to go where God said you would go. And he doesn't want you to become who God said you would become.

BUT slap somebody and say, "The devil is a liar. I am going live full and die empty."

EVERYTHING that the Body of Christ is going through, everything that your family members are facing, everything that you as an individual may be fighting is because of your destiny. It is because of the impact that the devil knows you are going to have on the lives of others.

YOU possess a one-of-a-kind combination of passions, skills, and experiences.

THERE is something you can bring to the table that no one else can.

No one else can make your contribution for you.

And if you relinquish that power, then it will never see the light of day.

And you will always wonder, *What if?*

IF YOU are going to live full, you have to live fearless.

ESTHER was **fearless**.

Her God-given assignment was to approach the king, to secure the deliverance of her people.

And she was determined to do what she was destined to do. And so she said, "If I perish, I perish. But I must see the king!"

And she fulfilled her purpose.

She lived full and died empty.

TELL SOMEBODY, "Live full, die empty."

IN order to be fearless, you must let go off your fears. Fear will cripple you and prevent you from moving forward.

AND I say "moving forward" because movement is not progress. I can move (**show them**).

And still have not progressed.

BUT if I get out of my comfort zone and take a leap from here to here (**show them**), I would have progressed.

BECOME aware of the things that you fear in life and be determined to overcome them.

AND you can overcome them by filling your brain with images of what you want your future self to look like.

IF YOU know what I am talking about, say, "Neighbor, I see me in the future. And I look better. I see me walking in favor and prosperity too."

HIGH-FIVE three people and tell them, "My future looks better than this!"

SAY, "Neighbor, I am going to walk better than I am walking right now. I am going to talk better than I am talking right now. I am going to look better than I am looking right now."

FOR God has not given me a spirit of fear but of love and of power and of a sound mind!

TELL your neighbor, "Live full. Be fearless!"

IF YOU are going to live full, you have to live with **u**nwavering faith.

SHADRACH, Meshach, and Abednego had **unwavering faith**. They refused to bow to the king's idols.

And even at the point of being thrown into a fiery furnace, THEY said, "Our God whom we serve is able to deliver us. But even if He doesn't deliver us, we will not serve your gods."

TELL your neighbor, "I am not serving any other God than the King of Kings and the Lord of Lords. I AM not serving any other God but the Lion of the tribe of Judah."

SAY, "Neighbor, I am not serving any other God than the Am that I Am."

TO LIVE full, you must have unwavering faith.

UNWAVERING faith is to trust God with your life more than you trust yourself.

Unwavering faith is to trust God's timing even when you are running out of patience.

IT IS about trusting God's decisions even if you don't like them.

YOU may not know where the road is taking you, but keep going!

YOU may not know if you are good enough for something, but trust God and go for it!

YOU may not know if you have what it takes, but still try!

Unwavering faith means that even when you question God, you still believe in Him.

Even when you are tired from everything that He has allowed to come your way, you still sleep with your mind at ease because you are confident that God knows what He is doing.

TELL your neighbor, "Live full. Have unwavering faith."

IF YOU are going to live full, you have to live your dreams.

THE Bible says, "And Joseph dreamed a dream, and he told it his brethren: and they hated him yet the more."

JOSEPH'S brothers had hated him because he was the favorite son of their father.

But once Joseph began to talk about his dreams, once he began to talk about his future, their hatred for him increased.

LISTEN. When you are gifted, you are going to be hated.

But don't let that stop you from living your life to the fullest.

BECAUSE your haters are going to become elevators that will lift you to a higher place of blessings and glory.

JOSEPH'S brothers questioned him by asking him, "Shalt you indeed reign over us? Shall you indeed have dominion over us?"

YOU see, Joseph's brothers were not so concerned about who he was as a seventeen-year-old dreamer.

THEIR concern was more over who he was going to become as a result of his dreams.

THEY were not afraid of his present.

They were afraid of his future.

AND they wanted to stop him from becoming who God said he would become.

THEY wanted to stop him from going where God said he would go.

THEY wanted to stop him from entering into his destiny.

YOU see, the enemy knows that your destiny is going to severely affect his kingdom.

THE enemy knows that if you live out your full potential, he is in serious trouble.

He will not be able to do what he intends on doing.

BUT JOSEPH was determined to live his dreams.

Destiny was upon his life.

So even when Potiphar's wife wanted to trap him, he ran for his life because destiny was calling.

DESTINY is calling somebody here today.

And God says, "Live your dreams!"

KNOW who you are in God and allow God to work through you.

STAY focused on your dreams, set goals, and let God divinely get you there.

IF you view all the things that happen to you in life, both good and bad, as opportunities, then you will operate knowing that all things are working together for your good.

IN fact, begin to act the way that you want to be.

And in time, you will become the way that you act.

Because as Aristotle says, "You are what you repeatedly do."

KNOW that your dream is possible.

You may be in a pit like Joseph was, but that is just a temporary inconvenience.

The enemy meant it for bad.

But God is going to work it out for your good.

YOU may be imprisoned by your circumstances.

But like Joseph, God is going to use the experiences of your prison to propel you to your destiny.

SOMEBODY IS going to start living their dream today.

Why not let it be you?

SOMEBODY is going to decide to live life on purpose.

Why not let it be you?

EVERY DAY people are improving their lives by the decisions they make.

Why not be one of them?

IF YOU are going to live full, you have to lead by example.

BE conscious of the fact that as you go through life, somebody is watching you for clues.

SOMEBODY wants to know how to make it over.

SOMEBODY wants to know how to get back up.

SOMEBODY wants to know how to still have joy when their life is filled with sorrow.

SOMEBODY wants to know how to have peace in the midst of a storm.

LIVE full and show somebody the way.

Lead by example!

The devil isn't concerned about how much you shout in church because he is waiting on you on the outside to see if your shout meant anything.

IF YOU are going to shout in here and live like the devil out there, you are only fooling yourself.

Because not even the devil is fooled.

AFTER God saved you from a life of promiscuity, drugs, crime, violence, backbiting, malice-keeping, wouldn't it be foolish to go back to being bound by that which He had saved you from?

SATAN'S kingdom isn't devastated just by our shouts.

It is more devastated by our lifestyle.

AFTER we get through hollering in church, we need to be able to rebuke the devil from our lives.

YOU SEE, your gift can put you in the ceiling.

But your lifestyle can pull you back down.

BECOME a finisher. Purpose in your heart to finish everything that God assigned you to do.

WE ARE not just patients where we only need God for healings, miracles, and deliverance.

WE ARE called to be disciples of Christ.

We are called to follow Christ.

We are to be obedient to His Word.

We are the salt of the earth.

SALT changes the flavor of what it touches.

We are called to change the flavor of the earth.

LEAD by example and become a finisher.

Finish what God started through you.

Finish realizing the vision that God gave to you.

Ensure that you finish your ministry.

You are too gifted to leave this world full.

WHEN my mother died, I realized more than ever that how you live is more important than how *long* you live.

She lived full and she died empty.

MANY people fear death, but you ought not to fear death.

Because nothing is wrong with dying.

But something is wrong with dying empty.

SOMETHING is wrong with dying and not fulfilling the purpose for which you were born.

THE fact that Elisha's bones caused the resurrection of a dead man is proof enough that God doesn't want us leaving unfinished tasks behind.

ELISHA had one more miracle to perform.

One more miracle was left on the inside.

AND SO God did not want the story to end with Elisha's purpose being incomplete.

Because God wanted to show us the importance of our purpose here on earth.

That dead man needed the anointing on Elisha's life to experience a miracle in his life.

SOMEBODY is waiting to benefit from the anointing on your life.

AND SO what we ought to be doing is crying out to God to make us FULL.

FULL and fearless.

FULL with unwavering faith.

FULL to live our dreams.

FULL to lead by example.

"Make me full, Jesus" should be our prayers!

YOU must know who you are in God.

People may not like you because of who you are in God.

IF you owned the biggest house, that wouldn't make them like you.

IF you drove the nicest car, they still wouldn't like you.

Because it is not about what you have.

It is about who you are!

BUT NOBODY can do what God has called you to do.

Nobody can operate in the anointing that God has placed on you, and that is why you need to fulfil your God-given assignment.

YOU must know your assignment and not be jealous of other people's assignment.

Because you can't do what God has assigned them to do.

And they can't do what God has assigned you to do.

IT IS important to note that one of the things that we do wrong is that we assign levels of significance to people with charisma and persona.

And we act as if we are connected to God through them.

But we are connected to God through Jesus Christ.

AND anybody who introduces you to God has to get out of the way so that you can have a personal relationship with God and do what God has called you to do without you feeling intimidated.

YOUR anointing is like Cinderella.

Nobody's foot can fit that slipper but yours.

YOU HAVE God to realize that the power of any church is not confined to the pew.

The power of any church is embodied within all the people of the church.

THERE is a uniqueness about you, just like your fingerprint.

AND no wonder the Bible says your faith has made you whole.

GOD says He will never give you more than you can bare.

That means that whatever comes your way, God has already gifted you to handle it.

TELL your neighbor, "You are gifted to handle it!"

YOU DON'T have to beg nobody or plead with nobody to handle it for you because God has already gifted you to handle it.

The power is within you.

GOD gifted you so that others will need you.

GOD is the head of the church.

And we are just members of the Body of Christ.

AND it is Christ as the Head who determines what the members of the body do…

OUR right hand can never decide what our left hand does.

It is the head that makes that decision.

IF YOU never had a brain, you couldn't taste.

Oh, taste and see that the Lord is good.

IF YOU never had a brain, you couldn't walk.

IF YOU never had a brain, you couldn't talk.

It is not coming from the mouth.

It is coming from the head.

TELL your neighbor, "I am called out to be blessed. But more than that, I am called to be a blessing."

EVERYBODY has a responsibility to share their gift with the Body of Christ.

WHO TOLD you that you don't have a place in the church? Is it because you haven't been in church all your life?

Well, the church has been looking for you because we have been sequestered and locked up within these walls.

AND SO God has to send some new people with new experiences SO some stuffed-up people can understand that they are not the only ones that God has called.

WE have people who like little groups, and they operate in their little groups.

But God has gifted people who are outside your group.

And you are going to be short-changed by staying within your group because there is a blessing waiting outside your group.

WE shouldn't confine ourselves to what we deem as our little group.

WE should allow our lives to be impacted by those who may not be in our little group, as they maybe the very one holding our blessing.

TOUCH YOUR neighbor and say, "Neighbor, I have a piece of your puzzle. YOU may have been trying to put the puzzle together without me, but check the empty space and see if my gifting doesn't fit."

Check the empty space and see if my arm doesn't fit.

WE are a part of the body of Christ.

And so we are in this thing together.

You need me just as much as I need you.

YOU better break up your clique, because your clique has been keeping you restricted and causing you to miss your blessing.

YOU are bigger than a few people.

God sent you to touch the lives of a lot of people.

GOD is bigger than what you want to do.

He has greater things for you than for you to just hang around a few limited people.

OPEN up your scope. You are not only local.

You also need to see yourself as global.

SHAKE your neighbor and say, "There is a whole lot in you that needs to come out."

YOU need to live full so that you can die empty.

SAY, "Neighbor, there is a whole lot in you that needs to be passed on to somebody else SO that you can live full and die empty. Neighbor, there is a whole lot in you that must be divinely imparted because God has commissioned you to life full and die empty."

TELL somebody else, "You are special. Don't let anybody limit you."

GOD sent me to tell you that he has called you out.

He has stepped over people in your family just to get to you.

He has stepped over people in your community just to get to you.

EVERYBODY that did time in prison is not in church.

But God went to your cell just to awaken you.

EVERYBODY in your class did not fall under God's vision because He called you before the foundation of the world.

HOW do you explain how you came through all of the stuff that killed people that you knew?

HOW do you explain that you didn't have the qualifications yet the door opened on your behalf?

HOW do you explain when you should have lost your mind, somebody kept your mind in perfect peace?

HOW do you explain how you came out when everybody else was down and out?

IT WAS because God had His hand on you before the foundations of the world.

TURN to somebody and say, "I've got a testimony."

He brought me out for a purpose.

He brought me out for a reason.

And I can't help but lift up the name of the Lord.

I am here for a purpose.

GOD has you here for a purpose.

And no matter how the devil tries to destroy your mind, YOU have it within you to say devil, "Get out of my face. Get out of my space. Get out of my mind. Get out of my house."

I have been called to be a blessing.

HOLD on to somebody's hand and say, "Neighbor, I was lost in sin. I was messed up. I was a nobody. But God stepped into my life and called me out for a purpose."

AND because of that, I am going to praise Him.

I am going to lift Him up.

IT's been hard. It's been rough.

But I see a cloud the size of a man's hand.

It is getting ready to rain.

It is getting ready to rain on my ministry.

IT is getting ready to rain on my life.

A fresh anointing is getting ready to rain down on me.

TURN to somebody and say, "Neighbor, this is my time. This is my season."

I feel an anointing. I feel a calling.

And this time I am going to say, "Lord, here I am. Send me."

Lord, send me. Send me to the lost and dying.

Lord, send me. Send me to the wounded and broken.

Lord, send me. Send me to the sick and diseased.

Lord, send me. Send me to the broke and depressed.

You are called out from a place of obscurity!

You are called out from a place of insignificance.

SAY, "Neighbor, we have been called to be a blessing."

SAY, "Neighbor, we have been called to go up higher."

SAY, "Neighbor, we have been called to function in the super-natural realm."

CELEBRATE with your brothers.

CELEBRATE with your sisters.

You are here for a reason.

You are here for a purpose.

Let the devil know that he can't stop what God is doing and is about to do in your life.

SAY, "Neighbor, I am glad I know you. I am glad I know you because you got something I need."

YOU got a word. Give it to me.

YOU got a miracle to impart. Give it to me.

YOU got an anointing. Give it to me.

YOU got joy. Give it to me.

GIVE me what God has gifted you for me.

THE world is waiting for you.

You are a world changer.

YOU have been called by God to be a world changer.

You are a world changer because the world is full of darkness.

And there is only one way to change darkness.

And that is by bringing in light.

And Jesus said whoever follows Him will have the light of life.

BE the one to take the good news of Jesus Christ to the world.

AND as you do so, you will change sorrow to joy.

You will change sickness to health.

You will change death to life.

HOW many world changers are here today?

IF you are a world changer, high-five two persons and tell them, "I am a world changer."

I am going to live full and die empty!

High-five seven persons and say, "Neighbor, you have been released!"

RELEASED to do what God has called you to do.

RELEASED to be who God has called you to be.

RELEASED to say what God has called you to say.

RELEASED to go where God has called you to go.

FIND three more persons and say, "Release!"

TELL SOMEBODY, "STEP. Step into your calling."

STEP. Step into your purpose.

STEP. Step into your anointing.

YOU are destined for greatness.

TO be great is to be outstanding.

And destiny is the purpose of God for your life.

So destined for greatness means the purpose of somebody here today is to be great.

IF YOU BELIEVE that is you, give God the highest praise!

WHO you are today is not important.

What is important is what you are purposed to do.

Because God can raise up a beggar from the dunghill and cause him to sit among princes and kings.

PROMOTION is coming to somebody today.

In the mighty name of Jesus Christ, you shall be great!

DAVID was a shepherd boy, but he was destined to be king.

MOSES was a murderer, but he was destined to lead the children out of Israel.

GIDEON was a wimp at a winepress, but he was destined to be one of God's choice warriors.

In fact, Gideon saw himself as a wimp, but God saw him and called him a man of valor.

> Therefore if any man be in Christ, he is a
> new creature old things are passed away. Behold
> all things have become new. (2 Cor. 5:17)

SOMEBODY here today is going to experience newness in their life because God wants you to live full and die empty.

GOD is the decider of destinies.

And the course of destinies can be changed.

All you need to do make a turnaround.

STOP living to please yourself. Start living to please God.

And watch God work in your life!

SOMEONE here today will see doors that have been slammed shut in your face reopened. Because God is changing your course of destiny.

IF YOU believe it, open your mouths and give God praise!

YOU ARE coming out of bondage.

YOU are coming out of a place of silence.

YOU are coming out of being unknown.

YOUR children shall rise up and call you blessed.

TECHNOLOGY shall not limit you.

Because what God has placed in you will change the course of time.

GOD is going to use you to blow the minds of those who put you down.

YOUR days of being overlooked are over.

You used to be the quiet one in the corner.

But God is going to place you at the head of the group.

THE very people who used to mock and jeer at you are going to call you great.

THE very people who used to criticize you are going to seek you out for answers.

Because God is going to give you new visions, new insights, new foresights.

LIKE Daniel, you will be the one to interpret dreams.

LIKE Moses, you will be God's mouthpiece.

LIKE Peter, you will be the one to say, "Silver and gold have I none. But in the Name of Jesus Christ of Nazareth, rise up and walk."

RISE UP and walk in your full potential.

RISE UP and walk in your purpose.

RISE UP and walk in your destiny.

YOU ARE called out to be a blessing.

TAKE THE LIMITS OFF!

You are too gifted to be hidden.

GOD is pulling you out of the shadows.

You are too gifted not to be on the choir.

You are too gifted not to be playing instruments.

GOD is pulling you out of your comfort zone.

You are too gifted not to be on the prayer group.

You are too gifted not to be on the Evangelism team.

You are too gifted not to be teaching or preaching the Word.

God has put His Word within you.

PUT your hands on your belly and say, "Thus saith the Lord, Word give birth."

THE Word of God that is going to come out of your mouth is going to set captives free.

THE Word of God that is going to come out of your mouth will cause lives to be transformed.

YOU ARE too gifted not to be transferring the anointing.

TOUCH your neighbor and say, "There is fire in my hands. Fire in my feet. Fire in my mouth. Fire in my belly. Fire! Fire! Fire all over me!"

TAKE THE LIMITS OFF!

It is your time to shine.

It is your time to shake up the place.

It is your time to turn the tables over.

Too much complacency in God's house.

Too much selling out in God's house.

It is your time to make an impact.

TELL YOUR neighbor, "No limits. No boundaries."

I see increase all around you.

Stretch forth. Break forth.

God is enlarging your territory.

YOU are better than you think.

You may not be the most educated, but you are anointed.

You may not be able to dress up like everybody else, but you are anointed.

You may not be able to live in the nicest of communities, but you are anointed.

THE anointing is going to cause you to do in a day what some people spend years learning to do.

And they still won't be able to master it like you.

GOD is going to cause you to solve problems that people have been struggling to solve for years.

SOMEBODY IS waiting on your next move.

SOMEBODY IS waiting on your idea.

SOMEBODY IS waiting on your testimony to get their breakthrough.

IF YOU believe it, shout out, "I am ready to do God's will! I am ready to be who He has called me to be! I am ready to go where He wants me to go! I am ready to live my live to its full potential!"

I AM ready because I am not satisfied with where I am at.

I am not satisfied with mediocrity.

I am not satisfied with the cold religion.

I am not satisfied with church as usual.

I want more. I want more. I want more!
USE me, Jesus. Use me for Your glory.
Use me, Jesus. Use me for Your honor.
Use me, Jesus. Use me to make a difference!

CHAPTER 15

Expect God to Do the Unexpected

Some persons were born to remain single, and some were born to be married. Finding out whether you were born to remain single or to be married is often one of life's greatest challenges, because who we were born to be does not always correlate with who we want to be.

I have always known that I was born to be married, by nature of my personality and by virtue of my caring spirit—none of which was my doing. It was simply based on who God had designed and purposed me to be, which has since been confirmed by the prophetic many times over.

The belief in the concept of a soul mate was birthed in me years after my marriage had failed. My failed marriage taught me many lessons to include the fact that marriage is ministry, and so who you are married to is not only dependent on whether the person is a Christian or not but more so is dependent on whether God wants you married to that person. Was that person handpicked by God for you? Is that person the right fit for you, based on what God wants to do individually and collectively in both of your lives? These are questions that you have to determine the answers to before you marry, as I have come to learn that although God permits marriage, being in His perfect will is far more comfortable, happy, and blessed than only being in His permissive will. It is His perfect will that secures our predetermined alignment for His glory.

After my marriage failed, I wanted nothing to do with the idea of being in a relationship. Ten years had passed before I found that I regained the feelings of wanting to once again share my life with a spouse. In fact, I often joked with my friends by saying if my husband-to-be had presented himself, I would not have seen him, because for those ten years after my marriage had ended, I directed my focus to the Lord, my immediate family, work, and ministry only.

Soon after I began feeling the need for companionship again, I began praying, asking the Lord to provide me with a husband. I prayed that prayer so many times to the point that it must have annoyed the Lord, because one day as I lay flat on my back in bed, praying and asking the Lord to provide me with a husband, he replied as audibly as if someone was physically in the room. He replied by saying, "You will marry again, but don't ask me again."

I was both comforted and numbed by God's response, as although I could now rejoice over the fact that I would marry again, I did not know how much longer I would have had to wait. And I had lost the rights to ask. For years after that encounter, I trembled with fear each time that I was tempted to ask the Lord about my pending marriage, and so I just left the matter with Him to make it happen in His own time and in His own way. After all, I had already learned the hard way that I was poor at choosing, so I might as well leave the choosing to God, who knows what is best for me and knows exactly what He wants for me and for the person that He would eventually make my spouse.

When my mom—my best friend, my sharing partner, my listening ear, my shoulder to cry on, my counsellor, and great supporter—went on to be with the Lord, it left a void in my life. I am a private person, and I don't let persons into my inner circle easily. And the truth is, neither did my mom, which was why we had bonded so tightly. So as far as I was concerned, no one would have been able to fill the void that she had left me with but God.

Mother's Day was celebrated about five days after my mother's passing, and for the first time in many years, I did not attend church on a Sunday morning, although I was in the island. I just could not or did not want to find the energy to attend, as the grief was still so fresh and real, and so I decided to stay home.

As I lay flat on my back in bed, talking things through with the Lord, a most beautifully worded text of encouragement came in from an unfamiliar number, and so I inquired who it was. When the person sent me their first name only, I mistook the person for someone else with a similar name. To prevent any further misunderstanding, the person sent me a photograph, and I was shocked. I had been seeing the person for years now, but I never had the occasion to speak with the person, neither did I know that was the person's name, but here the person was texting me. I did not quite know what to make of the gesture, but then many persons had been calling, texting, and visiting me since my mom's passing, and so I summed it up to the three things that brought people together—birth, death, and marriage.

As the days and months went by, the person kept texting, checking up on me, and sharing with me to the point that I found I started to develop a comfort level with the person. I found myself sharing openly with the person concerning things that prior to my mother's passing, I would have only shared with her. The comfort level that I was experiencing often left me wondering what was happening to me, because it was almost like the person was filling the void that had been left by my mom, plus some. I found myself in a strange and unusual place, and I often questioned the Lord about it.

After three years and counting, sharing almost every day, and sharing about almost everything, it had become clear that the person and I had bonded in a way that I had not bonded with anyone outside of my family, and more so, outside of my mom.

I am now convinced that God Himself had orchestrated the bond between us. In fact, the bond seems almost indestructible, because after the bond was formed, it was tested, and then it was reformed. And now it has been transformed. Could there be a writing on the wall?

God is just amazing in how He orchestrates our lives and how He works to meet the needs and fill the voids in our lives, plus some.

He does not always show up when we expect Him to, but He often shows up when we least expect it.

One immediate takeaway from this experience is that we should always expect God to do the unexpected, because when He does, our lives will never be the same.

The Sermon

But the angel said unto him, Fear not, Zacharias: for thy prayer is heard; and thy wife Elisabeth shall bear thee a son, and thou shalt call his name John. (Luke 1:13)

And Zacharias said unto the angel, Whereby shall I know this? for I am an old man, and my wife well stricken in years.

And the angel answering said unto him, I am Gabriel, that stand in the presence of God; and am sent to speak unto thee, and to shew thee these glad tidings.

And, behold, thou shalt be dumb, and not able to speak, until the day that these things shall be performed, because thou believest not my words, which shall be fulfilled in their season. (Luke 1:18–20)

And the angel said unto her, Fear not, Mary: for thou hast found favour with God.

And, behold, thou shalt conceive in thy womb, and bring forth a son, and shalt call his name Jesus. (Luke 1:30–31)

Then said Mary unto the angel, How shall this be, seeing I know not a man?

And the angel answered and said unto her, The Holy Ghost shall come upon thee, and the power of the Highest shall overshadow thee:

therefore also that holy thing which shall be born
of thee shall be called the Son of God.

And, behold, thy cousin Elisabeth, she hath
also conceived a son in her old age: and this is the
sixth month with her, who was called barren.

For with God nothing shall be impossible.
(Luke 1:34–37)

THE PASSAGE of scripture that we read speaks specifically of
two women who experienced the unexpected in their lives.

ELIZABETH, an eighty-four-year-old wife, was barren from
birth.

HER barrenness was a social stigma.

HER barrenness meant that she didn't meet her wifely
expectations.

YOU SEE, in her time, barren women were frowned upon by
society.

AS far as society was concerned, a barren woman was a useless
woman.

WIVES were expected to produce heirs.

And every husband wanted a child to continue his lineage.

HOWEVER, Elizabeth, AFTER having prayed for many years,
had not had her prayers answered.

And she had undoubtedly settled with being seen as a social
failure.

Even her husband, Zacharias, accepted the fact that his wife
would never provide him with any offspring.

But the unexpected was about to happen!

AT the point of impossibility, impossible because of her age,
impossible because of her barrenness, God stepped in and did the
unexpected in this couple's life.

IN FACT, for Zacharias, it was business as usual when he had
a divine encounter.

THE angel Gabriel brought the news to him that his wife,
Elizabeth, would have conceived and bear a son.

And that his son's name should be John.

BUT the news was far from what Zacharias had expected.

It was far from his expectations.

So much so that he told the angel that it was impossible.

ZACHARIAS did not expect God to do the unexpected.

ZACHARIAS had gone to the temple on that set day.

He was busy burning incense before the Lord.

He was busy offering up worship to the Lord.

JUST like so many of you here today, you have come to this temple to worship God.

YOU have come to this temple to offer up your highest praise to God.

Yet you are not expecting God to do the unexpected.

LIKE Zacharias, you have been praying for a long time.

You have been trusting God for a long time.

But when God failed to meet your need on *your* timing, you stopped believing. You stopped expecting.

BUT the unexpected is coming!

NUDGE somebody and tell them again that the unexpected is coming!

YES! ZACHARIAS told the angel that the news that he brought was one of impossibility.

HE said, "I am too old, and so is my wife."

IN other words, "I don't have any gumption left in me. Time has robbed me of my fertility. Time has robbed me of my faith. Time has sapped my strength. PLUS, my wife is not only old, but she was never fertile to begin with."

GOD was speaking to Zacharias through Angel Gabriel.

God's messenger was telling Zacharias that his prayers were heard and were being answered.

Yet Zacharias failed to believe.

MANY persons here today are just like Zacharias.

You have prayed for so long.

So much so that you have grown weary.

YOU are worshipping God, but you are weary.

YOU are praising God, but you are weary.

YOU see, it is possible to do what is expected of you and to not expect anything in return.

THE circumstances of life can do that to you.

YOUR circumstance can take your hope and leave you hopeless.

YOUR circumstance can take your joy and leave you joyless.

YOU say, "There is no way that God is going to show up on my behalf.

"There is no way that God is going to give me the money that I need to pay my bills.

"There is no way that God is going to restore my broken relationship.

"There is no way that God is going to heal my sick body."

BUT I will still show up for worship.

I will still show up for services.

Because it is expected of me.

SOME will even say, "If God doesn't do anything more for me, I will still serve Him."

And that is commendable.

BUT the truth of the matter is, God can't help but to always do something more for you.

AND that is why He sent me to tell you today that He is getting set to do the unexpected in your life!

HIGH-FIVE three people and tell them, "Expect God to do the unexpected!"

WHEN Zacharias expressed his disbelief in the news that Gabriel had brought, Gabriel made a profound statement.

He said, "I stand in the presence of God."

LISTEN.

God is always present when His words are being spoken.

God is always present when His message to His people is being delivered.

GOD serves as a witness that His word is being delivered to you today.

GOD serves as a witness to whether or not you believe His word.

TELL your neighbor, "God is present! God is here!"

AND He is witnessing everything that is being said and done.

HE sees your hearts.

HE knows your thoughts.

AND He hears your responses—silently or openly.

GOD is present! He is here!

SO the angel GABRIEL told Zacharias, "Because you have failed to believe what God sent me to tell you, from hereon until the baby is born, you shall be dumb. You shall not be able to speak."

TELL your neighbor, "*Now* is the time to believe!"

DON'T displease God because of a lack of faith.

"NOW faith is the substance of things hoped for, the evidence of things not seen."

AND faith cometh by hearing. And hearing by the Word of God.

TELL somebody else, "If God said it, you must believe it!"

Because without faith, it is impossible to please God.

TO receive the unexpected, you must have faith!

MARY was the other woman in this story who didn't fit in with the others.

SHE didn't fit in because she was a virgin who had found herself pregnant.

AND isn't this a remarkable contrast?

FIRST, we found an eighty-four-year-old woman who had been trying for years to conceive but couldn't.

And then God stepped in and changed her life story.

AND secondly, we find in the very same passage a very young woman who, at the time, wasn't at all interested in conceiving.

IN fact, she had never had sex a day in her life.

And still, God stepped in and changed her life story.

AND as I thought about this, the Lord said, "Tell My people."

That it doesn't matter how old or how young you are.

It doesn't matter what your status in life is.

It doesn't matter what your situation is.

HE IS GOD!

And everything that He does is for His glory!

HE says His ways are not your ways.

His timing is not your timing.

But for His glory, He will change your life story!

GOD said, "Tell My children."

He changes times and seasons.

He removes kings and sets up kings.

He gives wisdom to the wise and knowledge to those who have understanding.

IN FACT, God says, "IN righteousness you shall be established; You shall be far from oppression, for you shall not fear; And from terror, for it shall not come near you" (Isa. 54:14).

GOD says, "Indeed people will gather against you." But it shall not be His doing. "Whoever assembles against you shall fall for your sake" (Isa. 54:15).

AND "Behold," says God. "I have created the blacksmith who blows the coals in the fire, who brings forth an instrument for his work; and yet I have also created the spoiler to destroy" (Isa. 54:16).

AND that is why God says, "No weapon formed against you shall prosper, and every tongue *which* rises against you in judgment you shall condemn" (Isa. 54:17).

THE devil meant it for evil.

He meant for your situation to determine your ending.

But God is about to change your life story.

YOU thought you were no one of significance.

YOU thought your lack of wealth, your lack of education, and your lack of known accomplishments would have determined your ending.

But God is about to change your life story.

IF YOU believe it, shout out, "LORD, change my life story!"

CHANGE it from a place of barrenness to a place of fruitfulness.

LORD, change my life story!

Change it from a place of not enough to a place of more than enough!

LORD, change my life story!

Change it from a place of insignificance to a place of significance!

LORD, change my life story!

IT WAS business as usual for Mary that day.

That day when God changed her life story.

MARY, who was engaged to be married, had not known a man.

And she was from humble beginnings, engaged to be married to a man who was also of humble beginnings.

Yet God handpicked her to carry and to give birth to a promise.

A promise is a pledge, a vow, an assurance that which what was stated will come to pass.

THE birth of Jesus had been prophesied/promised by prophets in scriptures at least ten times, many years before.

AND Mary, a virgin, was handpicked by God to carry and to give birth to that promise.

MOST, if not all, of you seated here today have been hand-picked by God to carry and to give birth to a promise.

NO! Yours is not to carry and to give birth to the King of all Kings, THE Lord of all Lords and the Savior of the world BECAUSE that Promise has already been fulfilled.

BUT yours is to carry and to give birth to some unfulfilled promises in your life.

SOME unfulfilled promises that were prophesied over your life through the written word OR through the spoken word.

SOME unfulfilled promise which says, "The LORD will make you the head and not the tail, and you only will be above, and you will not be underneath, if you listen to the commandments of the LORD your God" (Deut. 28:13).

SOME unfulfilled promise which says, "You will lend to many nations but will borrow from none. You will rule over many nations but none will rule over you" (Deut. 15:16).

SOME unfulfilled promise which states, "In the last days, saith God, I will pour out of my Spirit upon all flesh: and your sons and your daughters shall prophesy, and your young men shall see visions, and your old men shall dream dreams: And on my servants and on my handmaidens I will pour out in those days of my Spirit; and they shall prophesy" (Acts 2:17–18).

SOME unfulfilled promise which says, "But unto you that fear God's name shall the Sun of righteousness arise with healing in his wings; and ye shall go forth, and grow up as calves of the stall" (Mal. 4:2).

SOME unfulfilled promise which says you shall have it if you ask for it.

> Ask, and it shall be given you; seek, and ye shall find; knock, and it shall be opened unto you. For every one that asketh receiveth; and he that seeketh findeth; and to him that knocketh it shall be opened. (Matt. 7:7–8)

ASK your neighbor, "What unfulfilled promise have you been carrying?"

It is time to give birth to your promise!

LISTEN. WHEN the angel Gabriel told Mary that she was chosen/handpicked by God to give birth to the most honorable promise, UNLIKE Zacharias, her response was in keeping with the things of the spiritual provisions of God.

MARY said to Gabriel, "How shall this be, seeing that I know not a man."

AND what Mary was actually saying here was, "Gabriel, I know that the birth of this promise is *possible* to God, but how is God going to do it since it is *impossible* to the flesh?"

YOU see, she didn't say, "Gabriel, that cannot be because I know not a man."

BUT rather, she inquired of the spiritual.

She asked, "How shall this be, SEEING that I know not a man?"

AND because of her response, notice the difference in Gabriel's response to her as against Zacharias.

GABRIEL answered her and said, "The Holy Ghost shall come upon thee, and the power of the Highest shall overshadow thee."

TELL your neighbor, "Your promise was conceived by the Holy Ghost."

The birth of your promise is *impossible* to the flesh. But the Holy Ghost shall come upon you.

And the power of the Highest shall overshadow you!

CAN you feel Him? He is coming upon you right now!

CAN you picture Him? He is overshadowing you right now!

AND the Holy Ghost is going to cause you to birth your promise.

BECAUSE with God, nothing shall be impossible.

THE enemy told you that you would never come out of debt.

But God is going to make you debt-free.

Because with God, nothing shall be impossible.

THE enemy told you that you will always be sick, but God is going to heal you.

In fact, He is healing you right now.

Because with God, nothing shall be impossible.

THE enemy told you that you will always be a slave to sin, trapped in a life of lying, cheating, and stealing.

But God is going to deliver you.

In fact, He is delivering you right now.

Because with God, nothing shall be impossible.

SLAP somebody and say, "It may be *im*possible to man, but it is possible to God."

"It may be *im*possible in the flesh, but it is possible through the spiritual."

Expect God to do the unexpected in your life!

NOW I want you to note something of great significance with me.

IT was an angel who brought the news of new birth to Zacharias about his wife, Elizabeth.

AND it was an angel who brought the news of new birth to Joseph and to Mary.

ANGELS were used to warn of the impending dangers of Herod, who wanted to kill the baby Jesus.

AND when you look in the scriptures, you will see that the Bible tells us story after story of angels involved in the work and will of God.

FOR instance, in Genesis 32, the "angels of God" met Jacob while he was on his way home, and Jacob declared, "This is God's army."

AND in the same chapter, Jacob wrestled with an angel of God's army for his blessing. And he got a name change.

In Daniel 6, we read the story of how God sent His angel to shut the mouths of the lions.

In Acts 12, we find the apostle Peter laying bound in shackles, in prison, awaiting execution.

AND as he lay sleeping, an angel appeared, not barred by such things as doors and iron bars.

The angel appeared unto Peter in the prison cell, shook him awake, and led him to freedom.

AND how can we not immediately recall that after the human death of Jesus on the cross of Calvary, as His body laid in the tomb, it was an angel of God that rolled away the huge stone that was guarding the entrance to the tomb, thereby setting in place the events surrounding the resurrection of our risen Savior.

AND we could go on and on in citing instances.

SO angels play an active role in the work of the Lord.

AND WITH that said, God told me to tell you that angels are on assignment working on your behalf even as I speak.

WHY do you think God told me to tell you to expect Him to do the unexpected in your life?

IT IS because of the things that He has already set in motion.

GOD has already commissioned angels to do for you what you could not do for yourself.

IN FACT, before this day even arrived, GOD saw your need and He reviewed your destiny.

And He assigned angels to your purpose so that you can experience the unexpected in your life.

YOU may not know this yet, but suddenly, like Zacharias and Mary, you are going to meet someone, perhaps an angel, whose impact on your life will change its course forever.

YOU may not know this yet, but suddenly, you will receive a phone call.

The conversation will lead to doors of new opportunities being opened unto you.

YOU may not know this yet, but suddenly, you are going to receive unexplained sums of money that God allowed to be sent to you to pay off some long overdue bills.

YOU may not know this yet, but suddenly, your doctor's prognosis is going to change because your test results will reveal that you have been healed.

YOU may not know this yet, but suddenly, your estranged husband or wife is going to return home.

YOUR wayward children are going to mend their relationship with you and with God.

SUDDENLY, God is going to give you an unexplained peace—the peace that passes all understanding.

SUDDENLY, God is going to give you inspiration for starting your own business.

SUDDENLY, God is going to give you insight and foresight.

God is going to speak to you in your dreams and visions and tell you the directions to take to overcome situations that you face.

I DON'T know who I am talking to, but suddenly, God is going to cause your enemies to become your footstool.

> He that dwelleth in the secret place of the most High shall abide under the shadow of the Almighty.
> Surely God shall deliver you from the snare of the fowler, and from the noisome pestilence.
> He shall cover thee with his feathers, and under his wings shalt thou trust: his truth shall be thy shield and buckler. (Ps. 91:1–4)
> A thousand shall fall at thy side, and ten thousand at thy right hand; but it shall not come nigh thee. (Ps. 91:7)
> For there shall no evil befall thee, neither shall any plague come nigh thy dwelling.
> For God shall give his angels charge over thee, to keep thee in all thy ways.

They shall bear thee up in their hands, lest
thou dash thy foot against a stone.
You shall tread upon the lion and adder—
The young lion and the dragon you shall
trample under your feet. (Ps. 91:10–13)

IF YOU believe that this word is for you, TELL somebody, "God is going to change my circumstance."

WHATEVER you are going through in your life was predestined so that the awesomeness of God can be seen.

IT was predestined for Elizabeth to wait until the age of eighty-four before conceiving to give birth to John the Baptist, the forerunner of Jesus Christ.

IT was predestined for Mary, a virgin, to conceive at a very young age and to give birth to our Lord and Savior.

JUST as it was predestined for Shadrach, Meshach, and Abednego to be thrown into the fiery furnace just so God could show that He would deliver them.

JUST as it was predestined for the Red Sea to be the only route of escape for the Israelites from Egypt just so that God could show that He can create dry land in the middle of a sea.

GOD specializes in making the impossible possible.

YOUR situation is an opportunity for God to show that no task is too great, no struggle is too difficult, no battle is too intense for God to handle.

FOR God has an army of angels who are ready to help in the fight.

SOME people may doubt the existence of angels.

But the Word is clear about this truth.

THEY are heavenly beings assigned to believers, and they not only take instructions from God but also wait for us to give them instructed assignments daily.

HEBREWS 1:14 says angels are "ministering" spirits sent to minister to the heirs of salvation.

WHO are the heirs of salvation? You and me!

ANGELS are a part of God's covenant promise of divine protection.

IF YOU believe that God is using His army of angels in the fight for you, TELL somebody, "I am going to be all right suddenly."

The angel of the Lord encampeth round
about them that fear Him. (Ps. 34:7)

IF YOU believe that your miracle is about to be realized, TELL somebody, "Suddenly, God is going to do the unexpected in my life."

Because God giveth power to the faint;
and to them that have no might he increaseth
strength. (Isa. 40:29)

IF YOU believe that today is your day to breakthrough, TELL somebody, "Angels are on assignment on my behalf!"

YOU may not understand what has been happening in your life physically.

But in the spiritual realm, changes are taking place.

IN the spiritual realm, battles are being fought.

IN the spiritual realm, demons are being defeated.

AND suddenly, you are going to move from nothing to something.

SUDDENLY, you are going to move from being nowhere in God to being somewhere in God.

IN FACT, God sent me to tell you that the angels are listening.

THEY have been working on the instructions of God.

But God also wants you to use your authority and release them to work in your life on your instructions.

ONE of the keys to releasing the work of angels in your life is to speak the Word of God.

ANGELS are powerful beings, but they don't just move because you want them to.

THE Word says, "They hearken unto the *voice* of God's Word" (Ps. 103:20).

AND that means that until you speak the Word of God, they will not go to work on your instructions.

TELL your neighbor, "Speak the Word."

> Plead my cause, O LORD, with them that strive with me: fight against them that fight against me. Take hold of shield and buckler, and stand up for mine help. (Ps. 35:1–2)

TELL somebody else, "Speak the Word."

> Make haste, o God, to deliver me; make haste to help me, O LORD...
> Let them be ashamed and confounded that seek after my soul: let them be turned backward, and put to confusion, that desire my hurt. (Ps. 70:1–2)
> For I am persuaded, that neither death, nor life, nor angels, nor principalities, nor powers, nor things present, nor things to come, Nor height, nor depth, nor any other creature, shall be able to separate us from the love of God, which is in Christ Jesus our Lord. (Rom. 8:38–39)

SLAP somebody and say, "Speak the Word."

> But my God shall supply all your need according to his riches in glory by Christ Jesus. (Phil. 4:19)

SLAP somebody else and say, "Speak the Word."

> Heal me, O Lord, and I shall be healed; save me, and I shall be saved, for You are my praise. (Jer. 17:14)

> For He was wounded for my transgressions, He was bruised for my iniquities, the chastisement of our peace was upon Him and with His stripes, I am healed. (Isa. 53:5)

IF you are ready for the unexpected, speak the Word.

> Yea, though I walk through the valley of the shadow of death, I will fear no evil: for thou art with me; thy rod and thy staff they comfort me. (Ps. 23:4)
> FOR surely goodness and mercy shall follow me all the days of my life, and I will Dwell in the house of the Lord forever. (Ps. 23:6)

SPEAK the Word and watch God do the unexpected in your life!

IF YOU believe that God is going to do the unexpected in your life, GET UP OUT OF YOUR SEATS AND COME!

COME here.

YOU KNOW, as a matter of principle, the unexpected is like me handing you this twenty-dollar bill and telling you that the best is yet to come.

YOU didn't expect that, did you?

WELL, that is how God is going to work in your life and in the lives of all of His people IF you just start expecting Him to do the unexpected!

ABOUT THE AUTHOR

Minister Denise Samuels is an international speaker and is known and loved for her strong messages of deliverance, hope, and divine healing. She was called of God at an early age and commissioned by Him to preach and to teach the gospel.

As the associate pastor at Faith Cathedral Deliverance Centre (FCDC), Minister Samuels has direct responsibility for supervising the functions of its thirty-six ministries. Minister Samuels served as a trustee board member for the Deliverance Evangelistic Association (DEA) 2012–2020. Prior to this, she served in many other capacities, to include ten years as facilitator for the Young Converts/New Members Class, president of the FCDC Business Club and as director of youth for over ten years.

Her service in media, which is fueled by her passion for seeing souls won for the Kingdom of God, spanned many years hosting television programs such as *The Bible Speaks*, *The Hour of Prayer*, *Community Connection*, and *Strength for Today* produced by Power of Faith Ministries International and the radio program *Reflections*, TBC Radio.

Minister Samuels is an internationally certified trainer and a human resource specialist with over twenty years' experience in the field. Prior to her current tenure as group human resource and administration manager at Kingston Wharves Limited, she held similar positions with the Interenergy Group and Transport Authority. Her credits include facilitating numerous seminars and workshops in change management, leadership development, conflict resolution, performance management, and ethics, team building, and interpersonal skills.

Minister Samuels holds a master's degree in business administration from the University of the West Indies, a bachelor's degree in business administration from the University of Technology, a diploma in theology from Cornerstone Christian University (Florida), and diplomas in human resource development and in management studies and business administration from the University College of the Caribbean.

She is a justice of the peace, a certified mediator, and a member of the Lay Magistrates Association, St. Andrew Chapter, Kingston, Jamaica.